THE
BOMBARDIER
story

THE
BOMBARDIER
story

**planes
trains
and
snowmobiles**

LARRY MACDONALD

wiley.com

John Wiley & Sons Canada Limited
22 Worcester Road
Etobicoke, Ontario
M9W 1L1

National Library of Canada Cataloguing in Publication

MacDonald, Larry
    The Bombardier story : planes, trains, and snowmobiles /
Larry MacDonald. — Paper ed.

Includes bibliographical references and index.
ISBN 0-470-83196-0

    1. Bombardier Inc.—History. I. Title.

HD9709.C34B65 2002   338.7'629046   C2002-905032-4

Production Credits
Cover design: Interrobang Graphic Design Inc.
Printer: Tri-Graphic Printing

Printed in Canada
10 9 8 7 6 5 4 3 2 1

Contents

Acknowledgements   vii

A Brief History of Bombardier Inc.   ix

Preface   xvii

Introduction: The Rise of A Corporation   xxi

Chapter 1   Armand Starts a Company   1

Chapter 2   An Excellent Ski-Doo Adventure   19

Chapter 3   Diversify or Die   37

Chapter 4   A Breakthrough Deal   55

Chapter 5   Making Subway Cars the Bombardier Way   69

Chapter 6	Becoming Number One	93
Chapter 7	Gravy Trains on the Horizon	109
Chapter 8	Turning into Aerospace	127
Chapter 9	Portrait of a Turnaround Artist	147
Chapter 10	Revolution in the Sky	159
Chapter 11	Bombardier Takes Wing	171
Chapter 12	Dogfight in the Clouds	185
Chapter 13	A Jet Takes Off From the Drawing Board	199
Chapter 14	New Generations	211
Chapter 15	Lessons in Strategic Governance	223
Chapter 16	A Prototype for the Twenty-First Century?	241
Chapter 17	The Challenges Ahead	255
Chapter 18	Bombardier Encounters Turbulence	269
Endnotes		*285*
Index		*305*

Acknowledgements

I would like to thank editor Karen Milner for recommending the topic of this book. As well, editors Ron Edwards and Elizabeth McCurdy deserve special thanks for helping to get the manuscript into shape.

I am grateful to Bombardier Inc. for granting permission to interview staff. The latter included: Laurent Beaudoin (Chairman), Robert Brown (President and Chief Executive Officer), Yvan Allaire (Executive Vice President and Chairman of Bombardier Capital), Jeremy Lee Jonas (Vice President, Strategic Initiatives), and John Holding (Executive Vice President, Engineering and Product Development). Michel Lord, Vice President, Communications and Public Relations, cordially handled the arrangements.

A number of persons outside of Bombardier agreed to interviews, and I would like to express appreciation for their time and comments. They include: Eric McConachie (Chairman of Montreal-based aviation consulting firm, AvPlan Inc.), John Hethrington (former Bombardier executive), and Ed Lumley (former Liberal Cabinet minister, now Vice Chairman and Director of BMO Nesbitt Burns Inc.). There were also interesting communications with other persons, such as former employee Wanda Pokrykus, aerospace MBA graduate René Armando Armas, and McKinsey & Co. consultants Luc Sirois and Hugo Sarrazin.

For material on Joseph-Armand Bombardier and the early years of Bombardier, I am indebted to Roger Lacasse's *Joseph-Armand Bombardier: An Inventor's Dream Come True* (1988) and Carol Precious' *J. Armand Bombardier* (1984). Historical material was also obtained from portions of Matthew Fraser's *Quebec Inc: French Canadian Entrepreneurs and its Business Elite* (1987) and David Olive's *No Guts, No Glory: How Canada's Greatest CEOs Built their Empires* (2000).

David and Diana Nicholson of Westmount made me feel at home in Montreal, providing not only accommodations, but also admission into their lively Wednesday Night Salon, a weekly discussion group in which estimable Montreal citizens have exchanged ideas for over two decades. David and Diana also put me in touch with people connected with Bombardier and turned over some Wednesday Night Salons to discussions on Bombardier.

A Brief History of Bombardier Inc.

1937

- Joseph-Armand Bombardier awarded patent for the sprocket device that makes the B7 snowmobile possible.

1942

- Joseph-Armand Bombardier incorporates his firm, L'Auto-Neige Bombardier Limitée, which is based in Valcourt, Quebec.
- Participates in the manufacture of tracked military vehicles.

1945

- Begins production of C18 snowmobile (for taking children to school).
- Ramps up manufacturing of the B12 snowmobile (for public transport, freight transport, mail delivery, and ambulance services).

1948

- Quebec government passes legislation requiring all highways and local roads to be cleared of snow; L'Auto-Neige Bombardier's sales fall by nearly half in one year.

1953

- Diversification drive capped by introduction of the Muskeg Tractor, an all-terrain vehicle used in the resource and construction industries to transport heavy loads over swamp and snow.

1959

- Ski-Doo snowmobile introduced; Bombardier becomes number one producer, a position it held until the 1990s.

1964

- Joseph-Armand Bombardier dies and leaves company in hands of his son, Germain.

1966

- Following Germain's resignation, Laurent Beaudoin becomes the chief executive, a position he retains for the next three and a half decades.

1967

- L'Auto-Neige Bombardier Limitée renamed Bombardier Ltd.

1969

- Listing of Bombardier shares on the Montreal and Toronto Stock Exchanges.

1970

- Acquisition program highlighted by takeover of the maker of the Rotax engines used in Bombardier's snowmobiles (and later in its all-terrain vehicles and watercraft).

1972

- Annual sales of Ski-Doos peak at 210,000 units.
- Creation of a financing subsidiary to provide inventory financing for Ski-Doo dealers (later extended to other products, railcar leasing, and commercial lending).

1974

- Soaring energy prices and economic recession decimate the snowmobile industry, prompting Bombardier to diversify into the mass transit industry starting with a contract to build over 400 cars for the Montreal subway system.

1975

- Headquarters moved from Valcourt to Montreal.

1976

- Integration of Bombardier's rail transit operations with MLW-Worthington Ltd., a manufacturer of locomotives and the LRC (Light, Rapid, Comfortable) railcar; company name changed to Bombardier-MLW Ltd.

1977

- Wins first US transit equipment order (for commuter cars in the Chicago South Suburban Mass Transit District).

1981

- Name changed to Bombardier Inc.
- Lands an order for 180 subway cars from transit authorities in Mexico City.

1982

- Wins $1 billion megadeal to make subway cars for New York City, transforming company into the largest North American maker of rail transit equipment.

1984

- Licenses the monorail design from Disneyland.

1986

- Commences diversification into aerospace manufacturing with the acquisition of Canadair, maker of the Challenger business jet.
- Awarded a $1.7 billion multiyear contract to service CF-18 jets.

1987

- Acquires the railcar designs of US companies Budd and Pullman.
- Signs commercial agreement with Alstom (then called GEC-Alsthom) for the marketing of a high-speed train in North America.

1988

- Launches expansion into European rail industry with the purchase of a 40 percent interest in BN Constructions Ferroviaires et Métalliques S.A.
- Launches the Sea-Doo.

1989

- Increases critical mass in aerospace with acquisition of Short Brothers.
- Obtains a contract to design and manufacture 252 railcars for transporting automobiles and buses through the English Channel Tunnel.

1990

- Becomes a provider of a family of business jets with the acquisition of Learjet Corp.

1991

- Test flight of the 50-seat Canadair Regional Jet, the first commercial jet dedicated to regional transportation.
- Initiates development of Global Express business jet.

1992

- Acquires automated subway maker, Urban Transport Development Corp.
- Gains control of de Havilland, maker of Dash 8 turboprop aircraft.
- Acquires the assets of Constructora Nacional de Carros de Ferrocarril, a Mexican manufacturer of railway rolling stock.

1994

- Wins contract to supply metro cars to the city of Kuala Lumpur in Malaysia.

1995

- Introduces Flexjet, a fractional ownership program for business jets.

- Line of Dash 8 turboprops expanded with launch of 70-passenger version; inaugural flight of the Learjet 45 business aircraft; becomes third largest manufacturer in the civil aerospace industry after Boeing and the Airbus consortium.
- Annual sales of the Sea-Doo peak at 110,000 units.

1996
- Reorganizes into five groups: Bombardier Aerospace, Bombardier Transportation, Bombardier Recreational Products, Bombardier Capital, and Bombardier Services (later disbanded).
- Amtrak chooses the Bombardier/Alstom consortium to supply train sets for its high-speed service on the Washington/New York/Boston route.
- Bombardier receives order from the Deutsche Bahn for 120 diesel-powered rail units.
- Unveiling of the Neighborhood Electric Vehicle.

1997
- Delivers 200th Canadair Regional Jet, 500th Dash 8 turboprop, and 400th Challenger business jet.
- Bombardier Aerospace launches a new version of the Canadair Regional Jet, the 70-seat Canadair Regional Jet 700.
- New York City awards Bombardier a $1.3 billion contract to build 680 subway cars.
- Awarded $2.8 billion multiyear contract for the training of NATO pilots in Canada.

1998
- Creates another operating group, Bombardier International, to pursue growth opportunities in foreign markets outside of North America and Europe.

- Bombardier wins $2.6 billion order from the British Virgin Rail Group for equipment and maintenance services.
- Bombardier unveils the Traxter, an all-terrain vehicle.
- Wins $1 billion contract to extend the Skytrain metro in Vancouver.

1999
- Robert E. Brown is appointed President and Chief Executive Officer of Bombardier; Laurent Beaudoin remains Chairman.
- Bombardier Transportation awarded a contract from the Chinese Ministry of Railways to supply 300 intercity passenger vehicles.
- The Long Island Railroad requests up to a thousand commuter cars—contract worth as much as $2.7 billion.

2000
- Bombardier signs with Delta Connection carriers to provide 94 Canadair Regional Jet aircraft, an order worth nearly $3 billion.
- Announces development of 90-seat Canadair Regional Jet.

2001
- Bombardier completes the purchase of Berlin-based Adtranz, catapulting Bombardier Transportation to the top of the global rail transportation industry.
- Acquires Johnson and Evinrude engine divisions of Outboard Marine Corp.

Preface

While gathering information for this book, I was frequently reminded of the parable of the elephant and the six blind men. One blind man felt the trunk and declared it was like a snake; a second felt the tail and said it was like a piece of rope; a third felt the leg and thought it was like a tree trunk; a fourth felt the side and argued it was like a wall; a fifth felt the ear and proclaimed it was like a fan; a sixth felt the tusk and pronounced it was like a spear.

Bombardier Inc. is certainly of a size to suggest an elephant. Just consider the range of its products. There are the rail transportation products, which include the Acela high-speed train and thousands of subway cars in Montreal, Toronto, Vancouver, New York City, and several other metropolitan areas around the world. Then there are the aerospace products, which include Canadair Regional Jet, Dash 8 turboprop, and the Global Express business jet. And then there are the recreational products, which include the Ski-Doo snowmobile, Sea-Doo personal watercraft, and Traxter all-terrain vehicle. And finally, there are the financial products, which include inventory financing, leasing, and commercial lending.

Not surprisingly, a variety of reports emanate from the field. Some staff at Bombardier, for example, confirm the existence of Bombardier's legendary family environment—they feel the company will take care of them if they take care of it. But others speak of a sink-or-swim environment arising from the dictates of rapid growth in their areas. Outside the company, there is a diversity of viewpoints as well: constantly in the headlines, Bombardier invariably attracts favorable and unfavorable commentary. Supporters think it is a company for the twenty-first century; detractors think otherwise.

In this book, I have attempted to provide a fair representation of the different viewpoints. And I wanted to do so without creating a compendium of coffee-break tidbits or blood-on-the-boardroom-floor scenes. I believe the story of Bombardier deserves a more elevated treatment because of its accomplishments and spin-off benefits in the socioeconomic realm. Even the critics admit the stellar track record—their contention is with other matters.

This book is both a corporate history and business case study. The corporate history portion provides a sequence of events that lays out the rise of Bombardier from its birth to the present, explaining how the company emerged as a commercial success. The business case study, interwoven into the corporate history, offers lessons and insights into the Bombardier formula.

As such, this book should be of interest to businesspersons, consultants, economists, journalists, policy makers, and commerce students at the undergraduate and graduate levels. It should also be of interest to future, present, and past employees (and their families), staff in companies that deal or compete with Bombardier, users of Bombardier's products, and existing or prospective investors in Bombardier's shares (as well as those investors wishing to obtain a better understanding of the circumstances that can generate long-term growth companies).

John Kay, a British professor who writes a column on management issues for the *Financial Times of London*, speaks often of the subtleties of corporate histories and business case studies. Because of the elephant and blind men problem, as well as the ingrained biases of any given chronicler, he believes such case studies can offer little more than an interpretation. They can only hope to illuminate aspects of the reality; they are necessarily incomplete in their portrayals.

As an example, Kay cites accounts of the Japanese penetration of the North American motorcycle market in the 1960s.[1] One study said Honda and other Japanese manufacturers enjoyed economies of scale in their home market and used this as a springboard for expansion into the United States. Interviews with Honda managers reveal a different story. Hearing there was limited public transportation in California, they brought some of their motorcycles over for their own use. But after discovering the reliability problems of domestic motorbikes and being constantly quizzed on the street about their smaller bikes, they set up a marketing campaign.

Which explanation is right? Kay says neither is true, just as neither is wrong. They are just different ways of looking at the situation, and both can add to our understanding. A story from the inside, for example, is useful for providing detail from the front lines; a story from the outside has the benefit of including a broader list of variables. I tried to keep such subtleties in mind during the writing of this book. Business outcomes are often a mixture of design and accident, of planning and serendipity. They reflect the interaction of internal and external variables—the interplay of the strategies formulated within the company and forces outside the company.

I had completely free reign with this portrayal of Bombardier. Although the topic was suggested by my publisher (the kind of invitation I like to get), they did not specify what the angle should be. And although Bombardier kindly cooperated by allowing senior executives to be interviewed, it was without any strings attached.

In this book, I referred to persons by their last names except for three main characters, Joseph-Armand Bombardier, Laurent Beaudoin, and Pierre Beaudoin. I referred to Armand by his first name to avoid possible confusion with the company named after him; I referred to Laurent and Pierre by their first names to avoid possible confusion between father and son.

They say where you stand depends on where you sit. So perhaps I should mention my background as an individual born and raised in Ottawa, who went to work for a dozen years as an economist before turning to business journalism about two years ago. As such, my rendition of the Bombardier story may have emphasized different aspects than if it were told by a businessperson from Alberta, a social worker in Toronto, or a Quebec employee of the aerospace industry. But I would like to repeat that I have tried to offer a balanced presentation of the perspectives and events. And hopefully, this portrait of the elephant will show more verisimilitude than a beast comprised of snakes, ropes, tree trunks, walls, fans, and spears.

Note: All dollar figures in this book are in Canadian currency unless otherwise noted.

Introduction:
The Rise of
A Corporation

Bombardier was under attack again. This time, the flack was coming from the president of Berlin-based Adtranz, the rail equipment subsidiary of DaimlerChysler AG. In 1999, he traveled to Toronto and made a speech in which he warned that Adtranz was coming to challenge Montreal-based Bombardier on its home turf of North America. His motive was retaliation: he did not like Bombardier's invasion of Adtranz's European markets. So he was going to put the upstart from the hinterlands in its place. "The major player in the United States of the future will be, I believe, Adtranz,"[1] he predicted.

In the spring of 2001, Bombardier acquired Adtranz: so much for the taunts of rival executives. The parent corporation, wishing to focus on reviving its main business of automobile manufacturing, accepted Bombardier's takeover offer. The purchase more than doubled annual revenues at Bombardier's rail

equipment division to $8 billion and created an integrated pro-
ducer with expertise in both rolling stock and propulsion systems. It also catapulted Bombardier into the number one spot in
the railway equipment industry, ahead of the rail divisions of
Franco-British conglomerate Alstom and German industrial giant
Siemens.

Bombardier's rise to the top began in 1974 with a contract to
build several hundred cars for the subway system of Montreal,
Quebec. The expertise gained on this project allowed it to win
some big contracts in the United States, notably a $1 billion deal
in 1982 to supply subway cars to the New York City Transit
Authority. Meanwhile, North American rail equipment manufacturers were falling by the wayside. The industry was in a long-
term decline after World War II because of the growing
popularity of airplane and automobile travel.

By the early 1990s, former greats of US rail manufacturing,
such as Pullman Co., had disappeared. Only one major domestic producer was still around: construction giant Morrison Knudsen Corp., builder of such technological wonders as the Hoover
Dam and San Francisco Bay Bridge. Under a dynamic new chief
executive, William Agee (the corporate star from Bendix Corp.),
Morrison Knudsen had launched an aggressive foray into railway
equipment manufacturing.

For a time, it looked as if the Boise, Idaho-based conglomerate was going to give Bombardier some serious opposition.
Undercutting closest competitors by an average 7 percent, the
company won six of the eight contracts on which it bid between
1990 and 1992, winning orders to make more than 500 railcars
with options on another 1,000. Bombardier's success rate on bids
meanwhile was going in the other direction, from two-thirds in
1988 to one-third in 1992.

Aiding Morrison Knudsen's cause was an increased requirement to buy from domestic sources as set out in the *Buy American Act*, and a shift of funding to state and local authorities that resulted in a greater emphasis on local production. In one case, Morrison Knudsen won an order by pledging to make at least 80 percent of each car in the United States, only later to be granted a waiver from a major technical requirement for which two competitors had previously been disqualified. In another case, Morrison Knudsen won a lucrative railcar contract from a northern Illinois commuter agency after receiving bonus points for promising to do more of the work locally. These bonus points, which reputedly were not fully disclosed during the call for tenders, offset Bombardier's higher marks in the price and technology categories.

What undid Bombardier's competitor was a failure to execute on its aggressive marketing. The sudden volume of orders overwhelmed its engineering and resource base, leading to misses on deadlines and quality standards. And not enough economies were found in operations to offset the aggressive bidding for contracts, resulting in cost overruns. These overruns were largely responsible for the catastrophic loss of $310 million US incurred by Morrison Knudsen in 1994, a loss the company could ill afford since it was still burdened with massive debt as a result of past troubles in its construction product lines.

Faced with the prospect of having to cover an ongoing shortfall between cost and revenues on its rail contracts, the company was in danger of going out of business. Agee was dismissed by the board of directors, a retreat from rail manufacturing ensued, and the remaining parts of the company were rescued through merger with another construction company.

That left Bombardier as the only substantial North American player. It was not only surviving but thriving, enjoying rising profits from several large and lucrative contracts. In the mid-1980s, a decision was taken to put these profits to work in a campaign to penetrate the European rail market. Just over a dozen years later, Bombardier emerged on top, a feat somewhat analogous to a soccer player from North America rising to star status in the European leagues.

All the know-how and skills were supposedly in Europe, not in the snowbound Canadian province of Quebec. The rail equipment market in Europe was over four times the size of the one in North America, and it was dominated by firms that had been around for over a century. Some were world leaders in research and development, while others had solid business relationships with state-owned railway operators. And nearly all were favored by greater government support and cooperation.

What made Bombardier's progression in rail equipment all the more remarkable is that it occurred while yet another progression was under way at Bombardier's aerospace group. In 1986, the company decided to enter the aerospace sector by acquiring business-jet maker Canadair Ltd. of Montreal. This was followed by acquisitions of several other ailing aerospace companies, including world-renowned Learjet. Turning around these floundering assets, Bombardier came out of nowhere to become, in a little more than a dozen years, the third-largest member of the civil aerospace manufacturing industry. Only US giant Boeing and European colossus, the Airbus consortium, are larger.

As in the upward climb of the rail equipment operations, the aerospace operations of Bombardier surged ahead while other players faded. For example, Fokker of the Netherlands, a stalwart in the regional airplane sector, collapsed in 1997 under the weight of a massive debt load and outmoded processes. In

Canada, ailing de Havilland was rescued by Boeing, but when the latter threw in the towel on its turnaround efforts in 1992, Bombardier stepped in and transformed de Havilland into a productive member of its aerospace operations.

Rising to top positions in the rail and aerospace industries are laudable achievements in themselves. What makes them more remarkable is that they occurred while Bombardier was defending a dominant position in a third industry: motorized recreational products. In the early 1960s, following three decades of developing and manufacturing tracked vehicles for travel over snow and muskeg, Bombardier entered the market for recreational snowmobiles and quickly claimed the top spot in a rapidly growing industry.

It held the top position until 1990 when Polaris Industries of Minnesota overtook Bombardier (if US antitrust authorities had allowed Bombardier to acquire Polaris in 1980, it would likely have remained on top). Bombardier countered by upgrading its Ski-Doo line and developing new products such as the Neighborhood Electrical Vehicle and the Traxter, an all-terrain vehicle. Bombardier also diversified very successfully into personal watercraft under the Sea-Doo brand, ending up with a market share of 50 percent by the mid-1990s. Although the upgrades and new products were not enough to allow Bombardier Recreational Products to catch up to Polaris in motorized recreational products (the Polaris diversification into all-terrain vehicles had been very successful), they nevertheless helped to close the gap.

Bombardier threw more resources to another flank in early 2001 by acquiring the Johnson and Evinrude engine assets of bankrupt Outboard Marine Corp. (a company that had made a bid to acquire Bombardier in the 1960s). The chairman and chief executive officer of Brunswick Corp., the dominant player in leisure boat manufacturing, had a few choice words for its new competitor. Bombardier is "a very capable company...," he said. But, in taking on Brunswick, "the world's best engine manufacturer," it would "take an act of God for Bombardier to succeed."[2] Bombardier was under attack again. Yet another rival executive was laying down the gauntlet.

Finally, it is worth mentioning that Bombardier was expanding into a fourth industry while the other initiatives in rail, aerospace, and recreational products were unfolding. Filling a void the banks were not ready to enter, Bombardier created a capital group in the early 1970s to provide inventory financing to Ski-Doo dealers. Later, consumer financing was added for Ski-Doo consumers. As new recreational watercraft and all-terrain products rolled off the assembly line, financing was extended to dealers and end users in those niches. There was also an expansion into commercial lending, leasing, and asset management in areas related to core competencies, particularly business jets and railcars. By 2001, Bombardier had $13 billion in assets under management and was the third largest provider of inventory financing in North America.

Training for his pilot's license on a sunny summer day in 1970, Laurent Beaudoin jumped into the cockpit of a small airplane for a practice run. As the plane accelerated down the runway, Laurent reached down to adjust his seat to a more comfortable position. Just as the wheels were lifting off the tarmac, he found a lever and pressed. To his horror, the seat snapped backward. Firmly strapped in, Laurent strained forward to reach the control panel. He was barely able to get his fingertips on the instruments and bring the plane back to earth. "I was just high enough off the ground to kill myself,"[3] he sheepishly laughed about the incident some years later.

It was a good thing that the aircraft did not crash. Otherwise, Bombardier might never have become one of the more remarkable cases of sustained growth in the corporate world. As the chief executive in charge during the years from 1966 to 1999, and afterward as the chairman, Laurent is primarily responsible for the corporation's stellar success. Without him, the story might never have emerged. Instead of becoming a global powerhouse, Bombardier might have ended up as a lesser light in Quebec. Or it might have disappeared altogether in a takeover or through insolvency during the vicious downturns of the 1970s.

Laurent has been described as a physically impressive man with Bonaparte-like features and a courtly manner. His "eyes are darkly Italian, his nose is aquiline, the chin is strong, the sculpted form of his head pro-consular."[4] In close encounters, he can be charming and personable. His gaze rarely wavers, and there is a sense of a probing, analytical intellect at work. Yet, he is not one to seek the spotlight. "Everything to do with public relations— being a statesman, acting as the spokesman—that did not come naturally to me," he once revealed. "I was not trained for that role, and at the beginning I tried to delegate those functions."[5]

Along the way, several lieutenants made valuable contributions. One was Raymond Royer, who joined the company in 1974 and left in 1996 to become chief executive of forest products company Domtar Inc. Royer was a tireless leader who espoused a philosophy of "managing by commitment." Another lieutenant was Robert E. Brown, the Royal Military College graduate who reached the top ranks of the Canadian federal civil service before joining Bombardier in 1987 at the age of 42. With quiet determination, Brown applied his skills in negotiation and organization to pilot Bombardier's aerospace group to a dramatic growth trajectory over the 1990s. A third major contributor was Dr. Yvan Allaire, the business professor and management consultant who played the role of an *éminence grise*—and then some

—dispensing advice on key issues, playing a key role in the decision-making process, and serving as the lead executive on several
projects and programs.

But, of course, the contribution of the founder himself,
Joseph-Armand Bombardier, must not be overlooked. From his
garage in Valcourt, in the Eastern Townships of Quebec, Armand
gave birth to Bombardier in the 1930s with the creation of the B7
vehicle, a snowmobile that carried up to seven passengers over
unplowed wintry roads. Later, in the 1950s, when all roads were
required by law to be cleared of snow, Bombardier developed and
manufactured tracked vehicles for traveling over muskeg and
other difficult terrain encountered in the resource extraction
industries. A rare combination of inventive genius and able entrepreneur, Armand built up his company through thick and thin
so that by the time of his death in 1964, Bombardier was a very
solid enterprise with considerable growth potential.

Through a combination of astute acquisitions and organic
growth, Bombardier has emerged as a global giant in the transportation equipment manufacturing sector. Just how big? In the
fiscal year to January 31, 2001, the company recorded revenues
of $16.1 billion and had a workforce of approximately 56,000.
If revenues from the May 2001 acquisition of Adtranz are
included, the revenues are closer to $21 billion, and the number
of employees is nearly 77,000.

Virtually without setback, growth has proceeded at an annual
compound rate near 20 percent since 1977, when annual revenues were approximately $250 million. Most of the growth
occurred in the two groups of Bombardier Aerospace and Bombardier Transportation (rail equipment). Of the current $21 billion
revenues, aerospace accounts for nearly half and rail for about 37

percent. The majority of the remainder is comprised of revenues from Bombardier Recreational Products, with the residual taken up by Bombardier Capital. Contributing no direct revenues but still performing a vital function is a fifth and final group, Bombardier International, set up in 1998 to assist the four other groups with their expansion drives into markets outside North America and Western Europe.

For the most part, profits have progressed in line with sales growth. In fiscal 2001, net income reached $979 million, up from $0.5 million in fiscal 1977. This performance has boosted the price of Bombardier's Class A and Class B common stock well over 200 times during the past 25 years, putting the annual compound rate of appreciation above 20 percent. Bombardier shares split two for one seven times over the period: in May 1985, October 1986, July 1987, January 1992, July 1995, July 1998, and July 2000.

Trading on the Toronto, Frankfurt, and Brussels stock exchanges, Bombardier's market capitalization surpassed $30 billion in the spring of 2001. The Bombardier family—the three daughters (Janine, Claire, and Huguette) and son (J. R. André) of founder Joseph-Armand Bombardier—own 80 percent of the 347 million Class A shares, a stake worth approximately $6 billion. Since the Class A shares carry 10 votes each compared to a single vote on each of the one billion Class B shares, the family retains control of the company through ownership of 62 percent of the voting rights attached to all shares of the corporation.

Bombardier has no shares trading on US stock exchanges. Some believe this is due to Security Exchange Commission regulations barring companies with multiple voting shares. However, companies with such voting structures established prior to 1979 can be grandfathered. Bombardier is, in fact, studying a listing in the United States, but the company has the luxury of taking its time because its shares already enjoy a high value on the Toronto

Stock Exchange, and cash flows from operations are available to finance investment needs. In addition, Bombardier already has a considerable following among major US brokerage firms.

So far, Bombardier seems to have largely escaped the afflictions that often beset conglomerate organizations. Notably, there is no discount in the stock market attached to Bombardier's shares for being a composite of parts. Most other companies in this category have market capitalizations less than the sum of the value of their parts. Not so Bombardier. Relatedly, there does not seem to be much evidence of what management experts say are two common problems with large and diversified companies: bounded rationality and opportunistic behavior. The first term refers to the loss of control that management experiences as the size of the organization increases; the second term refers to unproductive and exploitative actions by employees who become aware of the dilution in management control.

As Dr. Allaire describes it, Bombardier is "one of the few companies that managed both geographical and product diversification without major mishaps."[6] Outside observers note that this has been accomplished in part by using a rather unconventional approach. They "have shrewdly assembled their new Bombardier from the castoffs and failures of others...."[7] explained one. Royer himself commented: "We could make an offer for a company that's doing super well, but that isn't what we are interested in. What we look for is a company where something is missing."[8] Laurent, along with other members of his team, have consequently achieved legendary status as deal makers. "Some of his deals would put Monty Hall [host of the TV show, *Let's Make a Deal*] to shame,"[9] wrote one columnist.

Diversification and acquisitions are central themes in the Bombardier story, but they are certainly not the only ones. Another important topic is product innovation. Maintaining a stream of new products allows the company to continue growing even after existing product lines have saturated the market. Other critical themes include the use of a decentralized structure to promote an entrepreneurial culture.

Last, but not least, a key thread is Bombardier's relationship with the public sector. Canadian provincial and federal governments have created, like their counterparts in other countries, various programs to assist domestic businesses in the development of technologies, creation of jobs, penetration of foreign markets, and other objectives. Bombardier, like many other Canadian companies, has applied for and received benefits from these programs.

Bombardier's main industries of aerospace and rail manufacturing are characterized by high levels of government support around the world. Many foreign aerospace manufacturers are nationalized, supported directly by taxpayers. Those not state owned—such as Boeing, the Airbus consortium, and Embraer —still nevertheless are the beneficiaries of billions of dollars in subsidies via government grants and military spending. And in railway markets outside North America, there is a heavy commitment of public funds to help develop infrastructure and new technologies. Such government support around the world in the industries of aerospace and rail equipment often compels Bombardier to seek, as a way of leveling the playing field, a share of the assistance available from Canadian government programs.

Public assistance to Bombardier has nevertheless invoked criticism. Detractors, steeped in the doctrines of free markets and laissez-faire economics, disagree with government assistance on philosophical grounds. Bombardier just happens to be one of the more visible manifestations of an approach to political economy with which they disagree. Other critics are chagrined by issues pertaining to the distribution of government funds. For example, groups based in Western Canada complain that the federal government is funneling money away from their region to support Bombardier as part of an industrial strategy to bolster the Quebec economy and mollify separatist factions.

These may be valid differences of opinion on public policy issues, but some critics go beyond this to assert that Bombardier owes its success to government help. They point to funds Bombardier has received from Technology Partnerships Canada, a program aimed at promoting the development of new technologies and products. They point to sales of government corporations to Bombardier. They also point to the Export Development Corporation (EDC), a Crown corporation set up to support the efforts of Canadian companies in foreign markets.

A prevalent misconception about the EDC is that it relies on subsidies from government. It does not receive funding from government in the normal course of business but strives to make a profit as a financial intermediary, albeit of a different sort than a bank. The agency borrows at Government of Canada rates and lends the funds at a markup to foreign customers of Canadian firms. It also facilitates export transactions by guaranteeing private sector financing provided to customers of Canadian companies. Lastly, it administers, at the direction of Cabinet, the Canada Account, a government-funded facility that lends in exceptional cases to high-risk foreign customers and is able to provide below-market rates to counter subsidized financing from other governments. The only time subsidies are handed out, aside from the possible case of below-market rates, is in the event uncollectible debts accrue in the Canada Account (and in rare situations involving humanitarian considerations, notably the Paris Club write-offs of the debt of impoverished third-world countries).

While Bombardier has benefited from government assistance, there appears to be, as Edward Clifford said, "more to Bombardier than luck and handouts."[10] Not to be overlooked, to use his list, is Bombardier's: 1) business strategy, 2) risk management, 3) manufacturing know-how, 4) financial controls, 5) product development, 6) employee relations, and 7) customer service. Many companies have received government assistance in Canada but have produced disappointing results. Bombardier has been one of the most successful companies in the history of the country. It is not just a matter of getting aid, but of what kind of organization is in place to put it to work.

Bombardier, it may be argued, is a form of private-public sector enterprise, but one in which the taxpayers' contribution is relatively small in relation to the scale of its operations and the aid received by many rivals. As such, the assistance appears to have delivered more bang for the buck than most other attempts at public-private cooperation around the world. The story of Bombardier is worthy of examination for this aspect alone, but since much of the performance appears to be linked to the acumen of the company, its business side is also worth looking at.

1

Armand Starts a Company

The corporate logo of Bombardier shows a sprocket, a rather simple-looking wheel with several teeth around the circumference. The teeth are broad in width and flattened at the top, suggesting durability. Across the center of the sprocket is emblazoned the company's name.

There is much significance to this logo, for the development of the sprocket was a crucial step forward in Joseph-Armand Bombardier's quest to develop a vehicle that could travel reliably over snow. When the rubber-encased sprocket was interlocked with a rubber-belted traction device, it provided the necessary shock absorption and propulsion to power a vehicle through virtually all wintry conditions.

This important invention capped years of experimentation between 1925 and 1935, performed inside Garage Bombardier in Valcourt, Quebec during the winter months when few motor vehicles or farm machinery had to be repaired. It led to Armand's first major patent (granted in June 1937) and sales of the B7 snowmobile (B for Bombardier and 7 for the number of passengers) in 1936, mainly to doctors who wanted to reach their snowbound patients quicker.

Most important of all, the sprocket and belted track breakthrough led to the decision in early 1937 to close Garage Bombardier and focus on the full-time production of snowmobiles under the company name of L'Auto-Neige Bombardier (Bombardier Snowmobiles). Such were the humble origins of the transportation giant now known as Bombardier Inc. The sprocket on the Bombardier logo is hence highly meaningful as the device that launched the company.

The difficulty of motorized travel over snow is highlighted by the fact that man-made machines could fly through the air before they could travel over snow. It was easier to lift a machine into the air than to send it over snowy terrain. The Wright Brothers' first plane flew in 1903, while the first vehicle equipped for snow travel did not emerge until 1904.

In that year, Frenchman Adolphe Kégresse, technical director in the imperial garage of Czar Nicholas II of Russia, converted an automobile to a snowmobile by installing a track drive around twinned rear wheels and a set of skis at the front for steering. Returning to France after the Bolshevik Revolution of 1917, Kégresse sold the patent rights to his inventions to automobile pioneer, André-Gustave Citroën. Further development led to the Citroën Torpedo, a vehicle aimed mainly at travel over swamp and sand. It was tested in the Sahara desert, and as part of a publicity campaign in 1931, two expeditions of the Citroën Torpedos journeyed to China.

In 1913, Virgil White, a Ford dealer in New Hampshire, devised a track and ski unit for the Model T Ford and later for the Model A. These units enabled the vehicles to travel over unplowed roads in the winter. During the 1920s, he built and sold 25,000 of the conversion devices and patented the term "snowmobile."

In 1922, Armand, then a lad of 15 who was fascinated in all things mechanical, designed his first snowmobile: a four-passenger sleigh frame supporting a rear-mounted Model T engine with a spinning wooden propeller sticking out the back. He and his brother drove this dangerous and deafening contraption for a kilometer (just over half a mile) through Valcourt before their alarmed father ordered them to stop.

In 1924, Earl Eliason from Wisconsin invented a device he called the motorized toboggan, which consisted of a wooden toboggan fitted with two skis steered by ropes and pushed along by a steel-cleated track powered by a 2.5 horsepower Johnson outboard motor. Eliason patented his machine, and it was manufactured until 1960 by his company and later, the F.W.D. Corporation in Canada.

Another pioneering effort at fashioning a functioning snowmobile was made by Adalbert Landry and Antionne Moriset of Mont-Joli in the Gaspé region of Quebec. Their effort was another attempt to convert an automobile. They put skis on the front for steering, and a caterpillar belt over the double rear wheels for propulsion. In 1924, Landry traveled the nearly 600 kilometers (375 miles) from Mont-Joli to Montreal in his snowmobile to an automobile show, arousing considerable excitement along the way.

While Eliason and the two Quebecers were demonstrating their inventions in 1924, Armand had started an apprenticeship as a mechanic in Montreal after convincing his parents that he was more suited for that line of work than the priesthood toward which he had been in training. During the day, he soaked up the tricks of the trade, while in the evening, he took correspondence courses in electrical engineering and mechanics. He also began to teach himself English because most of the science and technology journals were available only in that language.

This was the extent of Armand's formal training. There were no courses in engineering or science at the college or university level to provide him with the knowledge of electricity, construction, metal casting, vulcanizing of rubber, and other subjects necessary for developing his inventions in years ahead. That knowledge was mostly self-taught, acquired through reading journals and the experience of several years as a hands-on mechanic.

He was indeed driven by an insatiable thirst to learn everything about mechanical devices. Traveling companions on his occasional vacation trips outside of Valcourt remembered Armand slamming on the brakes of his automobile and dashing across a muddy field to inspect some piece of farm machinery that had caught his eye. He was always curious about things mechanical. When he bought an airplane later in life, he took its engine apart to see how it worked.

Victor Plante, a friend who managed an automobile repair service in town, received several visits from Armand over the years that appeared to be more in the nature of research expeditions. Without even saying hello, Armand would start to poke around Plante's garage, stopping only to examine a new tool or mechanical part. "He was studying the piece so intensely with his eyes and his hands that he seemed to be talking to the metal," Plante recalled. "When he put it down, I had the impression he knew everything about it, its characteristics, and its use. Sometimes, with his mind totally absorbed in what he had seen, he would leave, completely forgetting the purpose of his visit and without even saying good bye."[1]

Dr. André Lefebvre got an interesting reception when he went to see Armand in 1939 to inquire about his snowmobiles. Before the doctor even had a chance to explain the nature of his visit, Armand had his head under the hood of the doctor's car, a 1929 Ford. "He was examining the motor," the doctor recounted, "an eight-cylinder, 85-horsepower job, of the same type he was using in his B7s. He wanted to know how the motor had behaved all these years, the repairs done to it, and how it sounded after running for 10 years. This seemed much more interesting than saying hello or finding out what I was there for."[2]

In any event, by the time Armand returned to Valcourt at the age of 19 to set up his own garage, the earlier attempts of previous innovators to design snow-going vehicles had met with limited success. The Eliason toboggans were functional, but they were more of a curiosity than a vehicle for use in everyday transportation. Meanwhile, the bulky belts used for rear traction in converted automobiles frequently slipped or broke off, often in the middle of nowhere, or they clogged up with snow and ice, losing traction. And often times, a problem arose in getting through deeper snow.

Over the late 1920s and early 1930s, Armand experimented with several prototypes. His first ones were similar in nature to the converted automobiles of other inventors. He sold a few to local businessmen such as the hotel owner who wanted to transport winter guests from the train station to his front door. Still, Armand was not satisfied, and he started work on a second set of prototypes based on the propeller concept from his adolescence. He gave up because of the inability to go in reverse, problems with the engine overheating, and the danger of the spinning propeller.

By the mid-1930s, Armand's attempts had not produced a satisfactory solution, but they had nevertheless yielded many insights into what the successful design would be. For one, the engine would have to be rear mounted to better distribute the weight of the vehicle so that the front runners would not be pushed down too deep in the snow. Second, breakage and slippage of the belt (as well as strain on the engine and differential) could be reduced by using rubber rather than metal belts on the rear wheels.

By 1935, Armand was able to combine these ideas with his sprocket device to produce a machine that finally resolved to his satisfaction the problem of traveling over snow. The prototype used a Ford chassis and other body parts, with skis in the front for steering. The engine was located in the rear with the hood facing backwards. Armand once nearly got a parking ticket for seemingly parking the wrong way. The propulsion system was based on two parallel rubber belts coupled together with carbon steel cross-links for strength. The belt was fitted around a rear unit on either side consisting of two Ford wheels and Armand's sprocket.

The following year, a new version called the B7 was created. A major change was the outward appearance. A lightweight cabin made of plywood, similar in shape to the Volkswagen Beetle profile, now sat on the chassis. A new drivetrain and rear suspension were developed. It included parallel bars that supported the wheels and was linked to the chassis by means of a leaf spring. Priced just above $1,000, about the same price as low-end automobiles of the time, enough of these B7 models were sold in the first year to encourage Bombardier to go into production mode.

From 12 vehicles in 1937, annual output increased to 25 in 1938 and to 50 in 1939. Rising above the ravages of the Great Depression in the 1930s, a viable business was in the making as the popularity of the B7 spread outward from the early clientele of doctors to include taxi drivers, bus operators, innkeepers, funeral directors, utility company workers, milkmen, missionaries, and traveling salesmen.

Every year, the B7 model would be improved in some way. The sprocket was made of stronger metal alloys and sheathed in a more durable rubber casing. To provide a smoother ride, the suspension system was further refined. By 1939, it consisted of soldered axles and springs in protective metal jackets, which prevented ice accumulation and allowed the front skis to better absorb the shocks of hitting hard objects.

A remarkable transformation was now under way. His automobile garage was turning into a manufacturing operation, and Armand was evolving from a mechanic-inventor into an industrialist. A preliminary task for him in this regard was to put together a group of workers and train them in manufacturing. In the first tier of employees were members of his extended family: four brothers and three cousins.

Another important function was marketing—getting the word out on the new mode of transportation. Before delegating this function to his brother Alphonse, Armand handled it himself. He hired garage mechanics as sales agents, and took his B7 on trips around the province to demonstrate its abilities. A favorite tactic was to visit local newspapers to get coverage. It nearly always worked. The vehicles were such attention grabbers that the editor usually assigned a reporter immediately. A giant publicity coup was scored when Armand backed his B7 all the way up the lengthy toboggan slide near Le Château Frontenac in Quebec City just to prove it could go anywhere.

Armand's fast-growing enterprise was an all-consuming passion. He was totally absorbed, working 16 to 18 hours a day for six days of the week. Even on Sundays, the day of rest for a devout Roman Catholic such as Armand, he would sometimes put in a few hours of work after church. There never seemed to be enough time. A few precious seconds were saved each day by bounding up stairways three or four steps at a time. This constant state of agitation often left him sleepless at night, but rather than just laying there, he would slip down to the shop and get some more work done.

He was the kind of businessman who had to be involved in every aspect of his company. Juggling the jobs of president, chief engineer, and head of production over the next 25 years, Armand's frantic pace did not always result in the most enlightened human relations techniques when dealing with employees. He could be brusque with those who needed to have things explained at length or who did not accomplish tasks as quickly or as proficiently as he thought they should. He rarely offered praise or encouragement and preferred to impose his will to get a job done rather than engage in persuasion. Invariably, relationships with those around him were strained; employees usually felt a degree of anxiety in his presence.

Armand was such a perfectionist that it was hard for him to stand by and watch someone else putting together one of his machines. He would at times nudge workers aside from their machinery to show them how to produce better results. He was so concerned about getting things done the right way that he had an open-door policy whereby employees were free to come visit him anytime if they had a work-related problem. The result was a steady stream of visitors from the shop floor. Instead of thinking things through for themselves (and risk the disapproval of their boss), employees found it easier to go see Armand, even if their problems were sometimes minor.

Armand might be in the midst of discussing a legal matter with his lawyer or a tax issue with his accountant, but he would usually drop everything to accompany the employee back to the shop floor to provide a solution. The visitor would be left alone in his office until Armand would reappear, often with grease up to his elbows, to resume the conversation.

His accountant, Jacques Bélanger, recalled one meeting with Armand when he suddenly stopped the conversation and strode over to a dismantled engine on a table. Armand seemed to have a solution to a mechanical problem he had been mulling over, and wanted to deal with it then and there. He told Bélanger that he was going to take a piece for drilling. On the shop floor, he approached one of his employees and told him to drill two holes in different spots. As the shop worker slowly turned the piece over in his hand, Armand snatched it back and went over to the drill and did it himself. Back in his office a few minutes later, he fit the piece into the engine, turned the ignition, and smiled as the engine roared to life. He then shut it down and returned to his chair to resume his discussion with Bélanger, amid the gas fumes.

Yet Armand's impatient and looking over the shoulder management style worked. Despite a number of obstacles, his business flourished and produced affluence for him and his associates. A main ingredient was his ability to pick people who would be able to work with him; the fact that employees in key positions had family ties likely also helped.

Moreover, although they and other employees may have been on edge, they respected Armand because of his brilliance in mechanical matters. He had an inventive genius that supplied the firm with many successful products. But they also respected his drive and his devotion to work and excellence; he did not demand anything more of his workers than he demanded of himself. And Armand was aware of his effect on his employees, earning a degree of forgiveness from them by apologizing periodically for the nervous tension and fatigue that led to his abrupt style.

Armand was not by nature as austere a person as the workplace would suggest. In moments of leisure, he displayed a gentle and kind disposition. Then, he was also a more relaxed individual, fond of playing practical jokes on close acquaintances. For example, during a hunting trip—one of his few regular leisure activities—he came across a buddy who had fallen asleep on his watch for moose. Armand quietly crept up and tied a moose tail to the end of his rifle. Upon awakening, his friend jumped to his feet, startled by the dangling tail. A roar of laughter burst forth from Armand and his assembled comrades.

Armand's *modus operandi* was to some extent a reflection of the nature of his business. Production runs tended to be small and nonstandard. The many innovative products coming out of his fertile imagination also had to go down a learning curve before their technology was stabilized enough for production. It was not an easy environment in which to delegate and decentralize. Armand's business manner was also to some extent a result of the many crises thrown up by the constant flux of the business environment. Indeed, these external events at times threatened the very survival of the company, no doubt delivering anguish and stress to the founder. In fact, the pressures produced bouts of insomnia and left Armand in a continuous work mode.

The course of a commercial enterprise is fashioned by the complex interaction of interior and exterior contingencies. There are variables within the company that are under the control of entrepreneurs, but others in the external world are beyond their control. As such, each business is an uncertain ship cast upon the waters, headed for an unknown destination. The bow might be pointed toward some specific point, but unforeseen currents and storms may push the ship onto hidden reefs and rocky shoals.

Not surprisingly, the life of the entrepreneur is usually one of peaks and valleys. There is the potential for wealth and esteem, but there is also the chance for interminable periods of despair, culminating sometimes in collapse and resignation. Whether the down times turn out to be permanent depends on the interaction of a multitude of variables within a company and outside it. Entrepreneurs may improve their probabilities by gaining more competence over the internal variables, but ultimately, every commercial venture has an element of rolling the dice to it.

The case of Armand and his fledging business provides one of the better illustrations of this dynamic, except Armand somehow seemed destined to overcome anything in his path. His determination and ingenuity made him seem like a force of nature. None of the external variables proved capable of holding him back for long; there were no hurdles or setbacks that could extinguish his indomitable spirit.

The first setback came early on, just when everything was looking great. As the 1930s came to a close, demand for the B7 was taking off. While some Quebec streets in and around urban centers were cleared of snow during the winter by this time, these were the exception. Many main and secondary roads in the snow-belt region were left unplowed, creating a market for dependable snowmobiles. And with signs that the North American economy was finally recovering from the greatest depression of the twentieth century, the future looked bright for L'Auto-Neige Bombardier.

Demand was, in fact, outstripping the capacity of the Valcourt plant and annexes, leading to a decision to build a new, modern plant with an annual production capacity of 200 snowmobiles. As construction on the building went ahead, the development of the B12—a 12-passenger version of the B7—moved toward completion. By January of 1941, the new factory was complete, and Armand was on the verge of becoming a wealthy man.

However, just two weeks after the inauguration of the new facilities, the Canadian federal government issued wartime rationing regulations to redirect national production away from civilian needs toward military requirements. In this environment, Bombardier customers had to demonstrate to the Department of Munitions and Supply that a snowmobile was essential to their livelihood. Otherwise, they would not be granted the necessary permit to purchase a B7 or B12. Under these severe restrictions, production at Bombardier facilities dropped from 70 units in 1940-41 to 27 in 1942-43.

Thus, while valuable time was ticking away on his 17-year patents on the traction and suspension systems for snowmobiles, Armand had to find a way to merely survive for several years. He found this path by responding to the military's interest in vehicles for winter battlefields. Over the course of the war, Armand redesigned the B12 to serve as a troop carrier (called the B1 by army engineers) in Norway. In May 1943, he put the finishing touches on his ultimate military machine: the Mark I. It was an all-terrain vehicle equipped with a 150-horsepower Cadillac engine and two-meter-wide traction treads on either side, each wrapped around four wheels and the sprocket device. The machine was used for reconnaissance and haulage in the swamps of Italy and the South Pacific.

The contracts to produce Bombardier's war machines went mainly to larger companies capable of volume production on tight schedules, but Armand was put in charge of supervising the manufacturing at plants in Montreal. He would have preferred the contracts to go to his firm in Valcourt, but the military could not wait while his operations were refitted. Nevertheless, the Valcourt plant did get some prototype work and subcontracts for parts, which helped keep it to going during the war.

In his dealings with the government, Armand realized he would be in a better legal position if he incorporated his company. One benefit, for example, would be limited personal liability in the event business transactions went awry. Consequently, Armand incorporated a company under the name of L'Auto-Neige Bombardier Limitée on July 10, 1942. Authorized share capital was set at 3,000 shares. At the time, the only shareholders were Armand, Secretary-Treasurer Marie-Jeanne Dupaul, and Armand's brothers Alphonse, Léopold, and Gérard. Shortly afterward, Armand's oldest son, Germain, and an engineer, Roland Saint Pierre, became shareholders as well.

During the war, Armand was to experience a bitter disappointment. Having Canadian and US patents on technical innovations used in the B1 and B2 models, he expected to earn a stream of royalties as the vehicles were manufactured and put into service. But the Canadian military refused. After some wrangling, Armand's lawyer extracted a concession from the military to pay $2,000 to cover all past and future claims. Armand was outraged. He refused to accept the offer and seriously considered suing. But quite weary of the protracted dispute by this time, he just let it go.

After the war, controls were dismantled and business improved for Bombardier's Valcourt operations. By 1945-46, production had soared to 230 units, yet again stretching the plant's capacity. Customers had to wait weeks, sometime months, for delivery. So another decision was taken to expand. In 1947, a much larger assembly plant was opened, with an annual production capacity of 1,000 units.

Two new models helped fill the plant with work orders. The 12-passenger B12 was popular in public transport, freight hauling, mail delivery, and ambulance services. Over 1,500 were sold between 1945 and 1952. The C18, a larger version of the B12, was first used by school boards in Quebec's Eastern Townships to transport children to school during the winter.

It now looked as if Armand was finally on his way. In 1947-48, company sales reached $2.3 million, and profits went to $324,000. Once again, however, just when everything was looking rosy, Armand's company was dealt a severe blow. Actually, it was two hard knocks: 1) the winter of 1947-48 was virtually snowless in Quebec, and 2) the provincial government of Quebec passed a law that committed government authorities to keeping highways and local routes open to automobile traffic all winter. As a result, L'Auto-Neige Bombardier's sales dropped by 40 percent to $1.3 million in 1948-49.

The snow might return the next year, but so would the snow plows. It was a grave crisis, and something had to be done. Armand decided that salvation lay in the development of new products. He retreated to his newly built research center in Kingsbury, not far from Valcourt. He worked at a grueling pace developing a snow-clearing machine and then passenger vehicles (the C4 and B5) for traveling over asphalt, gravel, and snow. But he came up dry.

However, perhaps the greatest disappointment was the failed effort to realize his long-held dream of creating a light and rapid vehicle for carrying one or two persons over snow wherever it might be, on or off the road. The main obstacle had been the size of the engines then available—they were too heavy and unwieldy. So Armand set about trying to design a small one that was powerful enough to handle the job. By 1949, he had his engine built and used it in several trial runs in what was a forerunner to the Ski-Doo of the 1960s. But the prototype never went to market because the engine was deemed too complicated for mass production.

As the company fought to pay off suppliers and forestall layoffs, the mood at the plant became increasingly grim. Tensions arose among the shareholders over the proper course of action. Armand's fruitless research and the ongoing decline in the company finally led him to accept the advice of his doctor to leave the business in the hands of his brothers while he rested in Florida for a few weeks. When he returned, the situation was worse, but at least he was rested and ready to accept the challenge again. And to reassure creditors, he invested more of his own money into the company.

Armand was now fully aware that his business would remain precarious as long as it depended on the vagaries of snow conditions. He realized that his company would have to diversify, not only to get through the present crisis, but as an insurance policy to cope with future eventualities. A one-product enterprise might enjoy rapid growth for a time, but it was vulnerable to collapse if its market went through a downturn. Some stability would be brought to the firm if it could branch out to other product lines serving different markets. That way, a disruption in a particular product line would not become life threatening as it would be offset by other products in other markets.

He finally got a break in his search for new markets. One of his brothers, Théophile, had a tractor that was constantly getting stuck on soggy parts of his land. So he and another brother, Gérard, took up the challenge of improving its traction for all types of ground conditions. They added a wheel in between the rear and front wheels, and draped a track over it and the rear wheel. It was a simple solution, but it was very effective. Upon returning from his Florida vacation, Armand helped Gérard with further improvements, and the Tractor Tracking Attachment was soon ready for sale to farmers. It was an immediate hit and brought a revival in company sales.

Meanwhile, Armand pushed ahead with research into all-terrain vehicles for the mining, oil, and forestry industries. He went on trips to remote regions to observe transportation needs. This led to a remodeling of the B12 to create the BT, which had a small cabin at the front and a large platform for hauling logs and other cargo. There were other machines, but the biggest winner was the Muskeg Tractor, which first rolled off the assembly line in 1953.

The Muskeg was developed after Armand witnessed the need for more effective methods of transporting oil drills, seismographs, and other supplies over the snow and swamps of the recently discovered Leduc oil fields of Alberta. Use of the Muskeg gained broad acceptance in other resource industries as well as in the construction industry for the building of telephone lines, roads, railways, and other infrastructure in regions with difficult terrain. It also became an international success. It could be found, for example, cutting weeds on the banks of the Danube and clearing sand dunes from roads in the Sahara desert.

What made the Muskeg and Bombardier's other industrial machines possible were a couple of key inventions in the research labs in Kingsbury. One was the design of a new rubber vulcanizing machine that permitted the production of a seamless and shock-resistant track. The other was the invention of an unbreakable and warp-proof all-rubber sprocket. With these inventions, the problem of breakages in the track and sprocket were resolved. Durability for all-terrain travel was achieved.

Of all his industrial vehicles, Armand derived the most satisfaction from the Muskeg. "The Muskeg moves easily in muskeg where it would be dangerous for anyone to venture on foot. It is our greatest success." wrote Armand in a specifications note.[3] The introduction of the Muskeg began a very profitable period for Armand's company. In 1958-59, it helped earn profits of $825,000 on sales of $3.5 million. Armand was now a multimillionaire. He had outlasted a series of setbacks to finally reap the rewards of a persistent and inventive talent.

But his greatest success was still to come: the invention of a lightweight snowmobile called the Ski-Doo, which was able to take one or two persons virtually anywhere there was snow. Armand originally saw the machine as a replacement to the dogsleds used by trappers, prospectors, missionaries, and other persons in the North. However, it became much more than that. The affluent 1960s turned it into a hugely popular recreational vehicle.

By the late 1950s, engine technology had improved to the extent that small and efficient engines were viable. Some models had become available on the market, leading Armand and his son Germain to renew their efforts to design a small snowmobile. Also encouraging them in this direction was the invention by Armand's son of a seamless, wide caterpillar track. Following experiments with several prototypes, their first "miniature snowmobile" went on sale in the fall of 1959. The name originally assigned was Ski Dog, but a typographical error on brochures changed it to Ski-Doo. Armand thought this sounded better, so the accidental name stuck.

As the marketing and distribution network was built up, sales accelerated each year, from 225 in 1959-60 to 8,210 four years later. The rapid growth brought on successive waves of expansion and reorganization at the Valcourt facilities. In 1962-63, the appeal of the Ski-Doo model was enhanced with a major upgrade: a fiberglass cab and a more powerful engine.

The market could have absorbed many more Ski-Doos, such was the rage for them. If Armand had been a less conservative fellow, he might have boosted capacity even faster to keep up with the demand. But he had taken to heart the lessons learned from past shocks—government rationing in 1941 and provincial legislation in 1948 requiring the plowing of public roads in winter. He did not want to place all his eggs in one basket and become dependent on one product again. To chase the Ski-Doo euphoria would require diverting resources away from the industrial line and letting its significance dwindle. Prudence dictated a policy of balanced diversification. Accordingly, he slowed down promotion of the Ski-Doo to prevent it from overtaking company resources at the expense of other initiatives.

Unfortunately, Armand was not around to see how well his company would prosper throughout the remainder of the 1960s. By the time his persistent stomach pains were correctly diagnosed as cancer, it was too late. He died on February 18, 1964, at the age of 56. Nevertheless, he departed at the pinnacle of his career, leaving behind a thriving, robust business, with profits of $2 million on sales of $10 million in 1963-64. And the firm was ready to take on whatever misfortunes lurked ahead in the unfathomable external environment. The manufacturing of the Muskeg and other industrial vehicles provided a solid revenue flow, while the Ski-Doo offered superb growth potential.

An Excellent Ski-Doo Adventure

CHAPTER 2

"Bombardier was actually not a part of my career [plan]," Laurent Beaudoin once said. "I was an accountant and I thought that, at the most, I would make a successful career for myself as a management consultant in Quebec City. I never thought I would be running a company this size."[1] Thirty-five years after his unanticipated career change, Laurent is still with the company. For most of that time, he has been the leading executive.

He was born in 1938 in Laurier Station, near Quebec City. The only boy and youngest of six children, Laurent would sit fascinated for hours in the office of his father, a grocery wholesaler. After obtaining a Bachelor of Arts degree from Collège Sainte-Anne in Nova Scotia, Laurent enrolled in commerce at the Université de Sherbrooke, where he met and fell in love with another commerce student, Joseph-Armand Bombardier's second daughter,

Claire. After they married in 1959, she quit her studies to become a housewife, as was the custom in those days, while Laurent went on to get his master's degree in commerce and a chartered accountant designation. The couple established a household in Quebec City, and Laurent began the work of building up his management consulting practice.

Looking for customers, he asked his father-in-law to give him a chance to turn around an ailing sawmill in which he had invested earlier and was about to let go bankrupt. Getting permission to go ahead, Laurent studied the situation and found that the buying policies were wrong, wood was being wasted, and too many bad debts were piling up. Six months after Laurent restructured the operation, it was making a profit—for the first time in five years. Soon after this impressive performance, Laurent was invited to join Armand's company in 1963 as comptroller. Laurent and his wife then moved to Valcourt, Bombardier's headquarters at the time.

Laurent's arrival coincided with Armand's preparation for his succession. The planning actually began some time before, in 1954, when a holding company, Les Entreprises de J. Armand Bombardier Limitée, was created with his two sons and three daughters as shareholders. Armand's shares in Bombardier were put into the holding company, thus transferring the capital gains accruing after 1954 to his children. This maneuver, known in estate planning circles as an "asset freeze," would fix the value of his personal assets at their 1954 level, thereby putting a cap on the succession duties his heirs would have to pay.

Minimizing the tax burden and providing for the financial security of his wife and children were not his only concerns. Armand also wanted to ensure that his life's work would endure after his death. In the early 1960s, he stepped up his succession planning and consulted an advisor on how his company should be organized in order to increase its chances of flourishing without him. The advisor recommended separating the ownership and management functions—letting the Bombardier children own the shares but creating a board of directors comprised of independent experts.

The advisor thought this would be not only a more efficient arrangement, but would also help minimize the squabbles that often break out in a family firm at a time of intergenerational transfer. However, Armand did not like this solution. He believed in family-run firms. After all, four of his five brothers had worked with him in senior positions for many years. Consulting with his offspring, he found they too did not want the separation of ownership and administration. So it was ruled out. But, in his will, Armand did request that some seats on the board be given to independent experts as a way of enhancing the family's judgment and direction of the firm.

He had also discussed succession plans with his brothers and other minority shareholders in Bombardier but was unable to reach a compromise solution with them. As his health deteriorated in 1963, he solved the conundrum by buying back their shares. In this way, he would gain complete authority over the company and would be able to dispose of his estate as he saw fit. And his eldest son, Germain, would be able to step smoothly into the president's role, thereby providing more assurance that the firm would continue in the direction he thought it should go.

Germain had been in training for the part quite some time. He had been a vice president of the firm since 1956 and had worked loyally alongside his father as an innovator in the research lab. In addition, he served as the executive in charge of Rockland Accessories, the wholly owned subsidiary supplying vulcanized rubber to Bombardier.

Assisting Germain would be three brothers-in-law: Gaston Bissonnette (married to Janine), who was in charge of sales at the Valcourt plant and later vice president of research and development;

engineer Jean-Louis Fontaine (married to Huguette), who was vice president of production; and Laurent Beaudoin (married to Claire), who was comptroller in 1963 and became general manager around the time of Germain's appointment as president. Armand's youngest son, André, joined the executive ranks after 1965, following his university studies.

It was perhaps a good thing that Bombardier shares were not listed for trading on a stock exchange at the time. With the driving force of the company gone, investors might be forgiven for being less bullish about the company, especially when the average age of the new team was under 30 and a prime selection criterion was a family connection. In fact, short sellers—who sell borrowed shares in anticipation of a decline in their price— might have seen an opportunity to ply their trade. As Kathryn Staley states in her book, *The Art of Short Selling*,[2] one of the prime criteria for identifying a short-sale candidate is the presence of several related persons in the boardroom.

But the short sellers would have lost their shirts if had they bet against Bombardier. The arrangements Armand made for his succession proved to be enduring, although perhaps not quite in the way he would have anticipated. Notably, in 1966, two years after becoming president, Germain quit the company and sold his shares, citing health reasons. Laurent, in his late twenties, moved up to fill the president position, where for the next three-and-a-half decades, he would guide the company to its incredible success, albeit through some ups and downs along the way. The other brothers-in-law, Bissonnette and Fontaine, were to play important roles too, especially Fontaine, who was still listed as a corporate officer in the year 2000.

Thus, Armand's succession plan might be seen as both a success and a failure. His company would be controlled by the family and go on to prosper, but without his eldest son. Germain's upbringing was perhaps the weakest link in the plan. To prepare his eldest son for carrying on the family legacy, Armand had taken charge of Germain's education (leaving responsibility for the education of the other children to his wife). He brought to this task the same approach as he brought to the plant floor—a stern nature intolerant of weakness and direct in criticism. This discipline was said to be a cruel imposition on such a sensitive young man.[3]

Supporting this interpretation is a portrayal of Bombardier family life in *Bombardier*, the video movie released by Astral Video.[4] A telling scene shows Armand being curt with the young Germain and then being kind to his three daughters. Later, his wife reveals to Armand that Germain feels unappreciated. She advises him to give her son more favorable attention, but when Germain later brings Armand's shoes to him, he is ignored.

Nevertheless, Germain was a brilliant student, soaking up lessons on mechanics from his father. He became so good that he was his father's equal in the realm of technical discoveries, winning numerous patents. But this emphasis on mechanics and invention did not equip Germain particularly well for the management of a rapidly growing firm with over 700 employees. Bombardier was turning into a large corporation, which called for skills in other areas. Moreover, Armand had kept a tight reign on his company right up to his death. He did not bring Germain much into the decision-making process as a way to ease him into the leadership position. So when Armand died rather suddenly, the full weight of running the company fell all at once on the shoulders of his son.

In addition to these background factors, Germain's departure appears to have been triggered by a difference of views over company direction. Laurent had become concerned that Bombardier was not fully exploiting the potential of the Ski-Doo line. In his first year as comptroller, he had tried to persuade his father-in-law to engage in more publicity and promotion. Once, when Laurent suggested spending $35,000 to market the Ski-Doo, Armand exclaimed: "I could buy a house for that amount!"[5] Later, after Germain had taken over the top job, Laurent continued to press for an aggressive marketing and expansion strategy.

When questioned years later about Germain's departure, Laurent's explanation hinted that the parting had not been amicable: "Germain…didn't have the capacity to run a large company. We were doubling in size every year those days and he couldn't take it. By 1965, he didn't agree with our expansion plans so he sold his shares to the family."[6] On another occasion, Laurent again candidly revealed: "We were running too fast and the risks were too high. [Germain] had neither the nerve nor the capacity to run the organization."[7]

After leaving Bombardier, Germain starting spending most of his time in Florida. He also got involved in a Quebec rubber company, which almost went bankrupt in 1986. Following a lengthy illness, he died in January 1993 in Montreal at the age of 62. At the time of his passing, Bombardier issued a short press release; the *Financial Post* ran a five-sentence obit.

The younger Bombardier son, André, is still with the family firm as a member of the Board of Directors and vice chairman of public affairs.

Virtually from the moment he joined Bombardier, Laurent advocated a more aggressive promotion of the Ski-Doo. The company could grow much faster and make greater profits by shifting resources toward this product line. The industrial line of snowmobile products might wane in significance as a result, but it was the price to pay for a chance to tighten the company's grip on a booming market.

As comptroller, Laurent had managed to get the ball rolling. Seeking to promote the Ski-Doo to the wider North American market, he began looking around for an English advertising agency. He consulted with a Université de Sherbrooke marketing professor who had graduated from the University of Western Ontario. The professor referred Laurent to a fellow Western graduate, John Hethrington, who was then an executive with a Toronto-based advertising firm, Spitzer, Mills & Bates.

On Christmas Eve, Hethrington received a call from Laurent asking him to put together a television and magazine advertising campaign by January. Hethrington accepted the rush job and asked if he could try out some of the machines so that he could get a better understanding of the product. A day or two later, a truck pulled up outside his home and unloaded two Ski-Doos. Hethrington hopped aboard and thoroughly enjoyed himself skimming over the snow banks and darting through the fields. He was sold. Now he was ready to design a North American marketing campaign for the Ski-Doo.

The annual advertising budget was only $32,000 in the 1963-64 season, but it rose steadily until it hit $5 million by 1969-70. In the fall of 1966, the marketing campaign went into high gear when Hethrington joined Bombardier as vice president of marketing. Laurent liked to whimsically introduce Hethrington, the only English-speaking and Protestant executive on the management team, to others as "an Orangiste from Toronto."[8] Hethrington recalls that Laurent as a manager was "very detail oriented" and did not "like a lot of yakity yak."[9] He also remembers Laurent combining a sense of firmness with fairness in his dealings with subordinates.

In 1967, the company name was changed from L'Auto-Neige Bombardier Limitée to Bombardier Limitée, partly in recognition of the fact that Bombardier was emerging as a North American firm. Under that new name, two major advertising campaigns were mounted each year. The smaller one was a pre-season warm-up occurring during July and August. The second ran from October to mid-December and used prime-time spots on television, usually following the evening news or sports cast. Television was an excellent medium for demonstrating the fun of the Ski-Doos, but promotion through magazines produced the most direct inquiries. Full-page magazine ads appeared in mass-consumer publications such as *Life* and *Look* as well as in sporting periodicals such as *Outdoor Life*.

Another way to generate publicity for the Ski-Doo brand was through special events. For example, in 1966, with the help of Bombardier, Ralph Plaisted, an insurance salesman from Minneapolis, assembled a team (which included CBS reporter Charles Kuralt) for a Ski-Doo expedition to the North Pole. Warm weather, however, caused the ice to break up before their destination could be reached. Two years later, Plaisted tried again, this time bringing along Jean-Luc Bombardier, Armand's nephew. They left on four Ski-Doos in early March in -51 degrees Celsius (-60 degrees Fahrenheit) weather. At times, the travelers found themselves perched precariously on floating ice floes; rushing rivers forced them to make detours that nearly doubled the distance. Eventually, after 43 days, they reached their goal, becoming only the second expedition ever to reach the North Pole overland (the first was led by Robert Peary in 1909). Actually, as their arrival was confirmed by the US Air Force, the Plaisted group was the first *confirmed* surface trip to the top of the world.

The excitement was not to end there. With the spring thaw fast approaching, Plaisted and his team had to hurry back. On the return trip, they were confronted with open rivers, which they traversed by revving up their Ski-Doo engines and skimming across. When a fierce blizzard blew up, they had to huddle inside their tents for days. On the sixth day, the weather finally cleared, and the retreat ensued at top speed; slowing down risked breaking through thinning ice. Fortunately, before any major mishap was to occur, a ski plane spotted them and landed for the rescue. Some equipment had to be left behind, as author Carole Precious noted in her biography of Joseph-Armand Bombardier: "But there was only room on the plane for three of the Ski-Doos, so somewhere in the middle of the Arctic there is a Ski-Doo parked with the key in the ignition. If you find it, you are welcome to keep it!"[10]

In addition to special promotional feats, there were opportunities to promote Ski-Doos by entering them into snowmobile races, which were gaining popularity in the 1960s. There was a lot of media coverage to be captured by a good showing at any one of the bigger contests, such as the World's Championship Snow-mobile Derby at Eagle River in Wisconsin. In 1968, Bombardier scored some victories on this front after it introduced the verti-cal-twin Rotax 600 cc, the first engine its Austrian engine supplier had designed expressly for the Ski-Doo. The Ski-Doo model con-taining this engine was called the Track N' Trail (or TN'T) because it was designed to compete on the racetrack and be a hot per-former on the trail.

A small batch of machines was made available for the 1967-68 racing season. To keep the engines out of the hands of the competition as long as possible, Bombardier specified in letters to dealers that machines containing the special Rotax engines were to be used only for the duration of a racing event. The few enthu-siasts permitted to race, along with a small racing team from the factory, subsequently cleaned up in the unlimited class across North America. The first-place finishes paid off handsomely: the next season, the TN'T line was sold out before the snow was on the ground.

However, the dealer network was the crucial element in sell-ing Ski-Doos to customers. Laurent and Hethrington worked together setting up and strengthening approximately 18 regional distributorships, which in turn controlled over 2,000 dealerships spread across the North American snowbelt. Each year, a sales meeting was organized for the distributors in attractive locations such as West Yellowstone or the Schloss Fuch hotel in Austria (not far from where Bombardier's engine supplier was located). During the meetings, there were educational sessions, and distributors got to try out next year's models. After the distributors had placed their orders for the new models, they went back to their dealers and passed on what they had learned.

The dealerships were backed by year-round support. Their own marketing efforts were buttressed with media advertising campaigns from Bombardier. Servicing and repair functions were supported with manuals and technicians. To minimize its own indebtedness, Bombardier insisted on getting paid in cash when filling orders from the dealers. But the company also offered the dealers a finance plan that paid for their carrying charges on inventories held between July and November, a measure aimed at getting winter promotion under way early.

During the affluent and leisured 1960s, snowmobiling became very popular as a winter sport and recreational pastime. The snowmobile manufacturing industry experienced frenzied growth, with sales rising from a few hundred units in the 1960-61 season to 60,000 five years later, and to 500,000 units in 1971-72. The popularity of the Ski-Doo transformed Bombardier from a manufacturer of specialized equipment into a mass-market producer that doubled its output annually throughout the 1960s. Over the mania stage from 1965 to 1971, Bombardier's annual production soared from 23,000 units to 210,000 units. Its revenues jumped from $20 million to $183 million, and its profits from $3 million to $12 million.

The snowmobile market first emerged in the mid-1950s when Edgar Hetteen and coworkers at Polaris Industries Inc. of Roseau, Minnesota commenced making "motorized sleds" as a sideline to their farm machines. In the winter of 1955-56, Polaris sold five of its Sno Travelers. Sales rose to 75 the following winter and to more than 300 in 1957-58, the year the company initiated the development of a network of dealers to sell and service the machines.[11]

To promote the concept of snowmobiling to a wider audience, Hetteen and three others arranged a snowmobile expedition across Alaska in 1960. With the help of the Polaris distributor in Alaska, the party hopped aboard three snowmobiles in early March for a trek from Bethel to Fairbanks, a distance of over 1,600 kilometers (1,000 miles). The trip took 18 days and had several harrowing moments. At one point, the wind was so strong that it blew the snowmobiles sideways along a stretch of ice and over a 21-meter (70 foot) cliff into hip-deep snow. On another occasion, Hetteen's machine emitted a choking pop and died in the middle of nowhere. He took the machine apart in the howling wind and bitter cold to replace an electrical coil. When he cranked up his machine for a test, he accidentally dropped his hammer into the spinning flywheel, stripping out all of the cooling fins. For the rest of the trip, he traveled on a hope and a prayer that the machine would not overheat and die.

When Bombardier entered the snowmobile market in 1959, it quickly became the dominant manufacturer. As a result of the experience of making passenger snowmobiles and tracked vehicles over the 1940s and 1950s, the company was able to develop unparalleled mass-production facilities for the Ski-Doo. In addition, Bombardier's research and development team pioneered a new design that was good enough to become the industry standard: the lightweight, front-engine model. It opened the door to the recreational, mass-market possibilities for the snowmobile.

Most rival models at the time were aimed at the utilitarian market comprised of trappers and employees of conservation, forestry, telephone, and electrical companies. Arctic Cat's first product line, introduced in 1961, was a typical design. It had a tubular steel frame and a rear-mounted engine that putt-putted along at top speeds between 30 and 50 kilometers per hour (20 and 30 mph). The early models of Polaris Industries, for their part, were designed and tested on the flat terrain of Minnesota where snow conditions varied little because of constant cold. Thus, they were challenged whenever used in hilly terrain or sticky snow.

Both Arctic Cat and Polaris were to nonetheless rebound by redesigning their models along lines of the Ski-Doo and pioneering some of their own technological advances. Arctic Cat, for example, introduced the glide-rail suspension system that considerably smoothed out the bumps of a snowmobile ride, while Polaris developed a revolutionary clutch. Both companies were to suffer at times from cash flow problems and often had to scramble to stay afloat. Arctic Cat, for example, received a timely loan in 1964 from a US governmental agency, the Small Business Administration; Polaris became a subsidiary in 1968 of Textron Inc., based in Providence, Rhode Island.

One of Bombardier's first snowmobile models in the early 1960s was the Élan, a workhorse targeted at replacing the dogsleds used by trappers and other workers up North. It did not have a lot of speed, but it was rugged. When the model was phased out after some 30 years of production, a longtime trapper lamented its passing: "I was always amazed on a cold morning, when the only red in my thermometer was in the ball, to come out to the cabin and pull the rope on the Élan and have it come to life. The Rotax would fire once, bang! and then bang! bang! and then faster bang! bang! bang! until it was purring like a kitten."[12]

Once fired up, it could not be killed, a very welcome feature for journeys over vast expanses of unpopulated geography. And it was like a Model T in that it could be taken apart and put back together again with a couple of wrenches. Further, there were a few extra perks to ownership: "It was the only machine that got hot enough to cook breakfast on the muffler," said the old trapper. "More than once, I made coffee on the idling Rotax. On long rides home, I would stick my hands, one at a time, through holes cut in the cowling to warm them." [13]

One of Bombardier's most successful Ski-Doo models was the Olympique, introduced in 1964. The stylized design, with the distinctive bright yellow trim, took advantage of the increased speed and performance provided by the Austrian-made Rotax engine. When the Olympique was discontinued in 1979, over 265,000 units had been sold. Canada Post commemorated the model in a special stamp.

Another popular line in the early days was the Blizzard. The 1970 models were Bombardier's first attempts at building pure racers. A distinctive part of their appearance were the air openings in the center and on the sides of the hood. In the quest for speed in the 1970s, fan cooling of the engine was replaced by "free-air cooling." That is, outside air was ducted through large openings in the hood and directed to cooling fins cast into the cylinders of the engine. By eliminating the cooling fan, some power was freed up for propelling the sled.

While Bombardier's snowmobile product lines were big sellers in the 1960s, they might have enjoyed an even greater success. Low barriers to entry in the snowmobile manufacturing industry allowed many suppliers to flood onto the market and meet

demand. Armand's patents on the sprocket and traction system
had expired in the 1950s, and the patents he and his son managed to attach to the Ski-Doo in the late 1950s and early 1960s
covered only selected components such as vulcanized rubber
belts. With few legal obstacles and an uncomplicated technology, it was thus relatively easy to set up a manufacturing operation and churn out units. Nearly every small machine shop or
widget manufacturer, it seemed, was trying to launch their own
version. A large number of snowmobile makers were subsidiaries of firms from other industries such as marine products,
aircraft components, farm implements, garden-tool makers, and
even bicycle manufacturers. By the early 1970s, there were over
100 suppliers.

One of Bombardier's responses to growing competitive pressures was to intensify its strategy of vertical integration. Owning
suppliers was seen as a way of not only ensuring the quality of
components but also of protecting against shortages and higher
prices. In 1969, Bombardier acquired plastic-parts manufacturer
Les Plastiques LaSalle Inc. and fiberglass-parts manufacturer
Roski Ltée. Afterward, companies specializing in foam rubber
seats, precision metal tools, and chrome plating were added. Even
a textile plant was purchased to turn out a line of outdoor clothing for snowmobilers.

In 1970, the biggest in this series of acquisitions was completed: the purchase of the Austrian firm Lohnerwerke GmbH.
Bombardier had to purchase this Vienna-based manufacturer of
tramways as a way to gain control of its affiliate, Rotax-Werk
AG, the supplier of the two-stroke Rotax engines used in the
Ski-Doo. Once acquired, the affiliate was merged with Bombardier operations under the name of Bombardier-Rotax GmbH.
Bombardier intended to dispose of the tramway operations but
hung onto them pending an acceptable offer. The resulting experience of managing an enterprise in another industry was to have

considerable ramifications later on, providing a springboard for a crucial diversification of product lines.

Another way Bombardier responded to the forces of competition was through industry consolidation—buying up rivals. The Moto-Ski brand from Les Industries Bouchard Inc. was putting up some stiff competition, so Bombardier bought it out in 1971. This reduced pressures on operating margins and increased market share. It also gave Bombardier a new plant in La Pocatière, Quebec.

To help finance the program of vertical integration and industry consolidation, Bombardier listed shares for trading on the Toronto and Montreal Stock exchanges in early 1969. Two million Class A shares, representing about 15 percent of the equity, were offered by the family holding company, Les Entreprises de J. Armand Bombardier. The Class B shares held by the Bombardier family were convertible into the Class A, a feature that allowed the family to release at its discretion more shares from its holdings.

Over the 1960s and early 1970s, Bombardier had received takeover offers from several companies, including Chrysler and Outboard Marine Corp. The prices offered were attractive; Laurent and the Bombardier family could have become comfortable members of the leisure class. But they were determined to keep Bombardier an independent company, believing in its long-term prospects. They had other considerations too. One was a desire to honour Armand's dying wish to build an enduring edifice.

Around the time of the initial public offering, industry observers were quite optimistic about prospects for the snowmobile market in the years ahead. One 1970 market research study, extrapolating the penetration rate of the Quebec market (200 snowmobiles per 1,000 households) to the whole North American market, projected sales of 450,000 units for Bombardier in 1975 and revenues of $500 million.

The optimistic sentiment had also spread to the president of Bombardier. Laurent was part of a panel of high-level executives who were asked by the *Globe and Mail* what Canada would be like in the year 2000. His forecast was: " The snowmobile in the year 2000 AD will compete effectively with jet-powered automobiles, helicopters, and hovercraft. Some of the vehicles will have miniature jet engines and will run on an air cushion at speeds of up to 300 miles per hour [500 kilometers per hour]. Other models will run on solar cell batteries or nuclear fuel."[14] Such was the bullish sentiment at the peak of the snowmobile craze.

Bombardier had climbed aboard the snowmobile bandwagon to such an extent that by the early 1970s, 90 percent of its revenues were derived from the product. Being so heavily concentrated was a somewhat risky policy given the possibility of market saturation and the vagaries of winter weather. Moreover, it had invested in vertical integration to the point where 90 percent of components were made in-house, magnifying exposure to the overall trend in the market for snowmobiles. But Laurent did not seem overly worried about his company's focus. When questioned in 1970 about the dangers of locking onto one product, he drew attention to IBM, Xerox, Kodak, and Coca-Cola as examples of successful one-product companies.[15]

It was not as if he was against diversification. There were attempts in the late 1960s and early 1970s to launch camping and motorcycle products. In addition, following the purchase of patents from a US inventor, Laurent and designer Anselme (Sam) Lapointe led a team that developed a personal watercraft for scooting over the water, similar to the way the Ski-Doo scooted over snow. The main difference was the method of locomotion:

whereas the Ski-Doo used a belted track, the Sea-Doo was propelled forward by an intake mechanism that sucked in water and pumped it through the craft.

The Sea-Doo featured a sit down design, fiberglass construction, and handle bar steering. It had a top speed of 55 kilometers per hour (35 mph) and was able to reverse. This product would let Ski-Doo dealers stay open year round. As such, it would help offset some of the risks of selling a single product line and reduce dependence on winter conditions. To promote awareness, Laurent, Lapointe, and 10 others made the first long-distance personal watercraft tour, riding the vehicles from Montreal to New York City in 1969.

But the Sea-Doo product line was shelved in 1970 because of several problems. The flat hulls were good for smooth water but gave a rough ride over waves and prevented the Sea-Doo from turning quickly. The Rotax engines required more refinement for marine conditions, and parts of the Sea-Doo body were susceptible to corrosion. To fix these problems would require diverting resources away from the snowmobile line. The competitive battle in this core market called out loudly for more reinforcements, while the still uncertain potential of the Sea-Doo market did not.

Bombardier eventually did develop a successful Sea-Doo product line, but not until the 1980s. In 1986, Laurent asked his son Pierre and Sam Lapointe's son, Denys, to lead a team in a redesign of the watercraft. The fathers had developed the first generation, now the sons were going to develop the second generation. New technologies were applied to solve earlier problems, and an improved Sea-Doo was released to a more receptive market. It was a big hit and a major contributor to profits in the 1990s.

Despite the aborted debut of the Sea-Doo in the late 1960s, Laurent and Bombardier were in top form as they entered the 1970s riding a wave of seemingly insatiable demand for snowmobiles. The media hailed Laurent as a business superstar. He and his company were held up as models; analysts could find only good things in their strategies and actions. But that was not to last. By the middle of the 1970s, Bombardier was teetering on the edge of bankruptcy and Laurent had lost his exalted status.

3

Diversify or Die

The story of Bombardier in the 1970s is dominated by *forces majeures*. Economic upheaval, mild winters, and soaring energy costs dragged the company down during the first half of the decade. Political currents within a resurgent Quebec helped to pull it back up over the second half. Through the ups and downs, Laurent Beaudoin learned useful lessons on diversification, product innovation, and other matters —lessons that launched the Bombardier growth trajectory of the 1980s and 1990s.

An early trouble to beset Bombardier was the abandonment of the fixed exchange rate between the Canadian and US dollar. For most of the 1960s, the Canadian dollar was pegged at 92.5 cents US, but it was unhinged in 1970 and allowed to float upward as a way to curb inflationary pressures. The appreciation continued for about a year until a rough parity was reached. This higher exchange rate made it more difficult for Bombardier to export Ski-Doos to the United States market; it effectively levied a surcharge that had to be passed onto US customers or else absorbed as a cost.

The storm intensified over the next three years. Unemployment rose, culminating in a doubling of the rate to 8 percent. Inflation and interest rates also soared, topping out near 12 percent (as measured by the Consumer Price Index) and 10 percent (based on the 90-day rate on commercial paper), respectively. All in all, the economic turbulence made it not only difficult to manage a business of any sort, but harder for people to buy things such as snowmobiles.

Such were the macroeconomic aftershocks of the "guns and butter" spending policies of the US government in support of the Vietnam War and Great Society programs during the 1960s. The spending, financed in large part by printing excessive quantities of paper currency, lifted the North American economy on a warm tide of prosperity in the 1960s but then led to a deep-rooted inflationary problem that required stringent medicine in the next decade.

Those businesspersons who had taken the flood at its tide in the 1960s were, contrary to the words of Brutus in Shakespeare's *Julius Caesar*, no longer on a voyage toward fortune. Instead, like the individuals chided for missing their opportunity, they too seem destined for a life bound in the shallows and miseries. In fact, some of those who had been left behind because of their conservative disposition now appeared to be on higher ground. It seemed to be a time for the words of Euripides: "Chance fights ever on the side of the prudent."

A business venture is a delicate balance between the levers in the captain's hand and vast currents beyond. One day, the sun shines brightly and the waters have barely a distracting ripple; the levers work perfectly and guide the vessel to its destiny. On another day, howling gales whip the waves to the height of buildings, the captain's hand chafes at the wheel, and his vessel becomes a straw tossed about on the surface.

Bombardier had sailed into a furious storm, the kind produced by the collision of several weather fronts. One of those fronts was the topsy-turvy macroeconomic fluctuations. Another was meager snowfall over three successive winters. And then, the most damaging of all was the energy crisis. By 1973, the Organization of Petroleum Exporting Countries (OPEC) had gained sufficient control over the supply of oil to be able to impose an embargo and drive up fuel prices fourfold. Dependent upon gasoline for power, the Ski-Doo machines were hit hard.

In addition to these brute forces, Bombardier had to contend with the maturing of the snowmobile market, of which it had the largest share at over one-third. One hundred suppliers were in the midst of a mad rush to crank out snowmobiles just when consumers were getting their fill of the machines. Thus, the saturation phase of the market arrived concurrently with the other hard knocks. Some agonizing adjustments were in store for the industry and Bombardier.

Few manufacturers were to survive the shakeout: by the mid-1970s, the number had dwindled from 100 to six. Bombardier was one of the survivors, but just barely. An indication of the severity of the troubles was provided by the trend in the price of Bombardier's shares. After peaking at $23 in late 1969, it cascaded downward, reaching a low of $1.70 by the middle of 1973. Another indication of the gravity of the situation was the trend in snowmobile sales. Over the first four years of the 1970s, industry sales plunged from a peak of 500,000 to about 170,000 units; Bombardier's sales fell in tandem, plummeting from 226,000 to 60,000.

Inventories of snowmobiles piled up. Bombardier's own stocks went from 10 percent of sales in 1970 to 33 percent in 1974. Not helping any was a burgeoning market for secondhand snowmobiles, which was siphoning off orders from manufacturers. Not of any help either were government regulations that limited snowmobiles to areas away from highways, parks, and other locations. Price wars broke out, which intensified whenever a supplier exited the industry and dumped inventories at pennies on the dollar.

In this environment, Bombardier's profits eroded steadily to the break-even point (on sales of $151 million) by the fiscal year ending January 31, 1973, and to a net loss of $7.9 million (on sales of $132 million) in the following year. The stress showed up in the balance sheet too. Attempting to maintain its structure of operations along with a number of subsidiaries, debt accumulated. Over the first four years of the 1970s, bank loans jumped from $5 million to $37 million, while long-term debt climbed to $23 million. Interest payments rose to $6 million, a burden that would be hard to sustain as long as red ink flowed in the company's ledgers.

Watching the downward spiral into the abyss, analysts bemoaned the failure to diversify. One said: "The failure to diversify is...noted and is perhaps the most crucial [factor] of all... In other words, the problem with Bombardier is that it is as much committed to the snowmobile as ever."[1] A second asserted: "A major problem has been the failure to diversify...."[2] The marketing vice president for the Ski-Doo division was in agreement with this assessment but supplied the excuse that diversification had not been possible due to the exigencies of keeping up with the insatiable demand for snowmobiles.

The push into off-road motorcycles was acknowledged as a legitimate diversification effort but was deemed destined to fail since the market was highly competitive and already dominated by entrenched suppliers, mainly from Japan. Bombardier had a highly rated motorbike, but it cost more than comparable models. But even if it was the most attractive model overall, how would it help deal with the problem of escalating energy prices? Motorcycles were just as sensitive to gasoline prices as snowmobiles. As an analyst noted: "And try though it does, Bombardier's management seems to have the unfortunate habit of picking products vulnerable to rising gasoline costs and a possible slump in the purchase of leisure durables."[3]

Out of the trauma of the decade emerged several lessons that were to underpin Bombardier's incredible success over the 1980s and 1990s. That Laurent was able to learn these lessons and combine them with his business school training was a testament to his tenacity in the face of prolonged adversity. His experience evokes the words of the poet Horace: "Adversity has the effect of eliciting talents, which in prosperous circumstances would have lain dormant."

He may have owed some of his staying power to the fact he was linked to the firm's owners through family ties, but Laurent surely was also a person who had the nerve to bear up under difficult circumstances. He was the embodiment of the kind of person who Calvin Coolidge said would succeed because: "Nothing in this world can take the place of persistence. Talent will not; nothing is more common than unsuccessful people with talent. Genius will not; unrewarded genius is almost a proverb. Education will not; the world is full of educated derelicts. Persistence and determination alone are omnipotent."

A primary lesson Laurent took to heart, of course, was the value of diversification—of spreading risk over several product lines so that if one was to encounter a market disruption, the others could still carry the company forward. Joseph-Armand Bombardier knew well the value of diversification, but after his departure, the lure of the recreational snowmobile market had been too tempting for Bombardier to resist. To capture an exciting growth dynamic and deal with competitive pressures, it had concentrated nearly everything on the snowmobile.

But now, diversification was seen as the way to go. Product lines were to be like legs of a stool: three or four would provide the stability to withstand the vicissitudes of the external world. And although there would always be opportunities to diversify into new avenues, not just any would do. Various possibilities would have to be carefully examined to select those to which its skills could be applied. At the same time, a counterbalance to existing product lines would have to be provided. Thus, paradoxically it seemed, the diversified company would be pushing into new ventures, but, at the same time , it would still be sticking to its knitting.

There were several kinds of risk to hedge against. A very basic one was seasonal. The obvious solution was to make new products that could be sold at different times of the year. Another type of risk was the business cycle. The solution was to manufacture a collection of cyclical and non-cyclical products. One way to bring non-cyclical products into the portfolio would be to expand the customer base to include governments since they are less affected by business cycles and indeed, often choose to increase spending during downturns to help revive the economy. A third kind of risk was the maturing of product cycles. Protecting against this would require constant product development, a pipeline of initiatives in various stages of development; as growth in an existing product line slowed down, new products would be in the wings to pick up the slack.

Bombardier's own diversification program illustrates these concepts. As will be seen, it started an expansion in the mid-1970s into the manufacturing of subway and railway cars. In doing so, Bombardier was applying skills in the cutting, welding, and assembly of metal, which it gained earlier in the manufacturing of snowmobiles. Yet, the new field of endeavor provided a counterbalance to the snowmobile line. The popularity of subway and railway cars as forms of transportation could be expected to increase as energy prices rose, thus offsetting the impact on snowmobile sales. Moreover, as Bombardier was to find out, there would be less sensitivity to macroeconomic fluctuations since railway operators tended to be in the government sector and therefore enjoyed some immunity to business cycles.

In addition to the product mix, another consideration regarding diversification was the degree of vertical integration. To a certain extent, it is desirable to own suppliers of inputs as a way to obtain components that otherwise are unavailable or expensive to purchase. But extensive vertical integration increases the concentration on a single product and can make it more difficult for a firm to cope with market conditions, especially downturns. Reflecting back on his experience in the 1970s, Laurent observed: "You cannot react quickly enough, because as well as your main business, you have all these small ones that also have to be reorganized when their main customer gets into trouble."[4]

Bombardier's diversification drive was to address this issue. Over the late 1970s and early 1980s, many of the components and peripheral products produced in-house for the snowmobile line were shifted to outside producers. A big step occurred in 1983 when four plants making clothing, tracks, seat covers, and related items were sold to Camoplast Inc., a company formed by a group of former Bombardier employees. Afterward, Bombardier's in-house responsibilities were confined to making just the engine and the frame as well as controlling the key functions of final assembly, product development, and marketing and distribution. Everything else was outsourced.

Just as *forces majeures* can overwhelm the expertise at the core of a commercial enterprise, they can also align with those talents and help bring about a desired result. In the case of Bombardier, the effort to diversify got an assist from forces gathering on the political stage—in particular, the blossoming of nationalism within the province of Quebec.

In the early 1960s, Francophones made up 80 percent of the province's population but controlled only 26 percent of the financial institutions, 6.5 percent of the mining sector, and 22 percent of the manufacturing sector. To a certain extent, this concentration of ownership in the hands of an anglophone elite reflected cultural factors. Up until the early 1940s, Quebec was mostly an agrarian society under the influence of the Roman Catholic Church, an environment in which callings other than commerce were esteemed. For the best and brightest, it was an honor to be selected by the Jesuits or Holy Cross fathers for the *collèges classiques*, in which students would be trained for the priesthood or the professions of law and medicine.

But as Quebec evolved toward a more urban and secular society, Francophones increasingly began to feel that the anglophone business elite was an obstacle. For one thing, there was a tendency for the language of the workplace to be English, which made Francophones feel they were at a disadvantage in getting hired and promoted. Statistics confirmed their sentiments: in the early 1960s, nearly 80 percent of middle-level management positions were English speaking. If Francophones could not speak English, they would have to look outside the business world for work, or stay on the farm. (In the early 1960s, 91 percent of farmers in Quebec were French.)

Protest movements consequently started to gather momentum, several of which advocated the separation of Quebec from the rest of Canada. Some sought to radicalize the dialectic, and a rash of bombings put the citizens of Montreal on edge in the 1960s. The climax in extremist measures came in October 1970 when a British diplomat and a minister of the Quebec legislature were kidnapped and one was killed. In response, the federal government invoked the *War Measures Act* and sent the Canadian army into Quebec for several weeks.

While these outward manifestations of dissent underlined the need for change, the election of Jean Lesage as premier of Quebec in 1962 had already set the dynamic in motion. His election campaign slogan, "Maîtres Chez Nous [Masters of Our Own House]," neatly encapsulated what he and his Liberal Party were all about: the reclamation of the Quebec economy. A key plank in their platform, the nationalization of the hydroelectric industry, was carried out by natural resources minister René Lévesque who, in 1976, was to lead the separatist Parti Québécois to power in Quebec.

Lesage, with the assistance of economic advisor Jacques Parizeau (later to be finance minister in René Lévesque's government and then Quebec Premier), also set up two agencies that were to have far greater repercussions over the long run. The first to come was La Société générale de financement du Québec (SGF), an investment agency entrusted with a large pool of capital to encourage the development of francophone businesses. In its original incarnation, the SGF was financed half by the provincial government and half by the credit union, Mouvement Desjardins. But the credit union pulled out in 1973, leaving the agency entirely state run.

The second to come, in 1965, was the Caisse de dépôt et placement du Québec, the provincial pension fund set up as an alternative to the federal program, the Canada Pension Plan. Fueled by billions of dollars in pension fund contributions, the Caisse de dépôt became a powerful tool for strengthening francophone enterprise. It also functioned like a central bank in Quebec, buying up the bonds of the provincial government on occasion. For example, when Quebec bonds came under selling pressure because of a flare-up in separation fears following the 1976 election of the Parti Québécois, the Caisse de dépôt was there to buy up the unsold bonds and stabilize bond rates.

By the 1970s, these state run agencies had major stakes in many sectors of the Quebec economy. One of SGF's first investments was a 60 percent interest in the Marine Industries, a shipbuilding and turbine manufacturer. Another notable investment, however, was the formation of a steel company, Sidbec, which was an attempt to foster an indigenous steel industry to offset the influence of Ontario and foreign steel companies. As for the Caisse de dépôt, its vast holdings were put to use expanding many francophone businesses such as Provigo, a chain of grocery stores.

Within this environment of rising nationalism, the City of Montreal called for tenders in 1974 to provide more than 400 subway cars for its subway system, which city planners wanted to expand in order to handle an expected increase in traffic during the 1976 Olympic Games. Bombardier was invited to submit a bid to give some competition to Vickers Ltd., the British company that had supplied the rubber-tired rolling stock ordered in 1963.

At first, Laurent was not interested. But then he thought about what his company was trying to achieve: to diversify into another industry that would react differently to economic and energy crises. As Laurent said, "we wanted something that would be countercyclical to our existing product line."[5] Moreover, the company did have some experience in the mass transit sector as a result of the takeover of Austrian firm Lohnerwerke GmbH (to acquire its subsidiary making the Rotax engine). And it had the basic manufacturing skills—the machining, welding, and assembly of metal components—as a result of its snowmobile manufacturing operations.

Vickers had supplied the existing stock of subway cars under a license from the French manufacturer CIMT-Lorraine (later absorbed into the Alstom group). However, believing it could avoid royalty fees and handle the design work on its own, the company had let the CIMT-Lorraine license lapse. This gave Laurent his opening. Bombardier purchased the license and entered the bidding, positioning Bombardier as the supplier able to provide subway cars compatible with existing stock.

Among the benefits to the City of Montreal of having the same-design vehicles would be the scale economies of servicing and repairing the same make of cars. A main benefit to Bombardier was not having to invest in expensive research to develop new designs, allowing it to get product out faster and keep costs down. And instead of having to lay off people and close down the La Pocatière plant acquired in the takeover of Moto-Ski, Bombardier would be able to give a new mission to the facility.

Laurent was aware of the risk of jumping into a new industry. Although there were similarities in competencies, there was still enough of a difference to induce a feeling of uncertainty, accentuated by the fact that he was betting the company. The large project, which stipulated significant penalties for late or shoddy work, would easily put the company under in the event of a failure to perform. "But it was diversify or die."6

Under the leadership of the vice president of production, Jean-Louis Fontaine (married to Huguette Bombardier), a company task force was put together to prepare a bid. The team, backed up by technical specialists from CIMT, was comprised of staff who otherwise would have been laid off because of the downturn in the snowmobile business. In light of the risks and newness of the venture, as well as the desire to make it work for their own sake, the team members prepared thoroughly, studying every aspect of transit systems. Aided by their experience in the snowmobile manufacturing process, they costed everything in detail to make sure the company could offer a competitive bid and still make a profit.

The technical support staff from CIMT thought the cost of making the 423 subway cars would be no more than $70 million, but the Bombardier team's estimate was just over $100 million. So their estimates were rechecked. They still seemed right, so a bid of $118 million was submitted. Vickers came in with a slightly lower bid, but Bombardier still won. This provoked a controversy. With economic nationalism in the ascendancy in Quebec, it was easy for critics to allege political interference. But defenders of the deal argued that the Vickers bid was lower only because their costs were understated by including a coupling mechanism that did not meet specifications; when the appropriate component was included, the Vickers' bid exceeded Bombardier's by about $2 million.

For years, analysts told Bombardier it had to diversify. Now Laurent had taken a big step in that direction. Shortly after winning the subway contract, he made a trip to New York to tell his bankers the good news. Of course, at the time, the railway manufacturing industry did not enjoy a good reputation. Railways were losing business to planes and automobiles. Still, Laurent thought his bankers would be happy, if only because railway manufacturing seemed to have better prospects than snowmobiles. "The bankers were so pleased by what I told them," said Laurent, "that when I got back home, they sent me a letter telling me they were canceling my line of credit!"[7] The diversification was just too much of a risk for them. Laurent later found another bank in Quebec.

While winning the subway deal may or may not have stemmed from nationalist policies, Bombardier's next diversification move was more obviously assisted by government efforts. In 1975, Premier Robert Bourassa and his governing Liberal Party announced in the Quebec legislature that they had decided to move more toward a European-style industrial strategy of private and public cooperation.[8] Provincial government investments, supplemented with an estimated $1.5 billion from the federal government, went toward the creation of corporate giants in chosen sectors. At the top of the list were an aluminum smelter, forest products complex, and petrochemical facility. Bombardier was under consideration for a makeover into a transportation equipment powerhouse.

In early 1975, Les Entreprises de J. Armand Bombardier Limitée, the family holding company controlling Bombardier, made a successful offer—with support from the Caisse de dépôt and SGF—for the shares of Montreal-based MLW-Worthington Ltd. The company had been incorporated in 1902 under the name of Montreal Locomotive Works and had made over the years—with the technical assistance of its parent company American Locomotive Company (ALCO)—a succession of steam, diesel, and electric locomotives. When ALCO ceased locomotive production in 1969, the Canadian operations were purchased by another US company and renamed MLW-Worthington. Just a year before the takeover by Bombardier's holding company, MLW-Worthington sparked an outcry in Canada when the US government pressured its American owners to block the sale of Canadian-made locomotives to Cuba.

The acquisition of MLW-Worthington was deemed desirable for Bombardier in that it would deepen its reservoir of skills for the Montreal subway contract. It would also push Bombardier's diversification farther afield, into intercity rail transportation. Of particular interest in this regard was MLW-Worthington's development of the LRC (light, rapid, and comfortable) railcar, which looked like a promising growth opportunity. Highlighting the significance of the MLW-Worthington acquisition was the relocation of Bombardier's headquarters from Valcourt to Montreal.

The acquisition process was moved forward a few months later when Les Entreprises de J. Armand Bombardier Limitée sold slightly less than half of its MLW-Worthington shares to SGF, receiving an infusion of $6.8 million from the government investment agency. After this deal was finalized, the family holding company arranged a "reverse takeover" by exchanging shares in Bombardier for shares in MLW-Worthington. This cleared the final hurdle for merging the snowmobile and locomotive operations, creating a new entity named Bombardier-MLW Ltd. in August 1976 (but renamed Bombardier Inc. in June 1981). Jean-Claude Hébert, fresh from successfully turning around another company, was installed as chief executive officer to manage the new railway sideline, while Laurent concentrated on turning around the snowmobile unit.

The reverse takeover, by the way, explains a discrepancy in different accounts of the history of Bombardier. Technically speaking, Bombardier was acquired by MLW-Worthington and subsumed into that larger entity. But because the Bombardier holding company controlled the larger entity, it was, in spirit, a takeover by the snowmobile manufacturer. This explains why some accounts, including the official one from Bombardier, maintain that the birth of the company occurred when Bombardier was incorporated in 1942, while other accounts, such as the *Financial Post's* Historical Reports, say it occurred in 1902, the year MLW-Worthington was formed.

It is also worth noting that Bombardier nearly ended up in shipbuilding right after its entry into the locomotive industry. Bombardier made an offer for the 35 percent stake in Marine Industries Ltd. owned by the Simard family, with the intention of gaining full control through an exchange of Bombardier shares for the 60 percent block owned by SGF. However, the latter, perhaps not eager to have too many eggs in the Bombardier basket, held out for better terms. Unable to reach an agreement, SGF effectively scuttled the proposal by exercising its right of first refusal on the Simard holdings, purchasing a majority of the block at the same price Bombardier had offered.

In the short term, the diversification strategy was full of frustrations and disappointments. Like most other businesses in the turbulent 1970s, Bombardier encountered labor unrest as workers demanded higher wages to keep up with inflation. Work on the Montreal subway contract at the La Pocatière plant was halted for a while because of a strike. Bombardier managed to deliver some of the cars before the Olympic Games started in 1976, but it did not complete the order until 1978.

Labor strife at the locomotive operations in Montreal was much more pernicious, with lengthy strikes occurring in 1977 and 1979. The latter was quite bitter: nearly 1,000 members of the United Steelworkers of America were off the job for over six months. As the strike dragged on, Laurent announced that he would be compelled to move the Montreal operations elsewhere unless the dispute was settled. He accused the union of being manipulated by a small band of ideologues who were more interested in using Bombardier as a call to arms in the overthrow of the political and economic system. Eventually, an agreement was reached and the Montreal location was retained.

There was also some tension in the boardroom. With both Jean-Claude Hébert and Laurent in leadership positions, there seemed to be some ambiguity over who was in charge overall. Hébert, a businessman in his early 60s, had his ideas, and Laurent had his own. It would seem foolhardy for Hébert to challenge Laurent given his family connections, but Laurent's star was not exactly shining brightly after the slide of the 1970s. In any event, Hébert departed in 1978, leaving Laurent in full control.

In addition to the strife in the boardroom and on the labor front, there were some discouraging setbacks in the search for business. For example, in 1977, the Ontario government awarded a contract to build 190 Toronto streetcars to an Ontario firm even though Bombardier was the lowest bidder. The Ontario Transportation minister referred to a high unemployment rate in Ontario as the justification for disregarding normal tendering procedures. Jean-Pierre Goyer, then federal minister of Supply and Services, lambasted the Ontario decision as "playing into separatists' hands"[9] in Quebec.

Perhaps the biggest miss was the one in its home province, right after the premier of Quebec announced his government would favor made-in-Quebec products in its procurements. A $100 million contract to build 1,200 buses for various Quebec municipalities went to General Motors of Canada instead of Bombardier and its partner American Motors. The Bombardier team was thought to be the favorite because of the preferential purchasing policy and the fact that Bombardier had positioned itself for bus manufacturing by purchasing a half interest in an Irish bus manufacturer. Bombardier was also putting forward the appealing argument that it would be an agent for the transfer of bus technology to Quebec, whereas General Motors would just be doing final assembly work there.

But the General Motors victory was a case study in how a multinational corporation can overcome nationalistic purchasing policies. First, their bid was aided by a significant presence in Quebec: their automobile manufacturing plant set up many years before in Sainte-Thérèse employed close to 1,000. Second, as part of its bid, General Motors had committed to moving its Ontario bus assembly plant to Montreal, in which it would produce buses for the entire Canadian market, as well as spare parts for the North American market. Third, their buses would be $3.5 million cheaper, roomier by two more seats, and cost less than $3 million to operate over their lifespan. All in all, it was an offer hard to refuse. Unable to gain a toehold in this sector, Bombardier sold its interest in the Irish bus manufacturer a few years later.

Nevertheless, over the long term, the diversification efforts of the 1970s were a success. The Montreal subway contract allowed Bombardier to gain a body of expertise that was parlayed, as will be seen, into several more lucrative contracts in the mass transit equipment industry. And whereas existing manufacturers were trying to push their own designs or revolutionize mass transit with new techniques, Bombardier's orientation in the beginning within this market was to purchase the rights to known and proven technologies, then adapt or improve them for local markets. Market needs came first, and then the technology. Bombardier differentiated itself through marketing prowess and manufacturing proficiency instead of research and development. Only as the company gained depth in core competencies and amassed financial strength did it shift more toward substantive research and development.

In contrast to the success of the mass transit division, the locomotive divisions never did blossom for Bombardier. Soon after they were acquired, Laurent discovered a variety of problems. "We found out early in the game a bag of problems," he said. "Management, labor relations, equipment, engineering, service to the clientele, quality of product—you name it."[10]

In the mid-1980s, unable to win a sufficient number of contracts, production of freight locomotives was phased out, and several hundred workers were laid off. Further, after an initial round of orders for LRC passenger cars and locomotives failed to lead anywhere, Bombardier wound down the whole sideline. The acquisition of MLW-Worthington was hence a comparative failure, burdening the company with years of losses that were only offset by a much bigger success on the subway car operations.

One reason for the setback was leaping into the MLW-Worthington deal too quickly, without adequate investigation. Perhaps, if Bombardier had known what a bag of snakes it was acquiring, it would have bargained for better terms or simply gone somewhere else. A second reason was that Bombardier had entered a market with two well-entrenched suppliers: the loco-motive divisions of General Motors and General Electric. It was not a niche market.

This was a misstep from which Laurent learned lessons. He was to apply them and others learned from the 1970s to the building of the Bombardier empire over the 1980s and beyond. One of the lessons was the value of positioning a company to assist local and national governments in achieving their social and economic objectives. There was more to business than mak-ing good products at reasonable prices; there was also ground to be gained from being able to provide solutions to the challenges facing public institutions.

Up until the early 1970s, Bombardier was focused solely on getting consumers to buy snowmobiles. But by the late 1970s, it was also aware of the benefits of becoming an agent for technol-ogy transfer, job creation, industrialization, and other socioeco-nomic goals. In so offering to address the various needs of governments, Bombardier would be promoting its own diversi-fication agenda and entering into projects capable of offsetting the ups and downs of business cycles. Little illustrates this bet-ter than the giant contract Bombardier won in 1982 to build sev-eral hundred subway cars for New York City.

4

CHAPTER

A Breakthrough Deal

It was one of the most gratifying moments of Laurent Beaudoin's business life. On May 18, 1982, the Metropolitan Transit Authority (MTA) of New York City gave Bombardier a letter of intent to purchase 825 subway cars at a total price of $1 billion. The deal provided a huge validation of his corporate strategy of diversification. Bombardier would be kept busy during the recessionary period of 1982-83. There would be no repeat of the agony and near collapse of the mid-1970s.

It was also a shining moment for Laurent because his company was now taking its first steps into the big leagues. The work experience to come would make Bombardier even more expert in its field, and the higher profile would bring in more contracts. Furthermore, the profits garnered over the next several years would support expansion into new growth areas, allowing the company to become what it is today: a global giant in the transportation equipment manufacturing industry.

Laurent surely felt a tinge of pride in knowing that the deal was (at the time) the largest order in the history of the mass transit industry and would set a record for the largest export sale by a Canadian manufacturer. And then there were the tangible benefits of creating thousands of skilled, high-paying jobs when unemployment was at highs not seen in decades. It was a very welcome achievement for the company, Quebec, and Canada.

To win the order for the "graffiti-resistant" stainless steel subway cars, Bombardier beat out two other big rivals: French consortium Francorail and Michigan-based Budd Co. (owned by a West German corporation). The latter's bid had been slightly lower than Bombardier's, but its offer included contractual terms (special pieces of equipment) that effectively raised the cost above Bombardier's, according to Richard Ravitch, chairman of the MTA.

Under the terms of the contract to be signed, the cars would be delivered in stages over the next five years, and they would be based on designs licensed from Kawasaki Heavy Industries Ltd. of Japan. As well, to help the MTA pay for the order, the Export Development Corp. (EDC) would give the MTA a loan equal to 85 percent of the order. Lastly, Bombardier would agree to do 60 percent of the work in Canada and 40 percent in the United States.

Winning the deal had been a lengthy and arduous process. On signing the agreement in the early hours of May 18, the exhausted negotiators—Laurent, Ravitch, and others—filed out of the MTA's building in New York, too tired to think of little more than celebrating with some coffee and sandwiches at a neighboring all-night diner. People passing by saw a group of men huddled together at a table in the bright light of the nearly empty eatery. They might have thought the group were old buddies gathered for a bite after their weekly poker game.

The chain of events that led to this scene commenced several months earlier when the MTA had called for tenders on a smaller order of 325 subway cars. Kawasaki won that contract over the only other bidder, Budd. (Bombardier did not participate, perhaps believing that it did not stand much of a chance at that time.) But during the bidding process, Ravitch had become dissatisfied. He felt the prices offered by Kawasaki and Budd had been too high; perhaps there was some implicit collusion? But there was nothing he could do to bring the prices down. His only option was to accept one of them or else reject both. So he accepted Kawasaki's, the better of the two.

For the upcoming order of 825 subway cars, Ravitch figured he could do better. He lobbied the state government in October to alter legislation defining MTA's role. Specifically, he asked for and obtained a change that would permit negotiations with bidders, rather than just passively accepting or rejecting their bids. If the MTA could be more active in bargaining with suppliers, a better deal might be arranged for taxpayers.

He then encouraged other suppliers to come forward and make proposals for the second, much larger order. One company so encouraged was Pullman Co., but it refused. Francorail entered the bidding, as did Budd. Kawasaki did not, discouraged in part by the opposition of US unions after winning the first order. The early 1980s were a time of high trade friction between Japan and the United States, and both Kawasaki and the MTA feared the reaction that would follow if Kawasaki won again.

By the early 1980s, Bombardier had emerged as a force within the mass transit industry. The experience of building the Montreal subway cars had given it the basis for winning deals in several US locations. One of these, signed with New Jersey transit authorities, introduced Bombardier's work to the MTA, which took six of Bombardier's cars as part of a joint agreement with its neighboring transit system. Bombardier consequently received an invitation from MTA to bid in the second round.

In November, Bombardier's vice president of marketing for mass transit, Carl Mawby, traveled to meet with Ravitch in New York. He wanted to know what kind of facilities and expertise Bombardier possessed and if they were up to handling such a big job. Mawby responded with an invitation to visit their railcar plant in La Pocatière. Early the next month, a vice chairman and senior engineer from MTA flew to the village of 5,000, some 135 kilometers (85 miles) down the St. Lawrence River from Quebec City. Flying in over the vast expanse of snowy fields and clumps of dense bush, the two must have had their doubts momentarily. If so, they melted away when, their breath leaving trails of vapor in the cold winter air, the pair walked through the front door. Inside, they would never have guessed that just a few years before, the plant was rolling snowmobiles out the door. It was now a full-scale operation for the production of mass transit vehicles.

On their return to New York, the vice chairman and senior engineer gave Bombardier high marks. An invitation to further discussions was extended, and in late December, Laurent flew down to have dinner with Ravitch. Laurent did not act like someone salivating at the prospect of snaring a billion dollars; he did not rush to promise the moon. Instead, he straightforwardly told Ravitch that his company could not meet the MTA's deadlines if it had to design the subway cars from scratch. The only way it could do so was if Bombardier licensed the designs from another company, in particular Kawasaki.

Ravitch liked Laurent's candid and honest manner and what he heard. He knew the Japanese design was good, and the commonality with the 325 cars already on order from Kawasaki would have the benefit of keeping the MTA's training and maintenance costs down. Things were starting to look good for Bombardier. Compared to rival bidders, the company was displaying a greater awareness and ability to respond to the MTA's needs while, at the same time, moving toward a deliverable solution.

Around the same time, the federal government of Canada was becoming active behind the scenes, motivated by dire domestic conditions. On the one hand, there was double-digit unemployment, and on the other, there was the threat of Quebec separation posed by the election of the Parti Québécois. Bombardier itself was unhappy with losing bids for contracts in the provinces of Ontario and British Columbia for what seemed to be political reasons. Winning the New York contract would therefore show Bombardier and Quebecers the advantages of remaining within the federation, while helping to alleviate the unemployment situation.

Trade Minister Ed Lumley and Consular General Ken Taylor (of the Iran hostages fame) were the federal government's point men. Taylor was the Canadian diplomat on the spot in New York City keeping the Canadian government informed on the details of the commercial opportunity. Lumley was active behind the scenes in negotiations with Kawasaki to obtain the license to manufacture their designs, which was secured by December. Lumley also helped set in motion the loan from the EDC for 85 percent of the purchase price. This loan would be very attractive to the MTA since US cities were no longer eligible for federal financial assistance to upgrade public infrastructure. President Reagan, under pressure to rein in the US government's ballooning deficit, had cut off the loans early in his first term.

Bombardier submitted its proposal to the MTA in early March. A round of 25 to 30 meetings followed in which teams of engineers, lawyers, and managers pored over the MTA's specifications. Raymond Royer, president of Bombardier's mass transit division, remarked that the specifications were as thick as a Bible and contained a few unusual requirements such as doors that had to close airtight. Some of these unusual requirements were simply not possible, Royer had to tell the MTA.

In the final two weeks, Bombardier staff operated out of a "war room" in a suite of rooms on the 42nd floor of the New York Hilton Hotel, a dozen blocks away from the MTA headquarters on Madison Avenue. Ravitch and MTA officials let Laurent and Royer know that the Budd submission was no longer under serious consideration but that the one from Francorail was still on the table because of some attractive financing offered by the French export development agency. A guarantee was therefore made by the Canadian side that the Canadian EDC would match the French financing, resulting in the offer of an interest rate of 9.7 percent, 4 percentage points below what the MTA could get in the open market. This last commitment tipped the scales in favor of Bombardier and led to the signing of the letter of intent.

News of the victory brought a mixed reaction in Canada. Parti Québécois politicians gave rare praise to the federal government. For example, Rodrigue Biron, the minister for Quebec Industry, Commerce, and Tourism said: "...for sure they do some good things sometimes."[1] But the minister for Economic Development, Bernard Landry, was less effusive. "It's only normal," he said, "that ... we get some economic money coming from Ottawa to Quebec because it's our tax money."[2]

At the federal level, members of the official opposition party, the Progressive Conservatives, downplayed the breakthrough. They criticized the government for giving New York City an interest rate subsidy while refusing to give VIA, the government-owned national railway, any funds to improve its eroding service. They also pressed the government to make the same low interest rate loans available domestically to businesses and farmers.

Elsewhere, the reaction had negative overtones as well. The chairman of the transit commission in a western province sent a letter to a Vancouver newspaper deploring what he saw as a misallocation of resources. "What do we Canadians get in return?" he demanded. "A thousand jobs in the Montreal area building Japanese-designed subway cars. Domestic content about 60 percent. Fewer Canadian jobs than in building homes or hospitals and the like."[3]

Some members of the Canadian business community had complaints too. The president of the aerospace firm CAE Industries Ltd., for example, lamented using concessionary export financing in the markets of a fair-trading country. "The irony is that the US government itself does not make available this kind of subsidized predatory financing to its own industry,"[4] he stated. Moreover, he added, the generosity toward Bombardier came at a time when other Canadian companies were experiencing increasing difficulty obtaining adequate financing from EDC for their exports.

Laurent could not help stepping into the fray to explain the rationale behind the EDC loan. He declared at Bombardier's annual meeting in June 1982: "...the only thing the Canadian government did was match the financing offered by the French ...we've been losing contracts all over the world because of the French financing, and the Canadian government, for once, I think, did something right."[5]

But the most negative reaction of all came from the United States. In fact, spearheaded by rival Budd, it was quite vociferous. The actions of the latter and other parties at times threatened to kill off Bombardier's "deal of the century." Over the next nine months of legal challenges, it was a cliff-hanger whether or not the deal would hold up. Indeed, at one point, observers gave Bombardier less than a fifty-fifty chance of coming through.

To put it simply, jilted Budd was furious and on the warpath. The company felt it should have won the contract because it was the lowest bidder and would do 80 percent of the work in the US, as opposed to Bombardier's 40 percent. Moreover, it claimed,

Bombardier had received the benefit of a supposedly illegal interest rate subsidy from the EDC. According to international arrangements within the General Agreement on Tariffs and Trade (GATT) and Organization for Economic Cooperation and Development (OECD) at the time, the lowest interest rate allowed on such export development loans was 11.25 percent. Canada, a signatory, appeared now to be in violation of the agreement.

Budd launched a two-pronged attack. First, it initiated a court action seeking an injunction against awarding the contract to Bombardier while it applied to the US Export-Import Bank to obtain financing similar to what the EDC was offering. (In 1976, Congress passed legislation allowing the Export-Import Bank to provide offsetting financing when foreign firms were backed by favorable financing.) Second, Budd, along with US labor unions, petitioned the US Commerce Department and other government agencies to impose countervailing duties on Bombardier equal to the estimated interest rate subsidy.

On June 10, the MTA and Bombardier went ahead and signed the final purchase agreement, but with a clause that would allow cancellation in the event Budd was to receive offsetting financing from the US government. A few days later, the MTA and Bombardier agreed out of court with Budd that should the latter win offsetting financing, the MTA would vote on exercising its option to cancel the deal with Bombardier and renegotiate with Budd.

While awaiting the ruling on financing, US Trade Representative William Brock referred the illegal subsidy issue to the dispute settlement mechanism of GATT, a process that would take several months but which could sanction the levying of countervailing duties. Responding to the action, Canada's Trade Minister Lumley said he felt confident Canada would not be found in contravention of GATT rules because subclauses permitted the use of cut-rate financing to match other cut-rate packages.

Officials at the MTA did not sit on the sidelines as the challenges mounted. They actively lobbied in favor of the deal they
had just struck with Bombardier. At a meeting of the US Senate
financial committee, Ravitch defended the contract as taking to
heart the words of President Reagan who said not to depend
upon Uncle Sam for financial assistance, but to go out and get the
best deal they could on their own. "If the contract is not consistent with his policy, then let him say so,"[6] challenged the angry
chairman of the MTA.

And to US Treasury Department officials examining Budd's
application before the US Export-Import Bank, officials from the
MTA declared that Bombardier won the contract not just because
of attractive financing. They were also concerned about the ability of Budd to deliver acceptable cars within the time frames proposed. On previous orders, the MTA had found that several of
Budd's cars had developed mechanical problems. Bombardier,
with its licensing of Japanese designs, was seen as offering more
assurances of quality.

On July 13 Treasury Secretary Donald Regan concurred with
these and other arguments. As grounds for his department's decision not to award Budd any financing under the Export-Import
Bank, he conceded that noncompetitive financing had not been
the determining factor behind the MTA choice of Bombardier.
Their investigations had indicated that after adjusting for contractual terms, the Canadian bid was superior on price, delivery
schedules, and engineering. In addition, it was superior in terms
of providing work in the state of New York. (Budd had committed to purchase components worth $79 million US from New
York suppliers, compared to Bombardier's commitment to purchase $104 million US.)

This was a significant coup for Bombardier. Not only had a
major hurdle been cleared, but the judgment indicated to the
world that there was a lot more to Bombardier than government

support. It was a first-class manufacturing operation able to compete with the big players, providing quality products in a timely fashion.

However, the judgment did seem to imply that Canadian officials may have been manipulated by MTA representatives into providing a greater break on financing than required. According to the Treasury Department's report, MTA officials apparently played off the Canadian and French bids against each other: "It is clear that the French financial competition was never as severe as the Canadians believed and that more scrupulous attention to the exchange of Telex information with French authorities could have resulted in Canadian financing at no more favorable terms and conditions than those specified by the GATT arrangement."[7] But an interview with Lumley in 2001 suggests this conclusion was for public consumption; he emphasized that he had concrete evidence of a lending rate close to 9.7 percent from the French side.[8]

In any event, Bombardier was not yet out of the woods. Investigations were still in progress to determine if the deal with MTA was actionable under countervailing duty laws. It was thought that the finding of the Treasury Department reduced the chances of an adverse outcome since it established that the subsidies had not been the cause of injury to the US mass transit industry. The next week, however, the Commerce Department found that Budd's petition for countervailing duties warranted further investigation and forwarded the case to the next stage: investigation by the International Trade Commission (ITC) in Washington to determine the existence of material or potential harm to US industry.

On November 15, the final agreement for the EDC loan, consisting of more than $750 million, was signed by officials from the MTA, the Canadian government, and Bombardier. Ironically, by this time, commercial interest rates had fallen to be very nearly equal to the subsidized rate agreed upon several months earlier.

This meant that New York was not getting any subsidy on the loan after all. And it meant a vindication for Canadian government officials, whose bold move, along with Bombardier's, now appeared to be farsighted (or perhaps a stroke of good fortune). In the end, the EDC was to make a profit on its loan to New York City.

Still, ongoing investigations in the United States into countervailing duties were proceeding on the basis of the historical data, the actual subsidy offered back in May. Shortly after the EDC loan was signed off, the US Commerce Department announced their estimate of the subsidy (and consequently the size of the countervailing duties): $137 million US (later reduced to $91 million US). Now, all that remained before imposing the fine was a ruling from the ITC whether or not material damage had occurred to US industry.

Having perceived the possibility of such penalties, lawyers for Bombardier had astutely included a clause in the agreement with the MTA, making the New Yorkers liable. This made it far less attractive politically to impose the charges since Americans would be the ones hurt, not foreign citizens. Before the ITC could issue its ruling, a flurry of behind the scenes negotiations took place to find a way out that would not punish the Big Apple.

On February 10, 1983, Budd withdrew its petition, and fellow petitioner, the AFL-CIO, was ruled ineligible. The latter tried to resubmit its application, but the next day, it settled for a compromise solution, which involved the MTA taking out newspaper advertisements stressing a commitment to supporting US labor and industry, and promising to adhere to the 50 percent US content requirement of the *Buy America Act* on future purchases over the next five years (which turned out to be 90 commuter cars).

Thus, the ITC never did rule on whether or not US industry had been harmed, and multimillion dollar duties were never imposed. All the obstacles had been cleared some nine months after the deal was announced. Laurent and Bombardier, after some nail-biting twists and turns, could breathe a sigh of relief.

One obvious contribution to Bombardier's success was the maneuvering of Trade Minister Lumley and other Canadian government officials to assist Bombardier with securing the deal. Another was Bombardier's own attention to detail and smart legal footwork to make the MTA responsible for paying any possible countervailing duties. But behind these immediate factors was the Bombardier business model.

Eschewing research and development in favor of focusing on efficient manufacturing and marketing, Bombardier had the flexibility and orientation to put together solutions that met the needs of customers better than their rivals. There was no huge investment of time and resources in new products to be pushed onto the market. Instead, attention was directed to researching customers thoroughly, then licensing and adapting manufacturing designs to their requirements.

"We research the heck out of prospective clients...and by the end of the preparation procedure, we know as much about the client's needs as the client does,"[9] Royer told a reporter. Between the time a transit authority decides to upgrade its subway and the calling of tenders, there is usually a span of several years. During this period, Bombardier sends its people to be with the potential client as well as to offer whatever technical advice needed. Full-time staff are also assigned to gather intelligence on developments and trends within individual states.

Some critics deplored Bombardier's lack of research and development, but it was a necessary part of the winning formula. It kept costs down and avoided several risks. One was developing new products that did not fulfill market needs. A second was missing market opportunities because of the long lead times required. For a newcomer such as Bombardier, the best way to enter the market quickly was through licensing technologies and often improving upon them. It would be foolhardy to take on directly the well-financed research and development capabilities of entrenched members of the industry.

So Bombardier differentiated itself through a focus on flexible manufacturing and marketing, an emphasis that was enjoying considerable success by the time the New York contract was won. Only two of the six previous mass transit projects on which Bombardier tendered had been lost. By the time Bombardier was ready to start on the New York deal, work was nearing completion on three other contracts worth several hundred million dollars in New Jersey, Chicago, and Portland. A large contract with Mexico City, worth several hundred million dollars, was just wrapping up as well.

This track record was turning into quite an achievement. Most other North American firms in mass transit equipment manufacturing had withered away in what was thought to be a declining industry. Bombardier was not only surviving as a North America entity, but it was emerging as a growth company, beating out Japanese and European rivals that had amassed formidable expertise because of the greater population densities and government support within their home markets.

The decision to expand into mass transit equipment was now paying off big time. While snowmobiles were highly sensitive to the business cycle, mass transit vehicles were largely immune, depending more on the needs of city governments to replace dilapidated stocks of subway and commuter train cars. As such, the steady flow of orders from the mass transit side was allowing Bombardier to avoid a replay of the calamities of the 1970s.

For the fiscal year ending January 31, 1983, the company's earnings stood at $6 million ($1.12 per share) on sales of $551 million. Meanwhile, nearly all other firms in North America were piling up losses in the midst of a severe recession. Attribute this performance to Laurent's strategy of diversification and manufacturing under license, but credit also the team at Bombardier that carried through on the execution. Led by the president of the mass transit division, Raymond Royer, they undertook and successfully completed a Herculean task: supplying New York City and many other metropolitan areas with thousands of subway cars. How did they do it?

5

Making Sub-way Cars the Bombardier Way

To illustrate his approach to management, Raymond Royer, president of Bombardier's mass transit division in the 1970s and 1980s, once told a story about evaluating a candidate for a management position. Early on in the interview process, the candidate had mentioned that his heavy beard was an integral part of his identity. Toward the end of the evaluation, Royer said he would be prepared to make an attractive offer if the candidate would shave off his beard. When the applicant heard this, he told Royer to forget it; he was going to withdraw his application. As soon as Royer heard this response, he knew he had found his man. He was hired, whiskers and all.

This story is an illustration of the importance Royer attached to a having a set of values, beliefs, and principles in the management team of a corporation. Technical know-how and skills of leadership, communication, motivation, and control were important, but there was more beside these qualifications. By asking the bearded applicant to get rid of his facial hair, he was testing the applicant's honesty and integrity—his willingness to say what he thought and to fight for his beliefs. He did not want to hire someone whose word varied according to time or place. These were not qualities that would help create a bond with employees or with his superiors, for that matter.

Royer was brought into Bombardier in 1974 to build up the mass transit division. Previously, he had been a vice president at a rival snowmobile firm, Skiroule Ltd. Its US owner had decided to shut down the operation when the snowmobile market collapsed in the mid-1970s. Before joining Skiroule, he had prepared for the business world by getting several degrees: Master of Commerce, Bachelor of Civil Law, and Master of Accountancy. The latter was obtained at the University of Sherbrooke, Laurent Beaudoin's alma mater.

Three years younger than Laurent, he would become, with his boss, the driving force behind the spectacular success of Bombardier's mass transit division. The two were a dynamic duo whose styles complemented each other. "Mr. Beaudoin makes decisions very quickly while Mr. Royer is more of a long-term planner," said a colleague.[1] In 1985, in recognition of his achievements and abilities, Laurent promoted Royer to president and chief operating officer.

The task of setting up the mass transit division back in 1974 required the conversion of the La Pocatière snowmobile plant to railcar production. The skills of the factory workers—metal cutting, welding, and assembly—could, to some extent, be transferred over to the new product line, but there were still considerable differences in manufacturing processes to require extensive training of employees. A local school was purchased and converted into a training center. Hundreds of new people had to be hired, as well. Royer, for his part, had to fill the 21 managerial boxes drawn in at the top of his organizational chart.

Later, in explaining Bombardier's success, Royer was to declare: "One of the important keys to Bombardier's success is the clearly defined criteria on which our future managers are selected."[2] Those criteria had three dimensions:

1. technical knowledge and experience,
2. management abilities, and
3. basic qualities and values.

The latter dimension was so important to Royer that he preferred to describe his management philosophy as "Management by Commitment." In other words, it was crucial for management to commit to a set of core values, beliefs, and principles in the treatment of employees, which consisted of the following:

- creativity and entrepreneurship—the drive to search for new ideas and opportunities
- honesty and integrity—the propensity to say what one feels, and to refuse to comprise on fundamental beliefs
- thoroughness and discipline—possessing a spirit of precision in words and actions
- perseverance and determination—a disinclination to give up when one is right, and the humility to give up when one is wrong
- commitment and respect for others—a willingness to assume full accountability for one's actions, and the ability to work with a sense of team spirit

In short, by hiring the right managers, Royer preferred to create a corporation that got things done through its culture or value system. He did not want an organization with a vast compendium of written rules, staffed with administrative manager types who told employees what to do. Nor did he want supervisors who ran roughshod over their employees even though they might be technically brilliant in their field. These command-style structures were perhaps suitable for stable times, but for the topsy-turvy environment in which Bombardier was struggling to survive, there was a need for a more flexible and innovative approach.

It was incumbent on the managers to involve their staff in the effort to meet customer needs better than rival firms. They were expected to meet with their teams to alert them to the challenges facing the company and to elicit their participation in the setting of goals and policies. As one production planner said, "I've got a real feeling of involvement and real participation."[3] The overall objective was to unite thinking and action within the company, to get "everybody singing from the same song sheet."[4]

Having set goals and policies jointly, managers gave employees room to achieve their objectives, all the while ensuring they were fully accountable for the results. Freedom to do a particular job was desirable, but only in relation to the yardsticks of customer and shareholder satisfaction. There was to be no step-by-step micromanagement, but instead, a trust and commitment to let individuals get on with the job as they saw fit within the given parameters. "You're left alone to do the job," one program director said. "They give you the basic guidelines and the goal to achieve. How you get there is your problem. For me, it is very important not to have somebody looking over my shoulder all the time."[5]

An atmosphere of teamwork was a vital ingredient in the culture. The sharing of ideas and problems was the preferred way to go, not groups working in isolation and competing against each other. No warring tribes here, just an environment in which there are "people who want to help each other and are not afraid to discuss their problems to find solutions," as an employee in the purchasing department put it.[6] Given the emphasis on team spirit within Bombardier, it was therefore important to have managers who respected people and possessed high principles and integrity.

One tangible implementation of this framework was Royer's prime rule that manufacturing problems affecting more than one department should be discussed in a group (but the department with the problem would have full responsibility for executing the decisions). Another manifestation was Royer's bonus plan for managers. Rather than being tied to individual performance, it was tied to the performance of individual divisions. So, if the division was successful, all the employees in the division would be rewarded; if the division were to fail, nobody would get anything.

Managers' obligations to their employees included a commitment to their personal growth and development. Given the belief that a corporation is only as strong as the people inside, there should not be any restraints placed on managers and employees alike in their becoming better at what they do. In concrete terms, this meant career development was to be promoted through training programs. Once a year, managers would meet with employees to draw up individual development plans that would be activated over the course of the coming year. This process, aimed at developing quality employees, would help ensure that Bombardier itself became a quality corporation.

One employee appreciated working at Bombardier because "there's a deep respect for everyone." Another reported that: "You're not just a number here. You're people. I think what makes this company a success is that management considers everybody on the same level all the way down to the workers. I think that here, if you're asked to do something, you'll do it and you'll do a little more. Its just that little more that makes a difference." Yet another employee, a production manager, revealed: "Where I used to work, you used to run equipment instead of running people. Here it's more human. They get you involved. You participate in most of the decisions. It's a big family.... You always have a certain sense of belonging...it's not, 'You're paid to do such and such a job. Do it and shut up.' Here if you have an idea...somebody will listen to you."[7]

Out of this environment grew the Bombardier Manufacturing System (BMS), generally credited as a main factor in the transformation of Bombardier into a multinational giant. A real tower of strength, the system evolved under the aegis of Royer's able lieutenant, Roland Gagnon. As the driven and energetic manager responsible for the La Pocatière plant during the 1970s and early 1980s, he helped introduce several innovations that significantly enhanced the productivity of Bombardier's manufacturing operations. So much so, that Bombardier was able to perform the remarkable feat of turning back a flood of Japanese and European rivals in its industry.

"The Bombardier manufacturing system is not just a way of doing things, but also a way of thinking," Gagnon said. "It is a philosophy first, a way of organizing work, a way of transferring and using information...."[8] A key feature of the BMS was a move away from traditional, serial communications, in which a product passes along an assembly line through various stages of production. Rather than wait for the engineers to complete the design of the various components and issue instructions for the sequence of assembly, manufacturing got started on their task before this stage. As parts were defined by engineers, manufacturing staff started putting them together and got the sequence as they went along. "They can start early, meet in the middle and cut cycle time by half," as Gagnon put it.[9]

A second key feature of the BMS was the coordination of changes to product designs during the manufacturing stage. If manufacturing found a problem with the design, then a request for a change was sent to engineering. They did not make changes in isolation so that the process of getting a product from the drawing broad to the showroom did not deteriorate into chaos or involve lengthy delays from incorporating all manner of refinements. Revisions were only issued when a drawing was available as documentation.

To keep this control mechanism from holding up the production line, the engineering redesign function was speeded up. Nearly daily, there was a meeting between engineering and methods people to handle all requests for changes. And once sanctioned, a drawing revision went out to everybody simultaneously, indicating what action was planned. So they all reacted at the same time, dispensing with the linear way of communications (whereby a drawing revision was sent from engineering to methods to planning to production control and to purchasing).

A third key feature of the BMS was the breaking down of manufacturing processes into simple tasks, so simple that anybody on the factory floor could do any one of them. This reduced learning costs. New workers were able to achieve standard times for all actions and operations in less than half the time of traditional approaches whereby specialized workers carried out tasks at higher levels of complexity. It also reduced the number of job codes and associated squabbles over who got paid what. Finally, it provided flexibility to recover production delays because workers were easily transferred to where there were bottlenecks, which reduced the need to hire more people or pay for overtime.

In 1980 and 1981, Royer and Gagnon presided over the opening of a US plant in Barre, Vermont, an area to which thousands of French Canadians had moved in the 1920s and 1930s to work in the granite quarries. Many of them, however, were now more American than French in their culture. English was not only their main language, but they used English pronunciations of French names and words. A worker by the name of Grandbois, for example, called himself "Grandboys" and his employer "Bomb-bar-deer" instead of the French pronunciation "Bomb-bar-dee-aye."

Bombardier wanted a presence in the US market to capture more orders. But the company actually did not have a choice in the matter; it had to go if it wanted to fill New Jersey's $100 million order for commuter cars. Under the *US Surface Transportation Assistance Act* of 1978, *Buy American* rules were now in effect, which required, among other things, railcars (purchased with federal aid) to have at least 50 percent US content and final assembly done in the United States. Since New Jersey was purchasing railcars with US government assistance, Bombardier had to abide by these legislated conditions.

Meeting the 50 percent US content requirement was not a problem since Bombardier railcars were already past that threshold. But to meet the final assembly condition, the company would have to set up a plant in the United States. The La Pocatière plant, however, would still do the majority of the work: fashioning components, doing subassembly, and working on aspects involving advanced technologies such as the shell, electrical work, and engineering.

By 1982, Royer was 40 years old. Deeply engrossed in his work and putting in 12-hour days, he was still a bachelor with a fondness for fast cars. It was not all out of vanity that the mass transit man went for flash and dash in his mode of transportation; it was out of necessity, too. He had set up his command post above a snowmobile warehouse in Boucherville, in between the Barre and La Pocatière plants. To get to Barre, it took his turbocharged Audi about 2.5 hours. The distance to La Pocatière was much greater, but it took him only three hours because he could open it up a bit on the Quebec roads.

Around this time, Royer had become aware of a change in the North American market for mass transit transportation equipment. In the late 1970s, Bombardier rarely faced more than one or two rivals—usually US-based companies such as Budd or Pullman—in bidding for contracts. After 1981, there were eight to 10 other bidders, the ranks being swelled by Japanese and

European entrants. The size of the market was still the same, but the competition was intensifying as foreign firms discovered they could offer more attractive prices because of ongoing depreciation of their domestic currencies against the US dollar.

Royer was fearful of a repeat of what happened to the shipbuilding and automobile industries, in which Asian exporters had earlier overrun North American manufacturers. On a trip to Asia, he became even more aware of the urgency of responding to the challenge from overseas. He had seen how companies and workers there were much more motivated to win market share than were their North American counterparts. The social fabric in these countries was truly different: with so few social programs, people worked to eat rather than to buy a new television set.

Alarmed, Royer felt he had to alert his employees to the growing threat to the survival of the organization. He had to get them involved in the collective effort to meet customer needs better than other companies. He therefore decided to meet with all of his 1,350 employees in group sessions of 50 to 60 people. Royer personally conducted over 20 of these sessions, meeting and talking with every employee by 1985. The talk was about the competition, what they were going to do to be better, and what they were going to do to win orders.

In these "technical councils," which took the better part of four hours each, attendees were invited to express their views especially on four questions:

1. If we were Americans, how would we react to buying and using railway and subway cars made in Canada?
2. What is the difference between ourselves and our competitors?
3. How could we assess ourselves in such an environment?
4. How should we assess our results?[10]

This joint thought process proved to be very effective in uniting the company. By raising such questions, the focus was shifted squarely onto the survival of the corporation and what could be done to ensure that. Rather than asking how the corporation was going to ensure their jobs, employees were now more likely to ask how they could ensure the permanency of the corporation as a way to protect their jobs. They understood better the need to offer the best combination of price and quality and the necessity to measure their efforts on their ability to attract customers. They accepted that the main difference between themselves and their competitors should be the quality of the Bombardier people.

When Bombardier signed a licensing agreement with Kawasaki in 1982, a clause allowed Bombardier employees to visit the Japanese facilities to observe the organization and work methods. Considering the cost of such trips, most other companies would normally send only five or six employees, However, Bombardier sent 70 people in groups of four to six over a six-month period. In selecting the people for the visits, Bombardier took into account their responsibilities in the transfer of the Japanese technology, picking a cross section of engineers, technicians, supervisors, and union representatives.

By sending many more people to go to Japan than was called for, Royer was using the licensing agreement as part of the education process—of making staff more aware of the competitive situation in their industry. When the groups came back, there was a great deal more acceptance of the fact that Bombardier people needed to work closely together to win international contracts and that individuals and teams needed to be fully accountable for their roles and responsibilities. Seeing what they were up against, they knew they had to dig down deep to win the war.

In summary, Bombardier's emphasis on people became a key strength for the corporation. The culture of involvement and participation brought a sense of teamwork and cooperation. It created a two-way communication between managers and staff that enabled all sides to understand each other better. Managers could appreciate the concerns of their staff, and staff could understand the concerns of their managers. The corporation was neither at war with itself nor asleep at the switch: its attention and energies were directed outward.

And once the successes started coming in, they bred further successes. Pay became more attractive, and employees in the company stock plan saw their shares appreciate. Not to be overlooked was the psychological effect, the growing sense of confidence that comes from meeting huge challenges. It felt good to be working for Bombardier, to be associated with a winner.

Laurent was taking a huge gamble committing his company to the $1 billion railcar contract in New York City. It was such a big project that a cost overrun could have easily wiped out his company. Indeed, history pointed to the likelihood of such an outcome. The public transit system in New York had earlier been the graveyard of several other US transit equipment makers. While seeking profits and profile in the Big Apple, they paid the ultimate price by going out of business trying to make railcars that met the stringent requirements of the transit authority's army of engineers.

Analysts worried that the Ski-Doo company from Quebec had bitten off more than it could chew. The hard bargaining of Ravitch and his team had trimmed the price, winning a deal favorable to New York City citizens but giving the supplier less margin for error. Bombardier was now in the difficult position of having to build Kawasaki cars at prices lower than what Kawasaki was charging the MTA. And Bombardier had to do this with supposedly more expensive and less efficient North American labor, while paying Kawasaki a royalty fee estimated at over 1 percent of the contract value.

These worries were fanned in March of 1985 after Bombardier sent a 10-car test train to the MTA in New York for a month-long acceptance trial. There were problems applying the brakes and maintaining speed on hills. An executive from the subway operators union, the Transport Workers Union of America, bluntly labeled the cars "lemons." He concluded: "We're stuck with some real bad Canadian equipment. It is one awful train.... The Kawasaki train, that's a gem."[11]

To a certain extent, the braking problem reflected the operators' unfamiliarity with the new controls installed by Bombardier. But a Bombardier spokesperson acknowledged that the problem also reflected defects in equipment—some printed circuit boards to be specific. Whereas the Kawasaki cars were fitted with traction and braking systems from General Electric Co., the Bombardier cars were equipped with systems from Westinghouse Electric Corp. The problem was easily rectified with a simple adjustment to the Westinghouse electrical equipment. It would cost only a few hundred dollars for each car, and everything could be done on site. No significant delay or cost overrun would result.

But the concerns did not let up after these bugs were ironed out. When the first batch of subway cars were delivered in June 1985, the official inauguration ceremony was postponed because of equipment breakdowns. A couple of cars had to be taken out of service because of jammed doors and other unspecified problems during the first week running on the Bronx to Brooklyn line. And passing by several working-class high schools, the "graffiti-resistant" stainless steel trains were vandalized and marked up with graffiti just hours after commencing service.

A few weeks later, two new glitches, involving electrical parts —the converter and arc chutes—cropped up. All 30 of the Bombardier cars delivered to date were affected. The culprit was again

Westinghouse Electric, the manufacturer of both parts. These glitches were serious enough to induce the MTA to withdraw the Bombardier cars from service and refuse any more shipments until the faulty parts were replaced. It seemed like a major setback, but Bombardier and MTA officials were reassuring in their portrayal of the situation as "teething problems," the imperfections that inevitably surface when introducing new and complex equipment. Even a member of the subway operators' union was supportive this time around. In contrast to the blast delivered a few months earlier, this individual said the operators were not too worried because "there are bugs in all new trains."[12]

However, the office of a New York senator was not convinced. In October, after receiving some confidential information from MTA engineers concerning cracks in the undercarriages of the Bombardier cars, an aide to Senator Franz Leichter denounced Bombardier as a company "used to making snowmobiles," and offered the view that "Bombardier might be in over its head."[13] Even though MTA officials took pains to declare the cracks merely harmless veins or seams, Bombardier felt the pressure mounting. As its on-site teams of technicians made welds to the seams, company spokespersons indicated that Bombardier had committed to delivering a 10-car train that would run 30 straight days without a hitch. Otherwise, the MTA would be free to cancel the contract. Thus, Bombardier's megadeal for a while had the makings of a nightmare. It all came down to 30 nail-biting days.

But the naysayers were not aware that Bombardier was more than a snowmobile company. They were not aware of the strengths of the emerging Bombardier Manufacturing System. Nor were they aware of the skills of the Quebec workers in the Kamouraska region surrounding the La Pocatière plant, where an age-old tradition of woodcarving created manual dexterity skills superior to most other workers. Nor did they take into account the fighting spirit and acumen of the department's leader, Raymond Royer.

The 30-day period passed without any glitches, and by 1986, the deal of the century was completed according to final deadlines and quality standards. Bombardier not only accomplished the mammoth assignment on budget, but it also earned an estimated pretax profit of $100 million. Moreover, Bombardier turned a potentially ruinous situation to its advantage. The company's reputation was enhanced when it adopted a take-charge stance in addressing the electrical problems in the components supplied by a contractor. Rather than sloughing off responsibility, Bombardier showed that it was prepared to take responsibility and tackle any problem to get a high-quality product out to the customer on time.

Royer said the New York contract and the way it was handled became "a tremendous calling card." As a result, "The transportation agencies are confident, and say, 'When you have Bombardier products, Bombardier supports them.'"[14] After the New York business went through, Bombardier proved that, as the tune goes, if you can make it in New York, you can make it anywhere. Its plants were kept humming with work on two other megadeals, one with the US national rail agency, Amtrak, and the other with the Massachusetts Bay Transit Authority (MBTA) in Boston. An official with the latter agreed that the past record for quality goods and service was a factor in choosing Bombardier.

The New York contract was the start of a beautiful, long-term relationship with the MTA. When other portions of its aging fleet of 6,000 subway cars came up for renewal in years ahead, it awarded Bombardier more contracts. In May 1997, the company found yet another reason to love New York City when it was awarded a $1.3 billion contract to build 680 stainless steel subway cars. The president of the transportation group at Bombardier said it was a happy repetition of the 1982 deal and confirmed that Bombardier had emerged as the supplier of choice for the largest subway system in North America.

In May 1999, even this blockbuster package was topped when Bombardier announced an order worth up to $2.7 billion to supply commuter cars for MTA's affiliate, the Long Island Railroad. The number of required cars totaled more than 1,000, consisting of an immediate placement for nearly 200 vehicles and an option for over 800 more. With the previous deals for subway cars and a rail link system for John F. Kennedy Airport, this meant that every agency of the MTA had purchased Bombardier products.

Although Bombardier's performance on the 1982 New York contract helped launch the company into the big leagues of the mass transit industry, a few reports in the press seemed to imply that other factors may have been involved as well. In particular, a May 18, 1986, article in the *Atlanta Journal and Constitution* noted that Bombardier had made payments to the brother of Mayor Andrew Young while the city of Atlanta was considering a bid from Bombardier to build a monorail along a proposed extension of the Georgia 400 route.

At the time, the mayor's brother, a dentist, was openly advertising himself as an international business consultant who could steer foreign companies through the state's government bureaucracy. The publicity kit for his firm, Young International Development, listed Mayor Young as a reference. Among his first clients in connection with the Georgia 400 monorail project was a French rail manufacturing company then called Alsthom Atlantique, which was additionally interested in promoting a high-speed railway line between Atlanta and Savannah. In March 1985, the mayor of Atlanta visited the French company in Paris and expressed support for the idea. The retainer fee paid by Alsthom Atlantique to Young International totaled $15,000 US.

As a client of Young International, Bombardier had agreed to pay a lump sum of $10,000 US and $2,000 US per month. Negotiations were also under way that, in the event Bombardier was the successful bidder, the firm would get an additional fee based on a percentage of the Georgia 400 rail contract, estimated to be worth $150 million US. A Bombardier executive said that the mayor's brother was hired because he had already represented the French firm and "was the only guy who really knew much about" the Georgia 400 project. "One of the problems when you go into a new area is really getting to understand the local scene," said the executive.[15]

These details came to light only when court documents were filed in a bankruptcy proceeding. Creditors were pursuing a business associate of the Mayor's brother, seeking to garnishee his income, including money he allegedly obtained through Young International. One of the items in contention was the $10,000 payment from Bombardier. The business associate argued this money could not be taken because it was not a payment to him but to the firm. He claimed the mayor's brother was also involved in the receipt of the money, and that the money was collected for the purpose of donating to political campaigns. He described the situation thus: "Dr. Young and I indicated to the potential client ...that...it would be very good if...Dr. Young and I had an escrow account within which we could donate funds to political candidates running in October 1985. The company agreed that it was a good strategy and forwarded $10,000 here to Atlanta."[16]

Among the evidence included in court records was a document written for Young International by the associate, entitled: "The Georgia 400 project, A Formula for Success, Projected Light/Heavy Rail-Line." It identified key politicians involved in the Georgia 400 project, including Mayor Young. Submitted to both the Canadian and French companies, it declared in one paragraph: "As you are aware, private businesses generally persuade politicians to accept or deny participants in contracts of the Georgia 400 magnitude." In his deposition to the court, the business associate added: "What we find...with foreign companies, whether it was Canadian, French, English, or German, is that obviously we had very good rapport with downtown political interests by virtue of the presence of Dr. Young."[17]

Responding to the public reaction sparked by the news reports, the mayor's brother went voluntarily before the City Ethics Board for an opinion on whether he was acting improperly by representing foreign firms. The five-member board, which was created by the Atlanta City Council to hear conflict of interest allegations regarding city officials, ruled that the mayor's brother's actions were not in themselves a conflict of interest, although they cautioned him about giving the appearance of such. At that point, press coverage petered out, and the issue faded away. Neither Bombardier nor Alsthom Atlantique ended up with contracts to build monorails or high-speed trains along the Georgia 400.

Nevertheless, a bit more smoke appeared a few years later when the *Houston Chronicle* ran an article in May 1991 reporting that Bombardier had come under scrutiny as a result of legal troubles faced by its partner in the building of Houston's monorail line. The partner, Kiewit Construction Group Inc., was alleged to have engaged in bid rigging, racketeering, and fraud. A Bombardier official said they welcomed the scrutiny of their firm because they had nothing to hide. "I would be very surprised if anybody brought anything up at all. Bombardier is a very straightforward company," he said.[18]

The article also referred to earlier charges of impropriety levied against Bombardier when it sold 35 railcars to the transit authority of Philadelphia. According to a Pennsylvania Department of Transportation report, there was evidence of improper contacts between the company and the chairman of the Southeastern Pennsylvania Transportation Authority (SEPTA). For example, prior to awarding the contract, the chairman had accepted an offer to fly his daughter to her New Hampshire college on Bombardier's corporate jet. In addition, he had solicited, on SEPTA stationary, political contributions for a US congressman, which led to Bombardier purchasing a pair of tickets to the congressman's fund raising dinner. Finally, there was evidence that the chairman had worked for Bombardier in his capacity as a private attorney, providing a legal opinion on a question of patent law.

Bombardier denied paying the chairman for this service and termed it a professional courtesy. When the federal and state investigators completed their investigations of SEPTA's contracting policies, they concluded that this and other forms of contact with the chairman did not merit charges of wrongdoing. So Bombardier emerged unscathed. The *Houston Chronicle* reporter conducted her own investigation, searching through hundreds of articles on Bombardier in the US and Canadian press from previous years. She found little in the way of other irregularities. Most of the articles "focused on new contracts the firm had won, companies it had purchased, or lengthy profiles lauding the company's business style."[19]

When news broke of Bombardier's $1 billion contract with New York City in 1982, some of the talk in the pubs, bowling alleys, and barbershops revealed a degree of incredulity. How could a snowmobile manufacturer from the hinterlands of Quebec land such a plum? Many New Yorkers did not even know there was a province of Quebec, let alone a company called Bombardier. If anything, a bombardier to them was the guy in the bomber crew who dropped bombs on enemy territory. Or it was the beetle that entomologists say hoses down its enemies with a searing, blister-raising spray emitted from a swiveling nozzle located at its rump. (Actually, in terms of Bombardier's effect on its competition and critics, these bombardier images were not far off.)

But those really in the know, the analysts following the mass transit industry, saw the landmark victory as a natural progression from prior events. It was not surprising to them because they knew Bombardier was much more than a snowmobile manufacturer by the early 1980s. In fact, by this time, less than half of Bombardier revenues were derived from snowmobile manufacturing. The remainder came mostly from the production of a full line of passenger rail vehicles. Indeed, Bombardier was the only North American company then in a position to provide the four main types of mass transit vehicles other than buses: subway cars, self-propelled commuter cars, light rail vehicles (tramways), and intercity trains (LRC—light, rapid, comfortable—vehicles).

That Bombardier was no longer just a snowmobile company was evident in the many mass transit contracts won in the five years leading up to 1982. Leveraging the experience and competencies gained from the City of Montreal subway contract, Bombardier had gone on to win business in several other cities, mostly in the United States. The New York deal was the climax in a series of previous mass transit assignments, which included bi-level commuter cars for Chicago, tramways for Portland, Oregon, and rubber-tired subway cars for Mexico City.

But perhaps the most important of these earlier breakthroughs was the $100 million US job to build over 100 railcars for New Jersey commuters. Hailed as the largest US contract for public transit equipment in 1980, Bombardier beat out Budd Co. and Vickers Canada Inc. In a foreshadowing of the New York situation, Budd launched a legal challenge, asserting that Bombardier's bid had been higher. However, the verdict went in Bombardier's favor: when the two bids were adjusted to make them comparable, Bombardier was found to have the lowest price.

A key ingredient in Bombardier's winning in New Jersey appeared, again, to be the strategy of putting the market first and technology second. Bombardier's approach was to study the requirements of the customer thoroughly and provide a close-fitting solution. The company would not engage in costly research and push its own designs onto the customer. Instead, it would look around for the designs that could be licensed and adapted to the needs of the customer. In the New Jersey case, it was the acquisition of the designs of the Pullman company that helped to tip the scales. New Jersey's existing coaches were Pullman designed, so there would be, among other things, economies of scale in maintenance and training functions.

By foregoing the expense of research and development to concentrate on efficient manufacturing and marketing processes, Bombardier was beginning to emerge as a force within the mass transit industry. It was, as Laurent and Royer said, a Japanese-style approach of acquiring established technologies and gaining an edge by adapting them to market conditions or by making improvements to them. As Royer liked to say: "We put more of the accent on the D than on the R in R&D."[20] The benefits of this way of doing things included speedier entry into new markets, avoiding the risk inherent in designing new products from scratch, and lower costs from not having a full-scale research function. All the while, Bombardier would be accumulating technical skills that would eventually allow it to do independent research and development.

Yet, Bombardier often had to defend its lack of research and innovation. In response to the critics, Royer put forward a rhetorical question: "Do we gradually develop our own design and perhaps miss the market, or do we go after the market and make the best of it for Canadian industry?"[21] Another senior

Bombardier executive replied: "The risk that has been taken on the various contracts we've bid for has been minimal. It takes years to prove the technology. Bombardier cannot afford to do that."[22] Later, perhaps weary of hearing the complaints, Royer responded with a tinge of irritation: "We don't do the R, we just do the D. Why reinvent the wheel? Buying technology gives us more expertise, more jobs, more profits, with less risk. So what, we used somebody else's designs. Big deal."[23]

After the 1982 New York subway deal, talk in the streets was also about how Bombardier appeared to be riding on the coattails of the Canadian government, benefiting from the EDC export loan and subsidized interest rates. There lingered a feeling that Bombardier was a favorite son of the Canadian government, and that together the two had competed unfairly in the international arena.

But again, industry analysts were aware that Bombardier was actually one of the last mass transit manufacturers to be favored with export financing by its government. If other countries had not already departed from an international "gentlemen's agreement," it is unlikely Bombardier would ever have received such assistance from the Canadian government. Bombardier and the Canadian government were, in fact, reluctant participants in the breakdown of the guidelines arranged in 1976 by the Organization for Economic Cooperation and Development (OECD) on export financing.

Under the OECD's Arrangement on Guidelines for Officially Supported Export Credits, financing terms on loans offered to foreign customers were set at prescribed levels. But as world interest rates rose over the late 1970s, several governments, particularly in France and Britain, let the prescribed OECD rates lag commercial rates, making up the difference with subsidies. Other governments, particularly in West Germany and Japan, eased their export credit programs by extending loan terms. When a US consortium lost a bid to modernize a telephone system in

Egypt, the outgoing administration of President Carter announced that it was no longer going to abide by the OECD arrangement and would henceforth offer loans with maturities of up to 20 years to customers of US exporters.

This US action set the stage for another round of amendments to export programs in other countries. For example, Japan raised loan maturities to a maximum of 25 years. In January 1981, Trade Minister Ed Lumley announced a program that signaled that Canada was joining other major trading nations in subsidizing its exporters. A fund of nearly $1 billion would be made available over the next three years for the EDC to distribute to Canadian exporters in need of concessionary loans in "selected cases...when it is clear that our competitors are resorting to this form of export subsidization."[24]

For Bombardier, the new program came at a good time. The company was just then in the midst of a competition against a French consortium, led by Compagnie Industrielle de Materiel Transport (CIMT) and Alstom, for the right to build subway trains and rolling stock in Mexico City. Bombardier had succeeded in demonstrating that its technical expertise was at least on a par with the French team, and it looked as if the Mexicans were going to split the order between the two groups. But the introduction of a very attractive financing scheme by the French bidders appeared to be turning things in their favor.

The Canadian government had rejected the idea of subsidizing exports, so Bombardier was resigned to losing the deal. But by 1981, with other countries breaking ranks on the OECD agreement and Canadian unemployment soaring to record levels, there was a change of opinion among federal politicians. Giving impetus to the reversal in policy were the growing secessionist tendencies inside the province of Quebec. Separatist forces might be held back by the sight of Bombardier and other Quebec exporters receiving aid from the federal government. Quebecers would see some benefits to remaining within the union.

With Ottawa's change of heart, Bombardier now had a chance in the Mexican market. Bombardier was the first to submit an application to the EDC. Able to provide the Mexicans with more generous financing, Bombardier won its share of the business, in particular, a deal to supply the City of Mexico with 180 subway cars. "Without the new financing terms, there is no way that we could have taken the business away from the French," Royer said.[25] Bombardier had been competing on the world stage with one hand tied behind its back. Now it had both hands free.

6 | Becoming Number One

Laurent Beaudoin was not feeling well in 1987. A mounting pressure in his chest told him something was seriously wrong. His appearance was much changed, too. He looked gaunt and weary; the usual vim and vigor had faded. Alas, the flat-out pace of his work week had finally caught up to him.

The 1970s had been nightmarish. His company had been tossed about like a cork on swirling currents. Worker militancy and at least three labor strikes were particular sources of aggravation. Then came the 1980s, and the company fared much better with its diversification into mass transit, but just about every step forward was a battle. The process of bidding for contracts was lengthy and exacting. If a bid were successful, it would often be just the start of a succession of frustrations that included legal challenges and threats of trade retaliation. Then there was the relentless pressure to deliver quality products on time, an easy enough task in industries with standardized goods but more of a challenge when customized production was required.

In early 1988, at the age of 49, Laurent underwent heart bypass surgery. During his absence, Raymond Royer assumed the post of chief executive. After convalescing, Laurent felt much better and was eager to get back to work. He jokingly warned his colleagues that he would be even more impatient because the blood would be flowing through his veins faster.

The scrape with mortality finally did what relatives had long begged him to do: curb his workaholic tendencies. But not by much. It appears that his only real concession was to start taking one day a week off, spending some time Ski-Dooing, Sea-Dooing, and fox hunting near his house close to Lac Brome in the Eastern Townships of Quebec. A keen outdoorsman, he pursued his recreation as passionately as his business affairs. Years after his bypass surgery, friends and coworkers marveled at how he would ride his Ski-Doo at daredevil speeds across the ice and participate in daylong Sea-Doo excursions down the Saguenay River at speeds up to 100 kilometers per hour (60 mph).

Other than taking a day off every week, a rule not necessarily always observed, Laurent tried to pay more attention to his body's signals during the hustle and bustle of the business day. If that ominous pressure comes back in his chest, he is ready to ease up. "I listen to my body more," Laurent says. "When I get to the point where I feel the pressure more than normally, I try to be more careful."[1] And he was going to try and be more relaxed. As he told an interviewer in 1990: "I am trying not to be as tense as I used to be, to share my problems a bit more with the people around me."[2]

His personal crisis meanwhile was in stark contrast to the condition of his company. By the mid-1980s, Bombardier was in the pink of health. The New York City contract and other deals had generated steady and ample cash flow. And rising sales and profits had boosted the price of Bombardier shares on the stock exchange, enabling hundreds of millions of dollars to be raised through the issue of more shares. Bombardier was on the move, displaying a remarkable momentum in an industry thought to be in decline, one usually passed over by investors seeking growth companies.

The North American rail passenger car business had indeed been in a long-term slide by the time Bombardier came onto the scene. The peak occurred in the 1930s and 1940s when trolleys coursed through downtown streets and passenger trains dominated long-distance travel. Major equipment manufacturers hailed mainly from the eastern and midwestern parts of the United States. They included Budd Co. of Pennsylvania, St. Louis Car Co. of Missouri, and Pullman Standard Co. of Illinois. But, in the years after World War II, the advent of the automobile and the airplane took a heavy toll. Cities replaced trolleys with diesel-powered buses, and railways cut back dramatically on passenger service.

More and more time would pass between major orders for new railcars, and the few contracts that were awarded tended to go to European and Japanese competitors. They had gained an edge because their governments had continued to subsidize and expand their railway systems, providing a steady succession of business on which to hone manufacturing expertise and amass financial wherewithal. Later in the 1980s, the rising US dollar allowed foreign firms to reduce the price of their products in the US market. Also playing a role were favorable financing terms provided by foreign export promotion agencies.

For a time, new US entrants such as aerospace firm Rohr Inc. raised the possibility of a rebirth in domestic production. The company got a choice assignment to develop subway cars for San Francisco in the 1960s and later won a lucrative job in Washington. But since the transit authorities there wanted a design different from San Francisco's, Rohr had to develop a totally new railcar. A bid for work in Atlanta was unsuccessful because city officials were not interested in either the San Francisco or Washington designs. That is when Rohr decided to give up. The lack of standardized designs across subway systems proved to be too much of an impediment, just as it later proved to be an opportunity for Bombardier and its "tailored" approach based on licensed technology and flexible manufacturing.

Peter Lynch, a stock market guru from the 1980s, says that declining industries are often surprisingly fertile grounds for the emergence of a growth company.[3] Industry revenues may be on a downtrend, but as weak firms leave the scene, they turn their share of the market over to the stronger firms. Or they can be purchased at bargain prices. Indeed, all around, railway manufacturing assets were going for a song. Former giants such as Pullman were just clinging by their fingertips from the edge of the precipice. Their management teams were demoralized by a downward spiral of lost opportunities and declining capabilities. Part of the problem was their business models were based upon expensive research and development.

Yet, Laurent could see hope on the horizon—the industry decline was not necessarily a permanent affliction. As before, he still felt the long-term prospects were favorable in that rail transport could be a solution to the pollution, congestion, and energy consumption problems of airplanes and automobiles. Accordingly, Bombardier tightened its grip on the North American market in the late 1980s by purchasing the remaining designs of Pullman and Budd as they left the industry. But there were also some new developments to get excited about. One was the coming of a common market in the European Community (EC) in 1992, which would generate lucrative commercial opportunities for a variety of companies, including railway equipment manufacturers.

By the mid-1980s, Laurent was looking to parlay his victory in the North American subway sector into even bigger victories.

He was not a person to sit still, even after a heart operation. In business, he believed, you cannot rest on your laurels. There is a constant flux, an ebb and flow that spawns new sets of winners and losers. "You can never be stagnant," he said. "If you think you are pleased with a plateau you've reached, by the time you stop to think about it, somebody's ahead of you."[4]

In the 1980s, government officials in the EC nations had become concerned about the competitiveness of their industries. Companies from Japan and the United States were in many cases a lot more efficient than their European counterparts. A big reason was the fragmentation of the EC economy. Protectionist trade barriers and preferential purchasing policies within the community had divided the market and confined many companies to operating within their respective national markets. For example, the European market, which was about the same size of the US market, was supplied by 16 locomotive manufacturers; the latter had just two. As such, European companies could not achieve the economies of scale that their foreign rivals possessed. Furthermore, operating behind walls of protection, the Europeans had become high cost and indolent.

After some discussion, heads of state in the EC reached an agreement to create a common market within their community, to dismantle obstacles to the free flow of goods, service, people, and capital. The target date set for implementation was 1992. Of interest to Bombardier was the planned reshaping of the transportation sector, in particular the removal of restrictions on state railway operators that required them to favor local suppliers in their purchases of equipment. Freed of national procurement policies, the operators would be able to entertain bids from any supplier in the EC. This gave Bombardier an incentive to establish a presence there. With its well-honed manufacturing system fashioned in the competitive North American market, it should be able to grab tenders away from bloated manufacturers accustomed to cozier arrangements.

But the commercial opportunity was greater than this. For one thing, major portions of the European railway network were antiquated and had to be replaced. In 1990, Bombardier estimated that the annual replacement market in European mass transit was $4 billion. For another thing, the case for rail transportation was much stronger in Europe than in North America. More densely populated, Europe was experiencing greater problems of congestion on its highways and in its airports. In response, and at the same time to move toward a unified market, transport ministers in the EC had formulated plans to invest more than $200 billion over two decades to upgrade existing rail lines and build a new high-speed train network from Scotland to the Iberian Peninsula. Stretching over 30,000 kilometers (19,000 miles), the bullet train project would take over a quarter of a century to complete, making it one of the biggest public works projects since the automobile highway grids were built in the 1950s and 1960s.

One of the first steps in building the high-speed train in Europe would be the construction of the Chunnel, a tunnel under the English Channel linking England and France for the first time by rail. It would be the realization of a long-held dream, one dating back to 1802 when French mining engineer Albert Malthieu drew up plans for a tunnel link to be traveled by horse-drawn carriages. If it had not been for the Napoleonic Wars, the tunnel might have gone ahead. In 1851, a British engineer proposed placing a giant iron tube into the sea to create a passage. In the 1880s, digging of a tunnel actually began on both sides of the Channel, but once again, British and French fears over military use of the tunnel brought work to a halt. Digging recommenced in the 1970s only to stop again, the enemy this time being escalating costs and environmental worries.

In any event, by 1986, both Laurent and his second in command, Raymond Royer, had decided that a diversification into Europe was a wise move in order to position Bombardier for the opportunities to be unleashed by the arrival of the common market. Moreover, Europe was not only a much bigger rail market than North America, but it was also where most of the action was going to be over the next decade or so. Governments there were prepared to boost their railways more so than those in North America.

Given their goal of gaining a foothold in Europe, the question became how to set up shop. One way would be to build facilities from scratch, but this was ruled out. It would be more economical to simply acquire local manufacturers. As inefficient and underutilized producers in compartmentalized markets, they would be inexpensive to buy, while, at the same time, they would yield valuable relationships with local customers. And in some cases, the acquisitions would bring new and advanced technologies.

The opportunity for the first acquisition arose when the Société Générale de Belgique expressed a desire to sell a minority stake in the troubled Belgian manufacturer, BN Constructions Ferroviaires et Métalliques S.A. Bombardier, which already had a close relationship with the company as a result of licensing its light rail designs several years before, acquired a 40 percent stake in the 135-year-old firm for $13.5 million in March 1986. It was a good start for both. The Belgian company obtained a partner with the manufacturing expertise to help provide, in preparation for the common market, new impetus to its lines of locomotives, freight cars, and passenger coaches. Bombardier secured access to a leading research lab and a launchpad to boost marketing efforts on the continent. In 1989, Bombardier exercised its option to increase its stake to 90 percent, spending another $20 million to gain full control over BN's five factories spread across Europe.

Later in 1989, Bombardier spent $23.5 million to acquire the second-largest manufacturer of railway equipment in France, ANF-Industrie. The struggling, century-old maker of double-deck railcars, turbo trains, and passenger coaches enjoyed a long-standing commercial relationship with France's state-owned railway and was a partner in France's high-speed train system. It was also a rival to Bombardier's BN and a leader in the Francorail consortium that competed against Bombardier in North American markets. So the takeover would help rationalize the supply side of the market, keeping a lid on oversupply and ruinous competition. At the same time, Bombardier gained a new pool of technical skills and a major production plan.

ANF-Industrie was driven into Bombardier's arms by the prospect of increasingly fierce competition, resulting from the opening of borders within the EC. To survive, it was looking to Bombardier's manufacturing and marketing expertise; it was also looking to obtain the capital necessary to modernize its facilities (over $100 million was subsequently committed).

In 1990, all the shares of a British rail transport manufacturer, Procor Engineering Limited, were purchased. Renamed Bombardier Prorail Limited, this subsidiary specialized in making freight and passenger cars for the UK market. This smaller acquisition brought the total number of European subsidiaries in the expanding Bombardier empire to four: BN, ANF, Prorail, and the tramway facilities in Austria obtained in 1970. Together, the acquisition of the four units were bringing greater attention to Bombardier in Europe. In fact, according to one observer,[5] its profile was higher there than in its home country of Canada. Every time Bombardier bought out a European firm, it received wide coverage in the European press, whereas these transactions barely attracted notice in Canada.

In the summer of 1989, the first coup came: the signing of a major contract that potentially, like the New York City deal earlier, was capable of establishing Bombardier's credentials across a huge, new market. Bombardier was a member of a consortium that won part of a $800 million contract to supply equipment to Eurotunnel SA, the Anglo-French consortium set up to operate the Chunnel after its planned completion date of December 15, 1993. Bombardier's assignment—to design and build 252 single- and double-deck shuttle cars for ferrying buses and autos through the tunnel—would be worth $425 million. Product design and fabrication of the casings (exteriors and ceilings) would take place in La Pocatière plant in Quebec, while the final assembly would occur in the Belgian and French plants.

Instrumental in winning the business was the expertise acquired from building stainless-steel subways cars for New York City. The humid and salty air around the Straits of Dover required the use of corrosion-resistant materials. Also important was Bombardier's stake in BN. With the feeder railway line into the Chunnel passing through Belgium, the Belgian manufacturer effectively guaranteed participation in the Chunnel megaproject. The EC's common market was another two years away, so local producers still enjoyed preferred supplier status. As analyst Fred Schilling of brokerage firm BMO Nesbitt Burns declared: "They had the inside track."[6]

However, the Chunnel assignment was to turn into a bit of a quagmire. Eurotunnel's agent, TransManche Link (TML), introduced changes to the specifications, forcing Bombardier into redesigns that put its cars behind schedule and over budget. Many of the changes were related to security concerns to make the shuttles safer in the event of worst-case scenarios such as bomb attacks by extremist groups. But a real drag was a request to widen the doors for wheelchair accessibility. This alteration tacked on another six months to the process. There were also some delays in obtaining approvals from TML; for a while, the Belgian plant floor sat silent because Bombardier did not want to continue production while it waited for certifications from TML.

Bombardier filed a claim against TML for $746 million to cover the cost overruns related to the multiple specifications changes and delays, as well as for the harm to its reputation and stock value. (An attempt to raise $150 million through issuing new shares had to be abandoned.) Eurotunnel and TML officials balked at such a high claim, and for a while, they were at logger-heads with Bombardier. With the Chunnel project on hold and on the verge of lengthy arbitration and court proceedings, Bombardier shares continued to come under downward pressure.

The financial statements of Bombardier's rail group were slipping too. They showed operating losses in fiscal 1992 and 1993 of $23.9 million and $72.6 million, respectively. However, the company as a whole still posted profits of $133 million and $176 million respectively in those two years because of the strong performance of the aerospace and recreational products groups. The diversification formula was working as envisioned. One product group was down but the others were up and maintaining overall momentum in growth.

There was pressure on both sides to come to a quick resolution. The Eurotunnel bankers were not eager to extend further loans, and Bombardier would not receive any payouts from the project until vehicles were delivered. Toward the end of 1993, an out-of-court settlement was reached in which Bombardier received $381 million, comprised of $157 million in cash and 25 million shares in the Eurotunnel consortium. Bombardier's stake, later increased, was about 3 percent of the shares outstanding, making it one of the largest investors in the tunnel.

With the official opening of the Chunnel reset for the spring of 1994, delivery of the shuttle cars resumed. Although Bombardier had claimed its reputation had been tarnished, company officials at the European facilities put a positive spin on the completion of the Chunnel contact. "To say to everyone we completed such a sophisticated technology is a formidable calling card,"[7] said Christian Dotte, a production director at ANF-Industrie.

The shuttles were truly state-of-the-art machines. A computer network in each car controlled virtually every function, ranging from air-conditioning to exhaust regulation to wheel braking. New heights in safety were achieved. For example, each car was made so fire resistant that it could contain a blaze for a half hour. The challenge of integrating all the systems while remaining within weight requirements was met through the use of lightweight materials commonly found in airplanes. "It's technological know-how without precedent,"[8] said a senior executive.

After the Chunnel contract, there was a restructuring of Bombardier's European operations, an implicit admission, according to one observer, that poor planning and coordination among the four subsidiaries may have contributed to the Chunnel miscue.[9] Management ranks were trimmed, and autonomous units were brought under a new holding company, Bombardier Eurorail. Bernard Sorel, a veteran executive from Caterpillar Inc., was hired as president. It would be his job to unify the European units behind a company-wide vision and to tap synergies.

As for Bombardier's Eurotunnel shares, a steady succession of operating losses and scares over indebtedness pushed their price into a long-term decline after the Chunnel's debut. Chunnel traffic did not rise quickly enough to cover ongoing financial obligations. Bombardier's Eurotunnel shares, originally worth over $200 million, were quietly written off in the late 1990s.

Although Bombardier was to experience several setbacks in its European expansion, none was serious enough to halt the drive. In early 1995, Waggonfabrik Talbot KG of Germany was purchased for $130 million cash. Founded in 1838 and managed by the Talbot family through five generations, the company was a world leader in the design and manufacture of double-deck railcars and undercarriages for passenger and freight applications. The addition of the company's 1,250 employees to Bombardier Eurorail increased the workforce by 33 percent to 5,000. This acquisition was handsomely rewarded the next year with a $340 million order for 120 diesel-powered rail units from Deutsche Bahn AG, the German national railway.

In late 1997, Bombardier took over Deutsche Waggonbau AG, which before the collapse of East Germany in 1990, had been the world's largest maker of railcars. At the peak, it had 25,000 employees and 21 factories serving markets from Russia to Romania to China. After the collapse of Communist markets, the company went through a painful restructuring, shedding all but 4,000 of its workers, while nearly a billion dollars were poured into new buildings and equipment. The company was attractive to Bombardier as a launching pad into eastern bloc countries, where railway grids were sorely in need of upgrading after years of Communist rule.

With this acquisition, Bombardier reached the upper echelons of the European rail manufacturing industry, where it faced three main rivals: Alstom, Siemens, and Adtranz. Of these, Alstom was perhaps the most daunting. It was formed as a joint venture (originally under the name GEC-Alsthom) in the 1980s to pool the power generation and rail transportation businesses of two European industrial giants: Britain's Marconi (formerly General Electric PLC) and France's Alcatel Alsthom. In 1998,

Alstom's parents gave their joint venture its independence by floating just over half their respective ownership stakes on the London, Paris, and New York stock exchanges. Since then, Alstom's management team has redesigned the firm by acquiring new companies and divesting noncore lines. In 2000, just under half of its 140,000 employees were in the rail equipment divisions, which provide integrated systems of locomotives and rolling stock.

The transportation division of Germany's Siemens was a lesser threat. Bombardier was one of the first to invade Siemens' territory in the open markets of the 1990s, breaking through in 1996 with a contract to supply streetcars to Cologne, Germany. Bombardier won the contract by underbidding Siemens by about 25 percent, indicating the extent of the gap between Bombardier's and Siemens' cost structures. Consequently, Siemens commenced a campaign to get its costs in line with new market realities.

One plank was to shrink the wage bill. In 1996, 20 percent of the 13,700 workforce was declared redundant. A second plank was to pressure suppliers into lowering their prices. A third was to launch a drive to change its engineering approach, which, during the previous environment of guaranteed customers, tended to overengineer products and recover costs through inflated prices. Now, it was imperative to design products with cost parameters in mind.

Adtranz, with an initial staff of 25,000, was formed in early 1996 by the merger of the railway interests of DaimlerChrysler (then Daimler-Benz) and Swedish industrial conglomerate ABB. Ahead lay several years of losses as the amalgamation struggled to reduce overlap and deal with rising competition. Yet, in 1999, the president of Adtranz taunted Bombardier in a Toronto speech, saying his company would emerge on top in North America.[10] This outburst was sparked by Bombardier's acquisition of Deutsche Waggonbau, which was viewed as an invasion of

Adtranz's turf. Poaching was a two-way street, said the president, and Adtranz would henceforth be developing its presence in North America.

The competition was heating up to be sure, but by 1998, Bombardier had taken its place securely alongside the three heavyweights. And Bombardier now had over a dozen railcar factories spread across Europe. Even though it was one of the more efficient European players, it was still short of optimizing its operations. Millions of dollars could be saved by closing down some plants and shifting production to the more efficient ones. However, despite the supposedly unified market of the European Community, Bombardier was finding that local presence was still important in winning business. Because of this still fragmented market, Bombardier's rail operations enjoyed profit margins of only 5 percent in fiscal 2000, compared to about double that in its aerospace operations.

Nevertheless, Bombardier executives were content to make the best of the situation for the time being. The president of Bombardier Transport said the essential thing was to have "a number of properly sized operations that work well together."[11] That is, it was important to have plants that coordinated their activities within given constraints, to have a team that pulled together to seize market opportunities as they arose.

One such opportunity, for example, was the trend, particularly in Britain, toward deregulation and privatization of railway operators. Decades of public ownership and restrictive rules had left their mark: inefficient service and losses that never seem to go away. Consequently, over the 1990s, there was a move to dismantle regulatory frameworks and sell off state-owned railway assets to the private sector, which, guided by the profit motive, would have a strong incentive to end the inefficiency and waste.

However, many of the successful bidders for the railway operating franchises did not have their own service and repair shops. This presented an opportunity for firms like Bombardier, which could offer to provide service and repair functions more economically than the new operators on their own. And a big opportunity it was. In 1998, for example, Bombardier won a $2 billion deal from Britain's Virgin Rail Group, of which more than half of the payment was for a 15-year contract to maintain and service the equipment it had sold to Virgin Rail.

In the spring of 2001, Bombardier leaped ahead again with the acquisition of Adtranz. DaimlerChrysler was eager to dispose of its subsidy because of years of losses and a desire to focus on making automobiles. And Bombardier had the cash flow and financial strength to do the deal as a result of the runaway success of its aerospace divisions in the 1990s. Bombardier would thus become a fully integrated producer, adding electrical and propulsion skills to its expertise in rolling stock, placing it on a par with Alstom. The deal would more than double the annual revenues of their rail group to $8 billion, making it the largest rail manufacturing operation.

7

Gravy Trains on the Horizon

The railway industry was often depicted as a sector in long-term decline. Yet, engineers continued to develop new technologies that enhanced the attractiveness of rail travel. Laurent Beaudoin and his team were excited by what was on the horizon and keen to be one of the first to get there.

In this regard, Bombardier had acquired several emerging technologies and was working on bringing them to market. Here, it was not as much a matter of reading the market and jumping into mass production with a solution best tailored to the needs uncovered. The markets were still virgin, and there were not all that many designs to license. Instead, seizing opportunities required more of a commitment to research and development in order to bring the emerging technologies along. Historically, such a commitment had been a risk avoided by

Bombardier, but as it gained critical mass in operations, depth in engineering, and financial strength, it was a risk that could be embraced.

One of the new technologies was the high-speed train, also known as the bullet train. In May 1990, a bullet train on a special run southwest of Paris reached a speed of 515 kilometers per hour (320 mph), establishing a world record for rail travel. It was not that much of a stretch, actually. In regular service, this specially designed train, called the Train à Grande Vitesse (TGV), averaged approximately 300 kilometers per hour (190 mph). Such speeds slashed travel times dramatically within France. For example, the trip between Paris and Lyon took two hours instead of the four it took before. This also made the train faster than air travel. Since the rail terminal was closer to downtown, TGV passengers could get to their final destinations faster.

The TGV debuted in France in 1981. Now it transports more than 25 million passengers per year. Germany has a popular high-speed train as well, which is called the Inter-City Express (ICE). Other European countries have similar high-speed trains under development or in service, such as Spain's Alta Velocidad Española, which runs between Madrid and Seville. Japan, which also has high-speed rail service, pioneered the concept with the Shinkansen Bullet Trains in 1964. The Super Hikari, introduced in the 1990s, covers the 515 kilometers (320 miles) between Tokyo and Osaka in 2.5 hours.

Thus, in countries outside North America, rail travel is now experiencing a rebirth, particularly for medium-range distances where cities can be linked in less than three hours. At these distances, high-speed trains are attractive alternatives to the airplane or car, getting passengers to their destinations faster and usually with less hassle. Cars still have an edge on shorter distances, while airplanes are faster for longer hauls.

In most countries, railway tracks were laid with lots of twists and turns in order to bypass obstacles and to get through hilly terrain. When regular trains head into these curves at high speed, passengers feel centrifugal forces pressing hard on them. The lateral forces can be very uncomfortable, making riders feel like they are on an amusement park ride. Furthermore, food and drinks may be spilled. To avoid these problems, conventional trains slow down, which makes for longer journeys.

Current high-speed service solves this problem in one of two ways. First, as in France and Germany, dedicated tracks can be built without any curves, or with very long and gradual ones. In Japan, if there is a mountain in the way, the line goes right through it. The tracks, resting on concrete ties, are welded together to eliminate joints. Overhead wires and substations supply electricity to the lightweight and aerodynamic trains running over these specially designed tracks.

Second, rather than the heavy capital outlay to build dedicated lines and attain right-of-ways, high-speed service can be brought to existing tracks, as Virgin Rail in the United Kingdom has done, by incorporating trains with tilting technology that causes the cars to lean into curves and offset centrifugal forces. These types of trains may not be as fast, but the cost can be as much as one-tenth.

There is a third form of high-speed train travel that is still in prototype stage: magnetic levitation (Maglev). Siemens and Alstom, among others, have been doing work in this area. An engineless train is propelled and guided along an elevated monorail by magnetic repulsion. Gliding along the cushion of a magnetic field, there is no contact with the rail. Since the Maglev train is not held back by friction, cruising speeds of up to 500 kilometers per hour (300 mph), or almost twice the speed of conventional high-speed rail service, are easy to reach. In April 1999 a test train in Japan edged out the 1990 French speed record for train travel by attaining 530 kilometers per hour (330 mph).[1]

As early as 1978, Laurent and his team moved to grab a leadership role in North American high-speed train travel by signing a lease-purchase contract with US national passenger railway, Amtrak, to supply light, rapid, and comfortable (LRC) intercity passenger train cars. This was followed by two orders totaling $170 million from Canada's national passenger rail service, VIA Rail, for dozens of locomotives and nearly 100 coaches.

The LRC was a high-speed passenger train based on tilting technology. The lightweight aluminum-bodied passenger cars contained a hydraulic power banking system with electronic sensors that would stabilize the cars around curves and thereby neutralize centrifugal forces. Development of the LRC had started in the research labs of MLW-Worthington Ltd. in the 1960s. After Bombardier acquired the latter company in the mid-1970s, it continued to push the LRC technology through a joint venture with Dominion Foundries and Steel Ltd. and Alcan Canada Products Ltd.

When the first LRCs were ready for delivery to Amtrak in 1980, Bombardier showed off the units to an audience in Canada. Company executives at the demonstration were excited. Of the 4,500 coaches then in short-run service in North America, "about 1,500 of these could be replaced by the LRC," said Raymond Royer, then president of Bombardier's mass transit division. "It's ideal for those runs with lots of curves where the authorities don't want to rebuild the roadbed."[2] The trains would be able to take the curves at 195 kilometers per hour (120 mph), and they would deliver 180 kilometers per liter (500 miles per gallon) versus 2 to 4 kilometers per liter (5 to 10 miles per gallon) for a jet aircraft, company officials said.

Henry Valle, Bombardier's vice president of corporate development at the time of the product launch, was an LRC pioneer.

As chairman of MLW prior to its merger with Bombardier, he had been involved with the project since it was a back-of-the-envelope drawing. He was just as enthusiastic as Royer, declaring: "We think the LRC is as good or better than anything comparable on the market anywhere, and we don't think anyone anywhere knows more about high-speed trains than we do."[3] VIA officials were caught up in the mood as well. In 1982, they predicted that Canada would have a rail service as good as that in France and Japan.

Alas, such high hopes evaporated after the LRC trains went into service and were found to have a host of mechanical problems and design flaws. There were reports of wheels falling off, doors jamming shut, engines not restarting, toilets freezing up, difficulties with hand brakes, and emergency door handles breaking off. The hydraulic banking system proved to be problematic and had to be turned off for long stretches. During Amtrak's trial period, a demonstration LRC train broke down and had to be towed; during a press visit, the braking system sprang a leak. Amtrak subsequently returned its train sets, seriously setting back Bombardier's aspirations for export sales, the only way it would earn a return on its investment. In Canada, the VIA experience was not going well either. A Canada Transport Commission study listed a variety of problems and attributed 50 percent of VIA delays to the LRC. (Other sources said it caused only 27 percent of the delays.)

Bombardier officials defended the LRC. They said it had been developed on a shoestring budget with little government support ($30 million of Bombardier's own money plus $3.7 million from the federal government). However, the high-speed trains in Europe and Japan had been developed with billions of dollars in public funds. Because of the underfunding, Bombardier did not have the luxury of testing the LRC trains extensively in a controlled setting as the French and Japanese teams were able to do.

The LRC train was still a good train, according to Bombardier spokespersons; it was just going through the normal debugging phase common to any new technology.

Transportation critics,[4] however, claimed that the LRC, free of bugs or not, was still the wrong choice for VIA. The LRCs might be economical on the densely populated corridor running from Windsor to Quebec City, but because of the presence of freight trains and many level crossings, a speed limit of 145 kilometers per hour (90 mph) had been imposed on the line, just 12.5 kilometers per hour (8 mph) more than what conventional trains were already attaining. So, what good was having an LRC train with a capability of 195 kilometers per hour (120 mph) if it was restricted to 145 kilometers per hour (90 mph)?

Perhaps Bombardier and VIA envisioned the speed limit being lifted, but even if that happened, the critics charged, the LRCs were not necessarily the answer. At speeds greater than 145 kilometers per hour (90 mph), trains wear down rail tracks more rapidly so that a major upgrading of the line would be required. Moreover, given the relative absence of curves on the Windsor to Quebec City corridor, there did not seem to be any particular need for a tilting technology.

Thus, orders for the LRC dried up, and production was halted after 1984. Leadership in tilting train technology would pass to other countries, particularly Italy. As of the mid-1990s, the Pendolino model of Fiat Ferroviaria was dominant, accounting for approximately two-thirds of the tilting trains in service, under construction, or on order. The mountainous, yet well-traveled routes of Italy proved to be suitable for testing and supporting the technology. Countries choosing the Pendolinos included the United Kingdom, the Czech Republic, Finland, Germany, Italy, Malaysia, Portugal, Spain, and Switzerland. The spring-mounted cars of Patentes Talgo SA of Spain were enjoying some success too in Canada, France, Italy, Portugal, and Switzerland.

In any event, Bombardier decided to adopt a different tactic after the LRC disappointment. In 1987, it entered into a partnership with Alstom of France. Bombardier would promote its TGV in North America in return for Alstom promoting the LRC train outside North America. Under the agreement, Bombardier would be responsible for the general management and production of rolling stock for TGV projects in North America, while Alstom would act as project leader for LRC opportunities outside North America.

Encouraging Bombardier to remain in the race were studies indicating significant potential in North America. For example, the Carnegie-Mellon Institute estimated in 1990 that over $200 billion would be spent on fast trains in the United States by 2010. Amtrak identified 22 corridors where high-traffic routes could be built to connect large cities.

Bombardier subsequently launched an intensive lobbying campaign in Canada and the United States, spending millions of dollars on the effort. In late 1989, Pierre MacDonald, a former military man, banker, and minister in the Quebec provincial government, was hired as vice president in charge of promoting the TGV concept. In his first year or so on the job, MacDonald and his staff made more than 300 presentations to politicians, bureaucrats, and business groups in Central Canada, proposing a TGV link between Montreal and Toronto (later to be extended at either end to Quebec City and Windsor). The benefits would be thousands of construction jobs as well as alleviation of air and road congestion. In addition, there would be the convenience to travelers of reducing train time between Canada's two major cities from 4.5 hours to 2.75 hours.

The overall cost for the proposed project was estimated at $7 billion, of which Bombardier was asking provincial and federal governments to pay 30 percent. The cost was so high mainly because of plans to construct new tracks, which would be straighter and more resilient. But a Swedish-Swiss multinational company, ABB (later to become part of Adtranz), emerged to offer an alternative service at a price tag of $3 billion, with minimal government support required. Its proposal would retain the existing track and use tilting technology to reduce traveling time between Montreal and Toronto to three hours, just 15 minutes longer than what Bombardier was proposing.

Politicians and transportation experts gathered into task forces and commissions to study the two proposals. By 1993, they returned a thumbs-down verdict on both proposals. Politically, it would be difficult to accept the Bombardier proposal at a time when governments were cutting back on services in an attempt to curtail ballooning deficits. Even if no subsidies were provided as in the ABB option, the concept of high-speed travel was still deemed impractical because of the fact that Canada had a small population base scattered over a large space. High-speed trains made sense in Japan and France because of their high population densities: in Japan, there were about 26,000 people for each kilometer (0.62 miles) of track; in France, there were 11,000. In Canada, the figure was close to 4,000. "We are talking about a technology that is designed to be economical with 10 million people at each end of it," said Michael Tretheway, a transportation economist at the University of British Columbia. "That does not sound like Canada."[5]

Concurrent with the lobbying campaign in Canada, MacDonald and other Bombardier staff made pitches to officials in the United States, where chances of acceptance were higher because of the existence of several densely populated, metropolitan clusters. Indeed, in the spring of 1991, a consortium that included Bombardier won a 50-year conditional franchise from the state of Texas to build and operate a high-speed TGV network joining Dallas, Austin, San Antonio, and Houston. The main condition was that the system had to be built without public money, a requirement the consortium hoped to meet by persuading the US Congress to change federal tax laws to allow them to raise $1 billion US through the issue of tax-exempt bonds.

As the consortium went about seeking financing in 1991 and 1992, Bombardier tried to use the Texas breakthrough to gain leverage for its TGV proposal in Canada. If the Texas job came through first, Bombardier warned, it might be pressured to build new production facilities there. But if the Canadian TGV were to come through earlier, the location of the new plants would likely be in Canada. But it was all for naught. The Texas consortium was not successful in obtaining permission to issue tax-exempt bonds, so when the target for raising the first allotment of capital was missed in December 1993, the consortium had to relinquish its franchise rights.

In early 1996, the dream of North American high-speed train travel was jolted back to life with two huge deals won by consortiums involving Bombardier. The first, in February, was signed with Florida state officials for a TGV service delivering speeds up to 320 kilometers per hour (200 mph) between Orlando, Miami, and Tampa Bay. What was significant about the Florida project was the commitment, for the first time, of state funds to a high-speed rail project. The amount would average $70 million US annually for 25 years. Before building was to start, there would be a three-year certification process covering detailed engineering and planning aspects as well as environmental analyses to determine best routes. However, just as the certification process was drawing to a close in 1999, Jeb Bush (son of one president of the United States and brother to another) was elected as the new Florida governor. Believing Florida taxpayers were footing too much of the bill, he withdrew state support, effectively scuttling the project.

The second megadeal in 1996 was announced just a month after the Florida deal made the news. A consortium led by Bombardier beat out five other bidders to win a $610 million US contract for 18 high-speed train sets to run in the northeast corridor of the Amtrak network, connecting Boston, New York City, and Washington. Bombardier's responsibility, consisting mainly of the supply of passenger cars with tilting technology, would be worth $440 million US. Its partner, Alstom, providing the propulsion systems, would claim most of the remaining value of the contract. Because of the tilting technology, existing tracks would be used largely as they were.

The so-called Acela Express would reach speeds of up to 225 kilometers per hour (140 mph), considerably less than in Europe or Japan but costing a lot less. Travel time would be cut by 10 percent between Washington and New York, and by 33 percent between Boston and New York. As a result, Amtrak forecast an increase in ridership of three million passengers annually, which would add $150 million to the bottom line each year. The survival of Amtrak hinged on this increase in revenues, as it would largely make up for the government subsidies that were scheduled to be eliminated in 2002.

The contract was critical to Bombardier as well. If it proved to be a success, Amtrak would open up several other of its corridors to high-speed train service. So the final business could be worth billions of dollars over the next 10 years. Moreover, it would be the demonstration project that Bombardier had long sought to prove that it was the company to turn to for high-speed train equipment in North America.

In awarding the contract to the Bombardier consortium, the president of Amtrak said: "It came down to a choice that was just not price but total package—financing, technology and commercial terms, guarantees about long-term performance, equipment reliability, and maintenance cost."[6] Probably the biggest selling point was the pledge from Bombardier and Alstom to obtain most of the financing for the project, an important offer since Amtrak was strapped for cash and might have difficulties obtaining reasonable financing on its own as a pubic corporation facing the threat of termination in 2002. The project also obtained $200 million US from the Clinton administration.

Work commenced almost immediately to meet a launch date for the fall of 1999. Some problems with wheel wear, said to be a responsibility of Alstom, were uncovered during testing, forcing a postponement of the launch date. This negative publicity was followed with more of the same in the spring of 2000 when it became headline news in Canada that the Amtrak deal had been won with the help of a $600 million US loan from the Export Development Corporation (EDC). In the eyes of some commentators, this took some of the shine off the Bombardier victory since the EDC financing did not appear to be offered as an offset to a financing package from another foreign government.

Then again, appearances are sometimes deceiving. Although the other bidders (of which Siemens was the runner-up) may not have offered special concessionary financing, they were likely to have benefited from substantial government assistance in the development and implementation of their high-speed technologies. Their technologies may have been proven, but that edge was derived in part from the experience of working on subsidized infrastructure projects in their home countries. So perhaps the EDC loan was an alternative, albeit indirect, way to counter high levels of government involvement in other countries.

The EDC, a Crown corporation responsible in theory to parliament through the minister for International Trade, also came under the spotlight. Critics charged that it was a huge gamble to lend so much money to Amtrak, an organization that faced the threat of termination in a couple of years should it not become profitable. But EDC officials countered that their agency operated as a commercial entity, raising its own funds on financial markets and covering its own bad debts arising from operations. (Although administered by the EDC, the Canada Account was a separate, government-funded program, the bad debts of which were covered by the Canadian government.) They had assessed the risk from a commercial point of view and deemed it acceptable.

The EDC's initial refusal to confirm the Amtrak loan or to provide details led critics to call an end to the Crown corporation's exemption from access to information rules. Some also called for audits by the auditor general of Canada. The response from EDC officials was that they were bound by confidentiality provisions that restricted disclosure of sensitive commercial information. "The corporation has always been exempt to reflect the fact that its operations would be constrained, if not rendered impossible, if it was expected to fully disclose,"[7] replied vice president Eric Siegel.

In the United States, an Amtrak spokesperson emphasized that the loan was fully disclosed in a *New York Times* article on March 16, 1996, just after the deal was signed with Bombardier. There was no attempt to hide anything. He added that Amtrak had won an award for the financial deal from the John F. Kennedy School of Government at Harvard University. In Congress, an aide to a transportation subcommittee dismissed the ruckus, saying: "I think it saved us money."[8]

In any event, the Acela Express was officially launched into regular service just prior to Christmas of 2000. Bombardier had navigated a series of setbacks and crises extending over a decade to finally emerge with a showcase of high-speed train travel in North America. It was an uphill path. The company had to contend with a trend in the 1980s and 1990s toward fiscal conservatism in the government sector, which lessened the chances of obtaining public funding of any amount, never mind the high levels in other countries. Also, Bombardier had to contend with lobbying by airline operators and other groups who would be disadvantaged by more attractive rail transportation.

Laurent's persistence reflects a deep conviction that high-speed train service is just a matter of time in North America, something that should ultimately take root and become pervasive. The logic of escalating population, pollution, and traffic congestion all appear to point to a shift in preferences over the long term for rail transportation. Furthermore, high-speed versions of train travel can offer a viable substitute to air and road travel between metropolitan areas within 800 kilometers (500 miles) of each other. And now that government budgets are showing surpluses in the 2000s, chances have increased for greater public funding of rail infrastructure projects. All in all, if everything comes through, a huge market, worth hundreds of billions of dollars, awaits, something perhaps worth pursuing with dogged determination.

Another technology with promise is automated metros—subways operated without drivers. Cars on these systems are controlled by a central command station equipped with banks of computers, surveillance cameras, and a handful of technicians. There also are no ticket agents. Passengers buy passes from vending machines at metro stops. About the only employees on the line are security patrols who do spot checks to ensure passengers have boarded with valid passes.

"A shift to fully automatic operation may well prove to be the next major advance in metro technology,"[9] writes transportation analyst William Middleton. A Brussels-based body representing transit professionals and manufacturers, Union Internationale des Transports Publics (UITP), issued an assessment of automated metros in 1997. The main conclusion was that they made economic sense and provided more frequent and reliable service: "A totally automated metro is less expensive in both investment and ongoing maintenance costs than a metro system with drivers. It also offers a much more attractive service quality."[10]

So far, there is only one automated metro in North America: the Skytrain in Vancouver. It was one of the first in the world, commencing operation in 1986. It runs underground in the city core, then on ground level and elevated tracks beyond. During rush hours, Skytrain cars come along every two minutes, and during off-peak hours at least every five minutes. Four more automated metros are located in France and another two in Japan. One was recently built in Kuala Lumpur, Malaysia.

The main supplier of equipment behind the Vancouver and Kuala Lumpur projects is Bombardier, a position that began with subcontract work on the Skytrain in the 1980s. The involvement then deepened with the purchase of Urban Transportation Development Corp. (UTDC), the company that originated the proprietary Skytrain technology. The UTDC was created in 1974 by the Ontario provincial government to promote mass transit over automobile expressways as a solution to traffic congestion on Toronto streets.

It was originally a small research organization of 40 persons entrusted with finding a transit mode that was cheaper than subways yet avoided the unreliability problems of mass transit systems based on mixed traffic grids such as buses and streetcars. Within a dozen years, UTDC had mushroomed into a world-scale supplier of urban transit systems with more than 1,800 employees, two manufacturing plants, and nine subsidiaries. Part of the growth was based on supplying equipment to the Skytrain in Vancouver and, on a lesser scale, to UTDC's smaller systems in Detroit and Scarborough, Ontario. The other part of UTDC's growth was based on supplying conventional metro equipment, mainly for Toronto's GO Transit, a commuter train system.

In 1986, the Ontario government decided to privatize UTDC. By then, the corporation had consumed over $160 million of public funds, and its new technology was experiencing problems winning market acceptance. The Vancouver, Detroit, and Scarborough contracts had required the Ontario government to put up $519 million in indemnities and bond guarantees to get the three customers to accept the risk of buying into a new technology. Yet, even with the offer of such insurance policies, there were no more takers. Two options, both politically unpalatable, loomed in the not-too-distant future: pouring more capital into UTDC, or announcing mass layoffs.

The UTDC financial accounts of the previous four years showed it had garnered a profit of $21 million on revenue of $560 million, although some analysts believed accounting principles had been stretched to inflate profitability. Nevertheless, two main bidders lined up, both from Montreal: engineering firm Lavalin Industries Inc. and Bombardier. They were given full access to the books in order to formulate their bids.

Bombardier ultimately decided against doing a deal because, for one thing, the Ontario government would not agree to cover the risk of the $519 million in guarantees extended to UTDC customers. If the equipment malfunctioned and triggered those guarantees, the owner of UTDC would be responsible for the payments. That was too much for Bombardier to accept. Lavalin consequently bought 85 percent ownership of UTDC (the government retained 15 percent) for $30 million in cash and notes.

A few years later, however, UTDC was up for sale again. Profits had evaporated as parent company Lavalin sank into financial difficulties and declared bankruptcy in 1991. Wishing to save jobs and the accumulated base of technology skills, the Ontario government took control of UTDC, paying wages for several months while searching for a new owner. This time around, the price would be a lot lower. While struggling to stay afloat prior to bankruptcy, Lavalin had diverted $25 million in cash and assets from UTDC's balance sheet and had let facilities depreciate.

Bombardier won the bidding over AEG Westinghouse Transportation Inc. of Pittsburgh, Pennsylvania, by promising to invest $30 million and maintain existing employment levels; the government promised a $17 million subsidy to pay for the cost of fixing up the mistreatment of facilities by Lavalin. Analysts applauded the takeover: Bombardier had not panicked and did not try to outbid a rival during the 1986 auction; the willingness to walk away from a risky deal was later rewarded with much better terms. For a bargain price, Bombardier became a supplier of conventional metro equipment to Toronto and environs, the third-largest mass transit market in North America (after New York City and Chicago). Other benefits were being able to present a united front in Canadian bids for international projects and the growth potential implicit in new technologies.

In 1994, the gamble on new technology hit a jackpot. A consortium led by Bombardier won a $1 billion contract to build an automated rapid transit system in Kuala Lumpur. Bombardier's portion amounted to $600 million and entailed delivering 70 transit vehicles similar in design to those used on the Skytrain. Winning the 21 kilometer (13 mile) extension to the Skytrain at a price of $1 billion in 1998 was another important victory. Vancouver authorities appeared poised to select a cheaper, streetcar alternative, but BC Premier Glen Clark intervened in the late stages to endorse Bombardier's proposal to extend the Skytrain.

To win the contract, Bombardier agreed to build a plant in British Columbia to assemble the Skytrain vehicles, providing 150 full-time jobs. A commitment was also made to build the Centre for Advanced Transit Systems to develop and market automated metro systems worldwide. In effect, Bombardier and the BC government had entered into a form of public-private sector cooperation. By giving Bombardier the chance to further hone its skills on a public infrastructure project, the province was allowing the company to develop a deeper set of skills that could be utilized in foreign markets. It was also providing a demonstration project that would show off Canadian know-how on world markets. Thus, the province was acquiring not just the Skytrain extension, but also an opportunity to participate in the spread of the automated metro technology to other countries. As contracts multiplied, so would employment and revenues at Bombardier's assembly plant and research center in British Columbia.

In 1984, Laurent went to Disneyland and posed for a photograph with Mickey Mouse. He had just signed a licensing agreement to market, manufacture, and operate the Disney-designed monorail transit system. Monorails, also known as people movers, are kind of like smaller versions of automated metros. They run over dedicated rails and have sufficient electronic intelligence to function without vehicle and station attendants. Operators are concentrated in a control center from which they monitor and control network performance through computers and video displays.

Bombardier planned to make sales to other theme parks, but it was also interested in adapting and selling the Disney technology to new applications. One was as a transporter of people within airports. Another was as a circulator in areas of high-density pedestrian traffic in downtown cores. Able to transport people above ground in open or closed cars straddling or hanging from an elevated rail, Bombardier saw the people mover as a less costly alternative to putting in underground transportation systems in certain locations.

Sales were slow coming at first. Seven years after acquiring the Disney license, the number of customers could be counted on one hand. By 1997, however, the systems were starting to catch on, with over 20 airports using people movers. They were also catching on outside the airport sector as well (in casino complexes, for example). In all, over 80 people movers were in operation in various locations around the world that year. Adtranz was a big supplier (now that Bombardier has acquired Adtranz, it is *the* big supplier). Others include Matra, Mitsubishi, and Otis Elevators. Currently, most are performing research and development to enhance their offerings. Mickey Mouse would be pleased.

Since it was initiated in the 1970s, Bombardier's foray into rail manufacturing has been a remarkable success, built on capturing major contracts to make subway cars, acquiring numerous other rail manufacturers, and developing new technologies. Within 25 years or so, the company has risen steadily through the ranks of the industry, from the very bottom to the very top. Key elements fueling this march include the introduction of new manufacturing techniques, putting the market ahead of the technology, and private-public sector partnerships. Of course, not to be overlooked is the quality of people, culture, and management.

The trouble with all this success, however, was that Bombardier again was in danger of becoming a one-product firm, with rail manufacturing overshadowing everything else. Taking the lessons of the 1970s snowmobile debacle to heart, Laurent was ready by the mid-1980s to find another leg for the stool, a third industry that would restore a balance to the growth trajectory.

Where it all began.

La Garage Bombardier opened in 1926 in Valcourt, Quebec. Joseph-Armand Bombardier, mechanic-turned-entrepreneur, patented the B7 snowmobile in 1936 and incorporated his company L'Auto-Neige Bombardier in 1942.

After World War II, the products of L'Auto-Neige Bombardier were used for many purposes, including public transport, freight transport, ambulance and rescue services, and mail delivery, as shown here.

Joseph-Armand Bombardier. A prolific inventor, he obtained over 40 patents in less than 25 years. The mechanic-turned-entrepreneur laid the foundation of what would become one of Canada's biggest manufacturing companies, and a global powerhouse in transportation.

Ski-Doos then and now.

A prototype of the light vehicles that were the forerunners of the Ski-Doo snowmobile. Joseph-Armand Bombardier tested them himself over the winters of 1957 and 1958.

Today the name Ski-Doo is synonymous with snowmobile. Bombardier remains a leader in the global snowmobile market.

Sea-Doo personal watercraft lead the industry in sales, as well as in innovations such as sound reduction systems and environmentally-friendly technology that reduces emissions and fuel consumption.

Sea-Doo sport boats use jet-propulsion technology, providing stronger acceleration, superior handling, and greater safety than traditional propellor-powered boats. In 2001, Bombardier expanded their marine products, acquiring the engine assets of Outboard Marine Corporation (OMC), which include Johnson and Evinrude engines.

The final signing of the New York subway car contract on November 15, 1982, which launched Bombardier into the big leagues in the mass transit business: (left to right) Raymond Royer, then President and Chief Operating Officer of Bombardier; Laurent Beaudoin, Chairman and Chief Executive Officer of Bombardier; Richard Ravitch, then Chairman of the Metropolitan Transportation Authority of New York; The Honourable Gerald A. Regan, then Canadian Minister of State for International Trade; and The Honourable Edward Lumley, then Canadian Minister of Industry and Regional Economic Expansion.

Rapid Transit Vehicle for the New York City subway system.

The acquisition of DaimlerChrysler Rail Systems GmbH (Adtranz) in 2001 firmly positioned Bombardier as the world's number one manufacturer of rail transportation equipment, across diverse product segments such as intercity rail, regional and commuter trains, rapid transit systems, and light rail vehicles. Shown here are high-speed electric trains for Amtrak, USA.

The Canadair 415 amphibian is the most advanced firefighting aircraft in the world.

The Learjet 45. Bombardier leads the business jet market with a range of products, including Learjet, Challenger, Bombardier Continental, and the ultra long-range Global Express.

The CRJ700 70-seat regional jet. Bombardier is a world leader in the regional jet market. CRJ aircraft have revolutionized the airline industry and are now in service or on order with airlines worldwide.

(Left) Laurent Beaudoin, Chairman of the Board and of the Executive Committee of Bombardier Inc. The son-in-law of Joseph-Armand Bombardier, he was only 27 years old when he became President of the company in 1966.

(Right) Robert E. Brown, President and Chief Executive Officer of Bombardier Inc.

8
CHAPTER

Turning into Aerospace

Bombardier's diversification into aerospace manufacturing was made possible by the success of the mass transit group in the 1980s. While the recreational vehicles group of Bombardier was holding its own, the mass transit group surged ahead and produced rising inflows of cash and an appreciating share price, which supported several new issues of stock. Combined, these sources of capital gave Bombardier the wherewithal to embark on a series of acquisitions and investments. One option exercised was to plow funds into opportunities within the mass transit group. But as this group got bigger, concerns mounted that Bombardier was again becoming a one-product firm. As of the mid-1980s, therefore, Laurent Beaudoin felt the time had come to extend Bombardier's core competencies to new and counterbalancing product lines.

Fueling Laurent's drive to diversify was his desire to create a corporation that would endure, one that would outlive the Bombardier family, and one "where French-Canadians could be proudly in the manufacturing sector, maybe even internationally."[1] He did not want to follow the tradition of Quebec businessmen selling off their companies to outside interests. He wanted to remain independent and build a shared monument to the Bombardier family and French-Canadians (later, this evolved to include all Canadians).

The diversification into aerospace was accomplished by flouting conventional wisdom, observed one business journalist: "Few gurus would dare suggest diversifying by acquiring a string of nearly bankrupt companies. Yet, that is precisely how Beaudoin built his most successful business: the aerospace unit..."[2] Another journalist marveled at the deal-making prowess displayed. "Donald Trump's book, *The Art of the Deal*, could have been authored by Beaudoin,"[3] he said.

Hugo Uyterhoeven, a Harvard Business School professor who sits on Bombardier's board, attributes Laurent's success in this area to his conservative-aggressive makeup. He is a rare breed of "disciplined entrepreneur," says Uyterhoeven. "In his heart and soul, he is an entrepreneur, but he was trained as an accountant. These two conflicting traits have worked to Bombardier's benefit. Beaudoin...has always blended risk-taking with an accountant's prudence."[4]

Yet, Laurent's very first acquisition, the purchase of MLW-Worthington in the mid-1970s, was a disaster. The company looked good financially, but everything else was bad, as Laurent came to realize. There were rundown facilities, poor morale, and deteriorating customer relationships: "You can have a very strong balance sheet, but no business."[5] After several years of trying to fix things up, he had to throw in the towel and close down most of the operations. Nevertheless, from this dismal experience,

Laurent learned several important lessons that were to be effectively applied to the building of Bombardier's aerospace group.

A primary lesson was the importance of due diligence, which
involved a lot more than just going over the income statements
and balance sheets. It included an exhaustive study of the situation. The business in its entirety had to be checked out in
painstaking detail. Markets and competitive forces were high on
the list. So was gauging the culture and values within the target
company. Were they compatible with Bombardier's or at least not
likely to clash?

Another key lesson was to confine acquisitions and investments to niche markets. Chances of success were increased if the
expansion was into markets in which larger rivals were not interested and there was a good chance of emerging as the dominant
player. The drive to gain a competitive edge took different forms,
but central to the dynamic was building a critical mass after the
initial acquisition or investment, usually through acquisitions of
other members in the niche. Consolidating a number of companies into one entity could generate lower unit costs and help
rationalize the supply side of the market.

Laurent usually preferred to buy companies at bargain prices.
This usually meant purchasing a company with flaws, which
Bombardier could fix by passing on its own expertise in marketing, manufacturing, and other systems. And he preferred companies with growth potential, particularly troubled ones with
crippled balance sheets that did not allow them to commercialize embryonic but promising technologies. By taking over the
company and injecting capital, Bombardier could unleash the
growth potential.

Although it was not Laurent's express purpose, buying
companies when they were cheap also helped put Bombardier
in tune with macroeconomic fluctuations. A preference for
inexpensive companies led to a greater number of acquisitions

during downturns in the economy, just prior to the recovery coming along and lending a hand to turnaround efforts. Conversely, this approach tended to reduce acquisitions during upturns, when the economy was close to peaking.

When negotiating an acquisition, Laurent did not hesitate to walk away if something was not right. This kind of disposition was perhaps the most vital element of his approach. As he said, "I have resolutely followed one principle throughout my career, one that everyone in business should respect. That is, never want something at any cost. Whatever transaction you are planning, you should always allow yourself room for retreat."[6]

If an analogy can be used, Bombardier's style appeared to be more like professional golfers who focus on their game rather than letting the performance of rivals pressure them into chancier shots. Its game was about taking the safe shot and staying out of trouble. The better play was to lay up in front of the hazard rather than risk going in and taking a penalty stroke.

Laurent was never in a rush to do deals. Patience was indeed the key. "I look at opportunities as they present themselves in the market. It is important to have a broad view, to know the business and competition well, and to have a good idea of where you want to go. Then you just wait for opportunities. They will come around."[7] A competitor might rush to do deals and jump ahead in the race for a time, but the panic button did not get pressed often in the offices of Bombardier.

From one perspective, Laurent's diversification strategy could be described as opportunistic. "Sometimes the greatest plan is just reacting to short-term opportunities," he stated in an 1995 interview.[8] Indeed, Laurent often gave the impression that his diversification policy was more in the nature of just ambling along, grabbing openings as they arose. There were never any lofty dreams to take Bombardier into particular sectors; the diversifications came about from the interplay of chance and volition.

Prior to the move into aerospace, Bombardier had several other initiatives under consideration as possible avenues for diversification. One of them, the manufacturing of military vehicles, commenced in the early 1980s with an order from the Canadian Armed Forces to make 2,800 military trucks (under an American Motors license). Shortly after, Bombardier received an another order from the Canadian Armed Forces, this time to manufacture 1,900 Iltis military jeeps (under a Volkswagen AG license).

A year or so later, Bombardier parlayed the Iltis manufacturing experience into the export market by winning an order from the Belgian government for 2,500 units. However, to win the deal over other bidders, an aggressive offset agreement was arranged wherein the Canadian government committed Canadian entities to purchases of Belgian goods worth three times the amount of the Iltis deal. (The norm in Belgium was about one times the contract amount, while in Canada, it was closer to 60 percent.) On top of this offset agreement, the price of the vehicles sold to Belgium was set at about $20,000 each, about $12,000 less than what the Canadian Armed Forces paid earlier.[9] Some members of the European Community protested, but the deal held up.

By the end of the 1980s, Bombardier was no longer manufacturing military vehicles in quantity. Thus, this instance of public-private sector cooperation was not a success, certainly not on a level with that realized in the mass transit field. There, a chance to work on a domestic infrastructure project enabled the acquisition of technology and skills sufficient for the creation of a viable export capacity. In the case of military vehicles, an export capability did not result. Overcoming foreign expertise and preferential purchasing policies in defense spending was just too insurmountable a task. It was not a niche market in which Bombardier could seize a competitive edge.

Winning deals in global markets would require an unacceptable degree of lubrication by the government.

The second major initiative under consideration prior to the aerospace diversification involved a large-scale research study into the feasibility of manufacturing a microcar for urban use in North America. It would be a small car with a three-cylinder engine suitable for zipping around in the city. Likely buyers would be students and families wanting a second vehicle.

The objectives of the research study were to quantify demand for such a car, perform a detailed costing and engineering analysis, and prepare prototypes. Technical and financial support for making the car was sought through a joint venture with Japan's smallest automobile maker, Daihatsu Motor Co. The latter would make available its small-car design and several proprietary components, as well as financial support. Bombardier would provide plant facilities and equipment for the assembly of a microcar adapted to Canadian weather conditions. The company also anticipated receiving government support "as was given to other auto assembly projects in Quebec and Ontario."[10]

The Venus Project, as it was called, was scheduled to go into full production by 1991, with about 200,000 units rolling off the assembly line annually. In late 1986, however, preparations were called off. Market studies indicated uncertainties over the size of the market. And while research and negotiations with Daihatsu were in progress, the yen had appreciated substantially against the Canadian dollar, making the Daihatsu drivetrain and other parts more expensive. Moreover, as much as 35 percent of world automobile plant capacity was idle at the time, which meant that some of the big automobile companies would have the flexibility to enter the niche should Bombardier prove it was lucrative.[11]

While Bombardier was in the midst of pondering the microcar venture, Laurent was approached by Michael Culver (son of

David Culver, a former chief executive at Alcan Aluminum). As a principal in an investment boutique specializing in aerospace banking (and a former marketing executive at Canadair), he was interested in brokering the sale of Canadair Inc. to Bombardier. He gave Laurent a report to read and recommended putting in an offer. At first, Laurent was skeptical. He was not interested in Canadair because of its well-publicized troubles.

Canadair has a long history, mostly positive in the beginning. It began in 1911 as the Canadian subsidiary of British firm Vickers and Sons Co. It made flying boats in the 1920s for use by the Royal Canadian Mounted Police on the numerous lakes and inlets of Canada. During World War II, production shifted mainly to military airplanes, and in 1947, the company was purchased by US defense contractor General Dynamics Corp., which kept the factory floor humming during the 1950s producing F-86 Sabre Jets. The 1960s were also a successful decade, aided by the design and manufacture of two planes: the CL-41 Tutor Jet (used by training pilots and precise-flying teams such as the Canadian Forces Snowbirds) and the CL-215 Water Bomber (used for fighting forest fires).

In the 1970s, recession and the winding down of the Vietnam War hit Canadair hard: the workforce plummeted from 9,200 in 1968 to less than 2,000 in 1975. General Dynamics decided to close down the plant. But the federal government did not want to see a large piece of Canada's aerospace industry go under, so it bought Canadair with the intention of sprucing it up for resale to the private sector. While the sprucing up went ahead, there was the question of retaining a nucleus of the top 250 engineers. To this end, in 1975, President Fred Kearns initiated, with the approval of Jean Chrétien, then minister of Industry, a project to design and build a business jet for corporate executives. Called the Challenger, the aircraft design would be leading edge. It would feature a wide-bodied fuselage that would be the first to allow passengers to stand up and move freely about inside the cabin. Special reinforced materials would also be used to increase durability and the capacity to serve as a carrier for courier companies such as Fed Ex.

By the spring of 1978, the Challenger was ready for test flights and the certification process (testing by government inspectors). At a display ceremony for dignitaries, the guest of honor, the Honourable Jean Chrétien, donned a Montreal Expos' baseball cap and climbed aboard a tractor ready to tow the airplane out of the hanger. But Kearns persuaded him to let the experts do it.

This initial burst of excitement over the airplane, however, was short lived. Certification took a lot longer than expected, and work increasingly fell behind schedule and over budget. The 1981 annual report put the total cost of the Challenger program at $1.2 billion, nearly twice the original estimate. Only 33 aircraft had been delivered to customers instead of the projected 113, leading to losses. Not helping matters was the unfortunate timing of having a new airplane come to market in the midst of a severe recession.

With a continuing shortfall in revenue, borrowing from banks escalated, and government officials became concerned enough to appoint review committees. The financial troubles spilled into the public arena in 1983 when an investigative news program on CBC television, *The Fifth Estate*, ran a series of damning reports. In the federal election of 1984, the privatization of Canadair (and other Crown corporations under the aegis of the Canada Development Corp.) was a main pledge of the victorious Progressive Conservative Party.

In preparation for the sale to the private sector, Canadair's finances were reorganized by transferring $1.2 billion in debt off the books to a shell Crown corporation. In the spring of

1986, debt-free and starting to show profits, the company was put on the auction block. A top priority in the sale was finding a buyer willing to put resources into expanding Canadair's existing programs—of preserving, if not expanding, the base of skilled craftspersons and technologies.

Laurent, after reflecting for a month following Michael Culver's visit, overcame his initial reluctance and decided to put in a bid. Looking past the headlines, he agreed with Culver's assessment that Canadair had a good business underneath the weight of a massive debt load. Now that the debt was stripped out, it was an interesting proposition. In particular, there was an opportunity to expand into the niche of business jets, a market in which the competition would mainly consist of small firms that Bombardier would be able to take on.

Moreover, as Laurent realized, the acquisition of Canadair was consistent with Bombardier's diversification goals: core competencies could be applied to developing a product line in aerospace that would balance existing product lines. "Putting a plane together is similar to putting a railcar together," said one analyst. "You're basically installing electronics into a metal shell."[12]

Including Bombardier, five parties put in bids for Canadair. After the preliminary round of evaluation, only two were deemed to have the capital resources and operational competencies to meet the government's special objectives. One was Bombardier and the other was Canadian Aerospace Technologies, which was led by Justus Dornier of West Germany and his Canadian partner, Howard Webster of Montreal. They were invited to submit more detailed proposals.

After the detailed bids were reviewed, Bombardier was selected the winner. A number of factors were involved in Bombardier's victory, but some commentators thought one was the nationality of the two finalists. Several months earlier, the Canadian government had provoked an uproar when it sold

Ontario-based de Havilland Canada to US aerospace giant, Boeing. To sell a second Canadian aerospace firm to a group with a large foreign interest risked a rerun.

Bombardier paid $120-million cash up front and committed to paying royalties on the Challenger technology in one of two ways: a maximum of $170 million over 21 years (depending on the level of sales), or a $20-million lump sum within two years in lieu of the royalty stream. The latter option was selected by the government. To ensure Canadair's money would not be redirected away from its aerospace business, Bombardier agreed to issue shares to the government that would be redeemed dollar for dollar as spending obligations were honored. Another class of shares were issued to ensure promised levels of investment in research and development.

Some observers thought the deal was a steal for Bombardier, noting that the price was less than the company's $240 million book value and even lower than the purported liquidation value of $300 million (the receipts expected from closing down operations and selling off assets). However, there seemed to be some disagreement over the book value and breakup values of Canadair. Reports from investment dealer Burns Fry Ltd. and Industry Canada estimated a net worth between $70 and $85 million if Canadair was left operating on its own. As for the breakup value, a report prepared by accounting firm Peat Marwick Mitchell & Co. concluded that closing Canadair would have cost taxpayers between $250 to $350 million because of the requirement to pay off contractors as well as to cover severance pay, pension obligations, and related personnel matters.

Nevertheless, reaction to the sale was immediately favorable nearly all around. Businesspeople, journalists, and even Canadair's union were congratulatory. One of the lone voices of dissent was a member of the New Democratic Party, Steven Langdon. He charged that the Bombardier family was the beneficiary of billions in taxpayer dollars poured into the development of the Challenger jet. Barbara McDougall, minister of State for Privatization, argued that no company would willingly pay for the billions invested in Canadair. Those were sunk costs and the government had to accept what the company was worth on the basis of its estimated earnings potential, if it was to preserve Canadair. Others added that if Bombardier actually had paid less than breakup or book value, the difference could be viewed as the premium for securing Bombardier's commitment to further the goals of preserving the workforce and technology.

A week or so after the sale was announced, however, the general tone of approval was shattered by howls of outrage. A contract worth $1.7 billion over 20 years to maintain Canadian Forces CF-18 fighter jets was awarded to Canadair over the Winnipeg subsidiary of British Aerospace, even though the latter reportedly had submitted a better bid. Westerners took it as a sign of favoring Quebec over their region. The resulting furor was a factor in splitting the ruling Progressive Conservative Party and fueling the formation of the Reform (later Alliance) Party, which displaced the Conservatives as the official opposition party in parliament over most of the 1990s.

But brokerage analysts were still smiling. Bombardier's share price climbed strongly several months afterward as the market bet on the benefits to be reaped. In fact, the Canadair acquisition was immediately accretive to earnings. Profits exceeded expectations in the first six months due to an accelerated completion of backlogged orders. But it was the long term that was truly attractive. Bombardier had taken possession of Canadair just as the Challenger technology was taking shape. There was also a growth opportunity: the wide-bodied fuselage of the 12-seat business jet could be stretched into a 50-seat, short-range jet marketable to regional airline carriers.

In sum, Bombardier got a valuable growth prospect at a good price and risk thanks in large part to Laurent's *modus operandi* of waiting for opportunities and not wanting anything at any cost. Bombardier was willing to offer the government the best hope of meeting its objectives in return for takeover terms sufficiently advantageous to the bottom line. If attractive enough terms had not been available, Bombardier would have gone on to other opportunities.

"Everyone thinks we're such great strategists," said Laurent, "but it was by chance that we got involved in rail transportation [and aerospace]."[13] On another occasion, he added: "Without the decision of the government to privatize Canadair...I don't think we would have gone into the aerospace sector."[14] Fellow executive Yvan Allaire described the approach overall as: "calculated risk of entry into new industries essentially at the right time."[15]

Between 1989 and 1992, Bombardier pushed further into aerospace by acquiring three more aerospace companies. The first of these was Short Brothers PLC (called Shorts) in Belfast, Northern Ireland. Shorts was one of the oldest surviving members of the global aerospace manufacturing industry. It had branched out from making hot-air balloons in 1908 with an order for six biplanes from the Wright Brothers.

In the 1930s, the company made C-Class Empire flying boats, and during World War II, Stirling heavy bombers. After nationalization in 1943 by the British government, Shorts manufactured a variety of aircraft including Solent flying boats, 36-passenger SD-360 turboprop airliners, and Tucano turboprop military trainers. In more recent times, the product range was rounded out by surface-to-air missiles for the British military and subcontracts to make components for original equipment manufacturers.

Under the bureaucrats, Shorts was a perennial money loser. In the year prior to Bombardier's takeover, it had lost $267 million on sales of $500 million. The workforce of 7,500 had a history of labor militancy, and, composed mainly of Protestants, it sometimes was caught in the cross fire of Irish sectionalism. In the 1980s, Margaret Thatcher's Conservative party was in power with a mandate to privatize government corporations. Shorts was at the top of the list. When Thatcher put the company on the block in 1989, Bombardier saw yet another short-term opportunity to nab.

The sale of Shorts was like a replay of the Canadair sale. Bombardier paid $60 million for a corporation just relieved of more than $800 million in debt. Moreover, an order backlog of $2 billion was on the books, and the British government had committed to providing over $250 million to modernize the plant, train employees, and defray other costs. But that was not all. The British government was to cover any possible losses arising on contracts signed while under public ownership.

Bombardier had acquired yet another company at a knock-down price and at low risk, again as a result of the Bombardier *modus operandi* and a willingness to negotiate within the framework of the government's socioeconomic goals. A company run according to the preferences of the government might not make strict business sense, but Bombardier was willing to give it a try if the government was willing to ante up for past mistakes in the operation of its enterprise. In exchange, Bombardier would make a commitment to preserve jobs, retain Shorts as an integrated whole for at least four years, and to invest $60 million on a plant upgrade.

Aiding the Bombardier bid was weak interest in Shorts on the part of aerospace giants Boeing and Airbus. As in the Canadair case, Shorts' product lines were mostly in niches outside their areas of interest. The only other serious bid, from a joint venture

set up by General Electric Co. PLC and Fokker NV of the Netherlands, outlined a plan to break up Shorts and sell off the various
parts. So it lost out, although not by much. Prime Minister
Thatcher was at first disinclined to accede to Bombardier's
demands for debt cancellation and several hundred million dollars in transitional subsidies, but her minister John Major (and
future prime minister) pressed her. "We had a two-hour con-
frontation that ended in fierce rowing and I was determined to
resign if overruled," he said.[16]

Bombardier was not necessarily doing anybody a favor in
taking Shorts off their hands, for the acquisition dovetailed
nicely with its own interests. Shorts would provide admission
into the common market when the European Community was
created in 1992. It would also convert a potential competitor
into a co-conspirator given the fact that Shorts had plans to
design and build its own short-range jet for regional routes.
Besides world-leading expertise in lightweight materials, Shorts
would bring hundreds of qualified engineers and extra plant
capacity to meet the production levels implicit in the nearly
200 regional jet orders then on Bombardier's order books. A
few days after the Shorts sale closed, British Airways took an
option for 20 regional jets. Sir Colin Marshall, British Airways
chairman, said: "A significant dimension of the project is the
participation of Shorts, whose involvement with Bombardier in
the design, development, and manufacture of the aircraft contribute to work in the British aerospace industry and particularly to jobs in Northern Ireland."[17]

Still, the purchase of Shorts required courage. As a maker of
planes, components, and weapons for the British military, the
company was a frequent target of the Irish Republican Army
(IRA). During the first three years of operation under Bombardier, seven terrorist bombs exploded at the facilities and
caused approximately $5 million worth of damage (but no loss

of life). As Bombardier had refused to buy Shorts unless the British government covered the risk of terrorist acts, the costs were covered by the British government.

The second of the three aerospace acquisitions was the purchase of Learjet Corp. of Wichita, Kansas. The latter company was founded in 1963 by William Lear, a character not unlike Joseph-Armand Bombardier in terms of inventive genius and entrepreneurial bent. Lear pioneered the business jet market, introducing a six-seat passenger jet adapted from the Swiss fighter-bomber, the P-16. In 1967, experiencing financial difficulties relating to the costs of developing new models, Learjet was sold to the Gates Rubber Co., which injected capital and streamlined operations until profitability was restored in the 1970s. William Lear continued to be involved in the development of business jet models until his death in 1978.

During the 1980s, Learjet stepped up diversification of its production base by accepting more subcontract work on defense, aerospace, and commercial aviation projects. And specialized versions of the Learjet were also sold as military aircraft to Brazil, Thailand, and other countries. Nevertheless, by the middle of the decade, Learjet was in financial difficulty again, mainly as a result of the sensitivity of its still-dominant business jet product line to downturns in the economy. In 1987, Gates bailed out of Learjet, selling a controlling interest to a leveraged buyout partnership that included Learjet managers and Integrated Resources Inc., a New York-based financial group.

As the business jet market recovered, return on Learjet's operations improved, but its financial backer went in the other direction. Struggling with a transition from tax shelter services to insurance and investment services, Integrated Resources ran out of cash to service its financial obligations and was in Chapter 11 bankruptcy protection by early 1990. This put added pressure on the company to proceed with its planned disposition of Learjet (then with 2,750 employees and annual sales of $250 million US). Bombardier, sensing an opportunity to negotiate a good price, entered the bidding and gained control by agreeing to pay $75 million US and assume $38 million US in liabilities. The fact that Laurent had passed on the opportunity to buy Learjet three years earlier when it was up for sale highlighted his patient and low-risk acquisition approach.

When the sale went through in 1990, it was another vintage Bombardier deal: for a low price, it took ownership of several valuable assets including the Lear brand name, a global network of 30 maintenance and service centers, a testing facility, relationships with defense contractors, and several lower-end business jets that would complement the larger-end Challenger jet and yield the most complete family of business jets on offer. Learjet executives welcomed Bombardier as a source of stability and capital investment.

The third aerospace acquisition between 1989 and 1992 was the purchase of de Havilland, headquartered in Downsview, near Toronto, Ontario. Started in 1928 as a subsidiary of a British firm run by Geoffrey de Havilland, operations commenced with the assembly of the Moth biplane. During World War II, production shifted to a fighter version of the Moth and to a high-altitude bomber, the Mosquito. After the war, de Havilland recuperated from a trailing off of military orders by manufacturing a military trainer of its own design and a variety of bush planes, such as the world-famous Beaver and Twin Otter.

In the 1970s, development of the Dash 7, a commuter airplane for landing on short runways, went ahead. This action was not authorized by the parent company in Britain, which, having a similar product in the works, subsequently decided to wind down the Canadian subsidiary. But the Canadian government was unwilling to see part of the Canadian aerospace industry disappear. It stepped in and bought the Canadian plant in 1974. Later, under government control, the 34-seat version of the Dash 7 came to market and was a big hit until recession ravaged the regional carriers in 1982, setting in motion a lengthy string of losses.

In 1986, the Progressive Conservative Party privatized de Havilland by selling it to Boeing Corp. (By then, de Havilland had cost taxpayers nearly $1 billion.) Over the next five years, Boeing poured more than $400 million into refurbishing antiquated facilities and developing the Dash 8 series of regional airliners. By 1992, however, troubles still persisted. High labor costs and a militant union was a factor, as was competition from Brazilian regional airplane maker, Embraer. Its international sales were assisted by a government interest rate subsidy program called Pro-ex. Moreover, an economic recession had caused sales of the Dash 8 to tumble, leading to a slashing of the workforce from 6,000 to 3,700 by 1991. Unable to make a profit and wrestling with an entrenched morale problem, Boeing decided to get out.

It looked in the beginning as if de Havilland's rival, Avions de Transport Regional (ATR), a European consortium, would buy de Havilland, with the help of several hundred million dollars in assistance from provincial and federal governments in Canada. But the European Community antitrust agency rejected the proposed deal on the grounds ATR would end up with 67 percent of the European market.

Canadian authorities, principally the ruling New Democratic Party in the province of Ontario, in which de Havilland operations were concentrated, then scrambled to find another suitor. Overtures were directed toward Bombardier, which responded with a list of conditions. Officials thought they were too extravagant, so they went off looking for other takers. Finding none, they returned to Bombardier, and signed an agreement with Bombardier.

Yet again, Bombardier's willingness to bide its time and hold out for the right deal resulted in an inexpensive and safe acquisition. There had been a chance to buy de Havilland during the 1986 privatization process and later in competition against ATR, but Bombardier was willing to let others bid higher and take the assets. Its due diligence had indicated that the higher prices others were willing to pay were overvaluing the firm in relation to its potential, so Bombardier would not match them. The company only agreed to a transaction after favorable enough terms emerged.

According to the arrangement, Bombardier would take control by putting up 51 percent of a $100 million cash injection, with the remainder coming from the Ontario government. There was an option to buy out the Ontario government's share (which Bombardier later exercised to gain full ownership). The deal also specified that the provincial and federal governments would establish a reserve fund of $300 million to cover losses incurred by de Havilland in the first four years. This was supplemented with over $200 million in shareholder loans from the provincial government, repayable as de Havilland became profitable, and another $230 million in assistance from the federal government in the combined form of interest-free loans from research and development programs and export credits from the Export Development Corporation.

The Dash 8 line of 36- and 50-seat commuter aircraft, powered by engines made by Pratt and Whitney Canada Inc. of Longueuil, Quebec, was seen as a complement to Bombardier's 50-seat regional jet aircraft then coming to market. There might be some overlap in serving the regional airline market with two such product lines, but for the most part, they were expected to address two separate niches. The Dash 8 would be more efficient for routes under 500 kilometers (300 miles), while the regional jet would be better for longer routes. Economies of scale were also expected from gaining a seasoned sales force in the regional airline market and access to a state-of-the-art paint shop in Downsview.

Thus was created the Bombardier aerospace group—from three downtrodden companies. It seemed to be almost an accidental compilation of assets, yet at the same time, a remarkable display of shrewdness. Over the 1990s, the three provided a very powerful boost to sales and profitability as Bombardier applied its turnaround skills and rode a sustained upturn in the economy. They were to launch and nurture a fleet of commercial airplanes that became the envy of other aerospace countries. They were the source of perhaps Canada's greatest aviation triumph: the Canadair Regional Jet, which is currently revolutionizing commercial air service around the world.

9

Portrait of a Turnaround Artist

Bombardier's approach to rescuing troubled companies differed from the conventional notion of a turnaround operation. Shock treatments in the form of mass layoffs and radical restructurings were not on the agenda. Nor were High Noon confrontations with unions or attempts to bulldoze ingrained cultures into the ground. Instead, existing management teams were often left in place and given freedom to get on with the job within a framework of incentives encouraging entrepreneurial behavior. Technical, managerial, and financial support was usually offered, quite often in the form of funding for upgrading facilities and developing new products.

All in all, the approach was so, well, Canadian. Mr. Nice Guy in action, one could say. But it seemed to work. By the fiscal year ending January 31, 1994, the ragtag collection of aerospace losers acquired by Bombardier was generating earnings of $135 million on sales of $2.2 billion. Over the rest of the 1990s things got even better. So how did Bombardier pull it off? How and why did its gentle turnaround artistry succeed?

It began with the takeovers themselves. In the Short Brothers acquisition, for example, Bombardier asked for three months to investigate the situation before putting in a proposal. The company really did its due diligence and would not be rushed, even if it meant losing the chance to bid. For, by striking a good deal, the chances of a successful turnaround were increased.

If satisfactory terms were not offered, Bombardier did not hesitate to back away, as illustrated by the chance in 1996 to buy Netherlands-based Fokker NV, then the leading maker of turbo-prop regional aircraft. After parent company Daimler Benz pulled the plug on its money-losing subsidiary, the Dutch government kept Fokker afloat while it searched for a buyer. Bombardier was a leading candidate, but it could not get the Dutch government to agree to what it thought were reasonable terms for a rescue operation. At this impasse, the talks broke off. Several other companies continued to negotiate to purchase Fokker, but its position was too far gone. In 1997, the company was wound down.

Once completed, a Bombardier takeover was in itself enough to start the healing process. Even before any actions were taken, there was an improvement merely because customers would regain confidence in the products of the distressed company. Before, they would be worried that they might be left holding a product with no service or warranty guarantees in the event of an insolvency, so they would hold back from purchases. But with Bombardier's financial and management strength standing behind the company, this worry was removed, and sales revived. At the time of the Learjet takeover in 1990, Chairman and CEO Brian Barents welcomed the chance to join Bombardier because: "Our competitors have made hay out of the fact our parent is bankrupt."[1]

When Canadair was acquired, most of the original management team had departed in the aftermath of the media probes into the corporation's miscues, leaving a caretaker executive group in place during the privatization. In this situation, Bombardier found new leadership, appointing Donald C. Lowe as president. Tall and gray-haired, he was forthright and had a presence that suggested the archetypal CEO. But there was a lot more than image to Lowe. He had demonstrated his turnaround skills earlier as president of Pratt and Whitney Canada Ltd. and then at Kid Creek Mines Ltd. Moreover, as a result of his years working in the aerospace industry, he was well known and respected by Canadair senior staff. His appointment was credited with getting the relationship between Bombardier and Canadair off on the right foot.

After several months of study, Lowe and Laurent got busy on the Canadair turnaround. A major problem with the company, in their eyes, was an overly bureaucratic structure. Numerous management layers made decision making lengthy and tedious. And responsibilities were too widely diffused. Employees and managers typically reported to three or four authorities in different areas, so nobody knew what they were responsible for. Lines of accountability were unclear, creating an environment in which staff were more concerned about preserving their jobs than taking action.

In response, Lowe and Laurent set up an organizational structure in which the main businesses—executive jets, water bombers, defense systems, and subcontracting—were "divisionalized" and turned into profit centers. Heads of the new units were given considerable independence to achieve goals. Where they once were just responsible for administering their divisions, they would now be responsible for managing their own marketing, customer service, product development, and cost structure.

They had more levers directly under their control, allowing them to act expeditiously in pursuit of goals, similar to an entrepreneur running a business. Pay was linked to performance, to how well they did on the bottom line.

Another important step was to bring in new business and diversify production at Canadair (as was done with the other acquisitions). New sources of revenues brought growth and stability to operations while spreading overhead costs over a greater base. The CF-18 maintenance contract was a first step in this direction. This was followed by the winning of several other contracts, notably the $1.7-billion subcontract from the Airbus consortium (members included French-based Aerospatiale and British Aerospace) to make components for their A330 and A340 models. Complementing these business-building initiatives were several in-house projects to create new versions of existing Canadair airplanes: a turboprop model of the CL-215 water bomber and the 50-seat Canadair Regional Jet.

This approach contrasted with Boeing's attempts to turn around de Havilland. Essentially, Boeing went in the opposite direction. Instead of broadening product lines, they narrowed the focus. Older lines, such as the Twin Otter, were shut down in favor of concentrating on the Dash 8 commuter aircraft. The plan was to enhance productivity by standardizing procedures and achieving long production lines on the Dash 8. Then, once profits started to roll in, the range of models would be extended into a family. However, the problem with this strategy was that de Havilland's growth trajectory would take longer to ramp up, be more vulnerable to market fluctuations, and bear higher per-unit overhead costs.

Furthermore, the Boeing approach involved subjecting existing production processes to more of a shock—taking away business and reshaping what remained. Not surprisingly perhaps, Boeing ran into problems with morale. The unions at de Havilland were more aggressive to begin with, but Boeing's approach did little to reduce militancy and win the workforce flexibility it needed to make the company profitable. By contrast, Bombardier's attitude of adding new businesses and products provided a basis for a happier workforce. In an growth environment, there were more opportunities for employment and promotion.

As for Shorts, when it became part of Bombardier, the day-to-day operations were left in the hands of existing management, led by Managing Director Roy McNulty. He and his team were given the capital, encouragement, and freedom to act on what they thought had to be done, with the understanding that it had to be validated by bottom line. The presence of Bombardier executives was limited mainly to meetings of the board. Otherwise, there were just a handful of mid-level Bombardier managers on site to help Shorts adapt to Bombardier's accounting and other systems.

McNulty gave an example of how the decision-making process was improved under Bombardier. The matter under consideration was whether or not to buy a vacant factory building to house the center for the manufacture of composite materials (used, for example, to build fuselages). According to McNulty, Bombardier executives gave approval after the proposal had been on the table for less than two hours at the director's meeting. By contrast, when the government was in control, the same proposition had been under deliberation for three years.

The other thing that improved was the physical plant and equipment. Shorts was a classic illustration of the tendency toward underinvestment under government ownership. Because government budgets typically group capital expenditures with current expenditures, large sums tend not to be handed out for upgrading facilities. They make government budgets look bad. Under Bombardier, however, hundreds of millions of dollars (including transitional subsidies from the government) were poured into a modernization drive. Labor-intensive machines dating back to the 1950s were replaced with more advanced versions, and computer-aided design and robotization techniques became more widespread. The end result was a boost to productivity.

When considering the purchase of Shorts, Bombardier examined more than the income statement and balance sheet. The company also did a thorough evaluation (as with other acquisition candidates) of Shorts' culture and value system. They talked to all levels of management and to union leaders. The interviewees were asked for an assessment of their organization and how they viewed their present and future roles. "When we look at a possible acquisition, the first thing we look at in-house is whether or not we share the same values," Bombardier president Raymond Royer once mentioned. "What we are trying to do is to see if there is a common understanding of what we are trying to achieve as a company and what the [acquired] firm...is trying to achieve."[2]

Bombardier was prepared to accept and respect differences in culture but not in core values. If the latter was the case, the offer to buy would be withdrawn. By refusing to get involved with companies whose core values were too much at variance, the risk of disharmonious and counterproductive mergers was minimized. In the case of Shorts, there was enough of a shared set of core values to proceed. Those values included a commitment to foster growth, respect for people, and a belief that the quality of a corporation was derived from the quality of its people.

With similarity in belief systems, it was relatively smooth sailing for Bombardier to discuss with Shorts' management what had to be done. From this process, for example, came the decision to abandon the executive dining room and spruce up the dingy cafeteria used by the employees. And a sophisticated training and management development program was set up, as well as a promotion policy based on hiring from within (as had been done at

Canadair). In effect, management and employees were entering into a commitment to support each others' growth. Managers would provide the setting for employees to get what they wanted as long as they provided what the corporation needed to sustain such an environment.

Substantial changes were also made in industrial relations. One of the conditions Bombardier had negotiated during the purchase of Shorts was that the seven separate bargaining units would be combined into one group to bargain for everybody. As well, contracts were to be elongated from one year to multiple years. Implementing these changes brought much needed stability to operations and considerably reduced resource requirements in the industrial relations area. Unions tend to resist such measures, but the unions at Shorts were aware that without Bombardier's involvement, the most likely alternatives were either a breakup of the company or bankruptcy.

When Learjet was acquired, the turnaround followed a pattern similar in many respects to Shorts'. President Brian Barents was not sacked, but was allowed to stay on and implement his turnaround plan. What Learjet actually needed most was money to bring its technology and product lines up to date. Saddled with debt and a bankrupt parent, there had been insufficient funding to do so, which Bombardier corrected. Within two years of assuming control, over $100 million was allocated for developing derivatives of two Learjet models.

By the time the de Havilland acquisition came along, another dynamic was contributing to turnaround efforts: horizontal integration. As orders for business and regional aircraft mounted, the new companies coming into the fold provided additional production capacity and new competencies. Work was allocated across the four companies according to their spare capacity and areas of specialization, capturing economies of scale from a more extensive division of labor.

As Bombardier Aerospace transformed itself into an integrated entity, Canadair emerged as the place for milling big aluminum components and assembling regional jets. Shorts' plant supplied special composite materials and fuselages for the business and regional jets. In addition to the assembly of propeller-driven aircraft and the Global Express business jet, the facilities at de Havilland made wings for the Learjet 45. Also, their state-of-the-art paint shop was where a number of Bombardier planes were sent to be touched up. The Learjet site assembled the smaller business jets and brought to the Bombardier group a network of service centers. And with 33 percent more good-weather days than Montreal, Learjet's Wichita site was also the flight test center for new airplanes.

The synergies that Bombardier captured contrasted with Boeing's attempts to generate synergies from de Havilland, not just on the production end, but also on the marketing side. For example, in putting together a family of business jets ranging from the six-seat Learjet to the Challenger to the Global Express, Bombardier created more scope for customers to trade up or down or to add new models to their existing holdings. By comparison, the Boeing-de Havilland connection produced less cross-fertilization between its big airliners and de Havilland's regional aircraft. There was just too much disparity between the two.

Horizontal integration, along with the policy of diversifying the production base at each subsidiary, had not only imparted growth to each, but product mixes were well positioned to weather market downturns. The spreading of risk at Shorts illustrated this. In 1995, besides making fuselages for Bombardier, it also made wings for Fokker regional aircraft, engine castings for

Airbus airliners, body parts for Boeing aircraft, antitank missiles, and equipment for Apache military helicopters. Ten years before, Shorts' survival was based mostly on the Short 360 "flying shed" propeller aircraft.

Horizontal integration was a useful tool for weaning the acquired companies away from their high degrees of vertical integration. With powerful unions on the shop floor, there was a tendency to have as much of the airplane built in-house as possible. Attempts to subcontract work out to more efficient suppliers risked strikes and labor disruptions, especially at de Havilland, where workers fought Boeing's remodeling attempts by filing grievances at the rate of over 1,000 per year. But through horizontal integration, Bombardier was able to offer offsetting work as a replacement for contracted-out activities. Indeed, by bringing in more new business than what was taken out, there was considerably more room to move to the optimal arrangement of in-house and contracted-out work.

Aiding this and other adjustments was Bombardier's sensitivity to employee relations. Learjet president Barents, in particular, was impressed with the way Bombardier got relations off to a good start. "They began the process not by coming in and asking questions but by explaining who they were and why they were interested in us."[3]

Mulling over the closure in 1992 of de Havilland's interior trim and seat shops in favor of outside suppliers, a Bombardier Aerospace executive explained how Bombardier typically approached such contentious issues: "We don't do anything without revealing it [in advance and] having a study and implementation plan. We're very thorough. That approach is going to pay dividends in dealing with employees."[4] Indeed, Bombardier's practice of opening up channels for communication and participation in corporate changes was such a breath of fresh air that Buzz Hargrove, head of the Canadian Auto Workers union, at one point described Bombardier's management as enlightened. "It's a good company to work for," he said.[5]

The attempt to get employees to buy into the company mission was also evident in the Shorts' acquisition. For example, to allay the concerns of the workforce, Bombardier invited representatives from the different unions to come to Canada and talk to Canadair employees. Further, they asked them to make arrangements with their counterparts in the Canadair union to be their hosts so that union people would be able to speak directly with each other.

But one of the most important contributions to turning around the floundering aerospace companies was the transfer of the Bombardier Manufacturing System (BMS) and other techniques from the mass transit divisions. In the case of Canadair, the transfer started with a five-year, quarter-billion-dollar expansion program called "Building Our Future." It included the addition of a new administration building and rearrangement of manufacturing layout to improve the flow of information and materials. Just-in-time (JIT) inventory control and new quality control methods were also introduced.

Prior to Bombardier's arrival, manufacturing at Canadair was much like it was elsewhere in the aerospace industry. New airplanes were very emotional products; engineers often got tears in their eyes when one of their designs made its maiden flight. As such, the focus was not very much on cost. Design engineers reigned supreme; they tended to draw up their blueprints with the idea of creating the best, most technically advanced plane in its category. When they were finished, the design was handed over to the manufacturing engineers and specialists with little regard for facilitating production.

In bringing design and manufacturing engineers together, however, the BMS achieved a greater consciousness of cost in the design of airplanes. For example, when development of the

70-seat Canadair Regional Jet was given the green light in 1996, 400 design engineers and 150 manufacturing engineers came together to discuss how they could build the right plane to the right quality at the right cost. The first thing on the agenda was building a model—not a plane model, but a financial model. "Our business is not making airplanes," said one Bombardier executive. "Our business is earning a respectable return for the shareholders. Airplanes are the means by which we accomplish that objective."[6]

The central player in the BMS is the methods department. Its responsibility is to work closely with the various components of the team as a coordinator. For example, it works closely with the engineering department to set up a manufacturing schedule and, with the procurement department, to advise on what tools to gather and how to plan the production line. The end goal is to put together a plane that will earn a profit. As an executive vice president of engineering in the Bombardier Aerospace group, John Holding declared: "We are not here only to make great aircraft. The Concorde is a great aircraft but it doesn't make money. Bombardier is here to make money."[7]

10

Revolution in the Sky

"What does it mean to leverage the type certificate?"[1] Laurent Beaudoin asked an advisor as he pondered the acquisition of Canadair Ltd. He was told, in so many words, that the type certificate was a document the government gave to the manufacturer of a new airplane model after it had passed through the certification process. In this instance, the type certificate belonged to the Challenger aircraft; the act of leveraging it involved stretching the size of the 12-seat business jet to a 50-seat aircraft for commercial passenger service.

The idea of transforming the Challenger "from a racehorse into a workhorse"[2] was attributed to Eric McConachie. In fact, many believed he deserved to be called the father of the Canadair Regional Jet. This product line, expanded to 70-seat and 90-seat versions in subsequent years, became one of Bombardier's principal growth engines over the 1990s and arguably the greatest aerospace achievement in Canada to date.

Today, McConachie is still going strong. In his seventies, the Edmonton-born aeronautical engineer is running a one-man aviation consultancy, AvPlan Inc., in Montreal. Over six feet tall (1.8 meters), he has a lone-wolf quality about him. Yet, he enjoys mixing at social gatherings, and his colourful language is laced with many quips and anecdotes. He obviously is a smart guy. His résumé shows advanced degrees in aerospace engineering: a Master of Science from the Massachusetts Institute of Technology and a Ph.D. from Stanford University.

Way back in 1953, McConachie joined CP Air to work on airplane evaluations. In 1958, he turned down a job offer from Boeing because he "had a maple leaf tattooed to his butt,"[3] accepting an offer from Canadair instead. There, as a senior executive in charge of marketing and sales engineering, he was responsible for (among other things) developing ideas for new airplane models, of which the CL-215 water bomber was one his more notable projects. In 1967, feeling frustrated with the slow pace of airplane development and marketing, McConachie "got tired of the crap"[4] and left Canadair to establish his own consulting firm, then called Aviation Planning Services Ltd., a forerunner to his present firm. For the next 20 years, he was in his element, carrying out more than 400 aviation studies for over 100 clients around the world.

Over the 1980s, he watched an interesting trend unfold in the US airline industry: the emergence of the hub-and-spoke system following the passage of the *Airline Deregulation Act* in 1978. In dismantling the Civil Aeronautics Board, the act phased out the administrative allocation of air routes and control over fares, opening the door to a intense free-for-all among hundreds of new and existing carriers. At one time, some individual routes had up to 40 airlines competing for business, usually at below-cost prices. Of the companies plying the no-frills, discount-fare strategy, People Express was one of the ringleaders, offering for a time a $99 US one-way, coast-to-coast ticket.

With their profits dissolving into losses, the incumbent carriers were locked into a struggle for survival. They were hit hard because of their high-cost, unionized workforces. They were also held back by the composition of their fleets. During the era of regulation, airline companies loaded up on large, 110- to 500-seat jets (the planes could fly with many empty seats on a route but would still be economic since returns were based on costs). Now, in the free-market environment of deregulation, many of those big birds were uneconomic because returns were based upon the number of seats filled, and those seats were increasingly departing empty as new airline companies emerged to siphon away business.

The development of the hub-and-spoke system was the strategic response that enabled many of the major incumbent carriers to regain their preeminent position. In essence, establishing a hub-and-spoke arrangement involved dropping numerous point-to-point routes and concentrating the remaining, more efficient part of the fleet at a major airport, to the point whereby the airline carrier would become the dominant supplier of flights out of that location. This system had actually started up during the period of regulation but never expanded because of legislated restrictions on dropping and adding routes. Examples of hubs are Delta Airlines in Atlanta, United Airlines in Chicago, and American Airlines in Dallas.

The hubs were advantageous to the major airlines because of economies of scale and scope. The benefits of scale derived from the concentration of labor resources and ground equipment (for example, aircraft pushers, baggage haulers, and maintenance equipment) at a single location, thus spreading their costs across more arrivals and departures. The benefits of scope derived from being able to provide service to many more cities with fewer aircraft and flight crews. For example, a hub connecting 20 cities to the east and 20 more to the west could provide same-day service to 440 city pairs with just 40 airplanes individually flying the routes between the hub and the connecting cities, whereas an airline providing direct flights between the 40 cities and hub would need far more—in the hundreds.

Regional airlines serviced short-haul routes in and around the hub-and-spoke system. They brought passenger traffic into the hub and adjacent cities, helping to fill up the seats of the major carriers operating out of the hubs. Recognizing the importance of the regional airlines, the major airlines entered into so-called code-sharing agreements to share reservation systems and revenues with them. Within this environment, regional airlines were to enjoy a renaissance, both in the United States and Europe (which was to deregulate, too). Many new outfits were started up, and some routes abandoned by the major carriers were put back into service by the regional carriers. As a result, demand for regional airplanes, defined as 20- to 110-seaters, was on the rise. Most of the suppliers were European makers of propeller-driven aircraft.

McConachie, in tune with the dynamics of the airline industry, saw these trends emerge. He also saw how the hub-and-spoke system, while great for the major airlines, created inconveniences for consumers. There was the abandonment of air service to many communities. And for those areas with air service, there were fewer direct flights to destinations. Travelers now were more likely to stop at a hub to transfer to another airplane. A flight that would have taken an hour or two was converted into nearly an all-day journey for many travelers (and sometimes there were missed connections or unscheduled delays). The free market might be presumed to rectify these inconveniences, but the obstacle was the state of passenger aircraft technology. The major airlines had big jets that were patently uneconomic for many point-to-point journeys in a free-market environment, while the regional airplanes had small planes that were noisy, slow, and could fly only short distances before having to land for refueling.

Aware of the capabilities of the Challenger airplane, McConachie saw an opportunity to push back the technological boundaries in favor of the consumer. As it was capable of speeds and distances of at least 50 percent greater than the average propeller airplane, why not, he reasoned, stretch the Challenger to expand seating capacity from 12 to 50 persons, thus turning it into a passenger jet? Stretching the plane was, after all, technically feasible since the Challenger, unlike other executive jets of the time, had been built with a reinforced, wide-body fuselage capable of two-by-two seating.

A stretched Challenger could improve service in many ways. Regional airline companies would be able to transport their passengers faster to their destinations, as well as open up longer routes and fly over hubs. The major airlines would be able to provide more service on small-load routes and on large-load routes during off-peak hours. In sum, McConachie sensed an opportunity to provide value in the marketplace: to connect more communities to the air grid and to reduce the number of those annoying stopovers. As such, there was a commercial opportunity to exploit.

McConachie did some "plotting and planning."[5] He submitted several unsolicited proposals to Canadair for a market study to estimate the demand for what he labeled the Challenger Regional Jet (the name was later changed to the Canadair Regional Jet). The reception was not always encouraging. Many personnel, busy enhancing and marketing the Challenger jet, were not interested. But he did find a receptive ear in executive vice president and chief operating officer Dick Richmond. He had been parachuted into the executive ranks at Canadair in 1980 as a Mr. Fixit to get the development of the Challenger back on track. He was a "grim-looking, no-nonsense...tough manager. He ruled with an iron fist...and...often dealt with a problem with the full force of his personality."[6]

When McConachie explained how the Canadair Regional Jet came to fruition, he cited the support of Richmond as one of the main reasons. The latter authorized the market research studies proposed by McConachie, starting with the first one in late 1984. One study, completed just prior to Bombardier's takeover, showed a superiority in operating costs. It estimated that the operating expense per hour on a 640-kilometer (400 mile) trip would average about $1,000 US for the regional jet, compared to $1,300 US for the then-popular Fokker F-28-4000 model. The main factor in the differential were fuel costs.

Michael Culver, pitching the idea to Bombardier of buying Canadair, told Laurent and his team about the potential of the regional jet. As part of that process, they arranged a lunch between McConachie and Bombardier staff, who, coincidentally were located just two floors apart in the same office tower in downtown Montreal. Laurent liked what he heard from McConachie and others. Indeed, with his proclivity toward entrepreneurialism, it was probably this growth opportunity that tipped the scales in favor of an acquisition.

On the eve of Bombardier's formal takeover of Canadair, McConachie gathered input from Donald Lowe, Bombardier's appointee to the position of president of Canadair, and forwarded a letter to Richmond summarizing a list of tasks that had to be undertaken to prepare Canadair management for their decision on whether or not to proceed with the regional jet. The list included preliminary specification and cost estimates, review of the regional jet concept with selected carriers, and preparation of a new brochure for presentation purposes. He wrapped up the letter with an offer: "In order to reduce the workload on your staff, I have suggested that Aviation Planning Services, in conjunction with our associated consultants, take on the bulk of the tasks...."[7]

McConachie got the green light. On October 31, 1986, he sent a letter to Lowe outlining actions taken to date. Of note was his visit to the Regional Airliner Association meeting, held October 20-22 in Las Vegas, to get a sample of interest in the regional jet. McConachie and his assistant had no official presentation scheduled, so they had to approach representatives during the coffee breaks and mealtimes, managing in this way to canvas informally 17 companies and leave preliminary brochures for follow-up. He also spoke to reporters from several aviation publications and managed to get some coverage. Overall, McConachie was enthusiastic and concluded with: "After you have assessed the foregoing I would like to discuss the subject further with you, since the initial evidence to date is that the aircraft could be a winner!"[8]

In a December 8, 1986 status report, McConachie passed on some preliminary results from his expanding market survey. Out of 78 operators contacted, 81 percent were interested in the regional jet concept. He also passed on some of the concerns raised by the operators. One was that the baggage compartment and seating pitch in the preliminary specifications were too small. McConachie reported that he had taken this feedback to the advanced design team (set up concurrently with his market survey) and was told that these problems could be addressed by making the fuselage slightly longer.

In all, the market survey, comprised of top-down and bottom-up assessments, took about 10 months to finish. In the top-down assessment, the regional jet was compared to competitive regional turboprops such as the Fokker 50, Saab 340, Dash 8, and ATR-42. In the bottom-up assessment, some 130 regional and major airlines were surveyed to gather readings on their interest. All the information was put together to generate a sales forecast of 900 regional jets within 10 years. On the assumption there would be one other significant rival in the regional jet market over the 1990s, Bombardier's sales were projected at approximately 430 units.

The results of the market survey were presented to the board of directors at Bombardier in September 1987. A month later, the board authorized the preliminary design phase and a campaign to obtain letters of intent from at least five carriers for 50 regional jets as a condition for the launch of a full-scale development program. In early 1988, Lowe hired McConachie as Canadair's vice president of marketing, putting him in charge of the team responsible for getting the targeted level of orders.

Soon after coming on board, McConachie was faced with news that two other aerospace companies were planning to launch regional jets of their own. Both Short Brothers of Northern Ireland (prior to being acquired by Bombardier) and Embraer of Brazil announced that they intended to offer alternatives. With two other rivals beating the same bushes, attaining the target of 50 orders would not be a slam dunk for Bombardier. In an attempt to lessen some of the rivalry, Lowe, McConachie, and others paid a visit to Shorts in the spring of 1988 to persuade them to team up with Bombardier, but they came away empty handed.

But it did not matter. A breakthrough came in a February 1989 when Lufthansa CityLine, a regional airline in Germany, became the official launch customer of the Canadair Regional Jet by placing an order for six units and options on six more. Once Bombardier had their first customer, others sitting on the fence jumped off. By the next month, Bombardier had 56 letters of intent. On March 31, the go-ahead was given to start production of the prototype models.

During the process of signing up customers, the marketing team uncovered further information on customer needs and passed it onto the design engineers, firming up the specifications and detailed cost studies. The initial price of the jet was set around $15 million US, which would be about $5 million more than a turboprop of similar size. However, the jet would reduce the time of a 500 kilometer (300 mile) flight by at least half, to under an hour. And with a range of 1,800 kilometers (1,100 miles), later increased to 3,200 kilometers (2,000 miles), it would have a much farther reach.

To accommodate 50 passengers, the Challenger would be elongated by inserting a 3.25-meter (128-inch) plug in the fuselage forward of the wing and a 3-meter (122-inch) extension aft. Retaining the General Electric CF34 engines in slightly modified form, the takeoff weight would increase only 10 percent. The wings would be lengthened 91 centimeters (36 inches) to support the greater length of the airplane. To accommodate more frequent flights as a passenger airplane, some changes would have to be made: for example, the wingbox would be strengthened, heavier-gauge wing skins would be used, and the landing gear would be reinforced and fit with larger tires.

Without the noise and vibration of whirling propellers, the ride of the regional jet would be a more comfortable one, something for which passengers would be willing to pay a premium, as McConachie found in his surveys. Space was not a problem either. With headroom of 185 centimeters (six feet one inch), four-abreast seating in two rows, and 78 centimeters (31 inches) of leg room, the regional jet would be as roomy as the economy class of most major airlines.

There was, however, one flaw: a low placement of the windows. Only the shortest passengers did not have to crane their necks to see out. Over a long journey, this could become uncomfortable for tall people. The situation brings a chuckle to McConachie as he looks back a dozen or so years later on. When the dimensions of the Challenger were set in the 1970s, he explained, the two top executives of Canadair, one short and the other wheelchair-bound, thought the placements were suitable from their perspective. "Hey, looks OK to me," McConachie imagines them saying at the time. This is how, he added with a grin, "decisions are made that bite you in the ass later on."[9] The flaw was tolerated on early models but was later addressed when Bombardier designed new versions of the regional jet with greater seating capacities.

Just prior to the decision to commence production of the regional jet, the Canadian and Quebec governments confirmed Bombardier's applications for financial assistance. A total of $86 million was provided to develop the new aircraft. The federal government would contribute half under the Defence Industry Productivity Program (precursor to Technology Partnerships Canada); the Quebec government would provide the other half through a loan from its industrial holding company, Société de Développement Industriel du Québec.

Even though Bombardier was getting government help, entering into the regional jet project was still a "gutsy move"[10] on their part, a bet-the-company step, in fact. Their cost studies indicated that they would need to invest $250 million of their own capital—half of their market capitalization—on a new product for which a market did not exist. There was, in fact, widespread skepticism within the industry that passenger jets on such a small scale were feasible. Several of the major airline companies "thought we had rocks in our head,"[11] recalled McConachie.

Nor was it a natural evolution to convert the business jet into a regional jet. Two different markets were involved. Business aircraft were built for immediate sale, cash up front. Regional aircraft were built out of a backlog of orders and required special financing. They were more like selling "a financial package with wings."[12] With airline companies placing orders for dozens at a time, the size of the loan often required a consortium of lenders instead of a single bank. And given the size of the financing, even slight differences in the interest rate, maturity, or other terms could overshadow the characteristics of the plane itself in landing a sale. That is, customers often decided more on the basis of the financing available.

Besides financing, there were differences in structural and maintenance requirements. Business aircraft might be flown for 400 to 500 hours a year, whereas regional aircraft were typically flown for 2,500 to 3,000 hours. Given these higher levels of usage along with higher standards for dispatch reliability, much stronger components and more servicing were required in the case of regional jets.

"But we have always been a growth company," said Laurent, "so when we realized that Canadair had plans to develop a 50-seat passenger jet, we asked a task force to look at it. Once we were satisfied with its findings, we pulled out some of the best engineers from Canadair, set them up in a separate building, and asked them to develop a regional jet."[13] A little over a decade after taking this leap, the rate of production at the Canadair plants was 12.5 regional jets per month.

11
CHAPTER

Bombardier Takes Wing

It is one thing to originate an idea. It is another to put it into action and realize its promise. After Bombardier had committed to the Canadair Regional Jet, the company faced the daunting logistics of setting up and continuously expanding a mix of inputs consisting of thousands of skilled persons, innumerable pieces of advanced equipment, and state-of-the-art physical facilities. This was in addition to building the Challenger and other business lines, accommodating several acquisitions, developing new generations of products, and fending off ever-rising competition. For most of the 1990s, the pilot flying these tricky winds was Robert Brown.

In February 1990, Brown took over as president of Canadair after Lowe moved to the deputy chairman position at Bombardier. Two years later, Brown became president of the Bombardier Aerospace Group, North America, and then in 1996, was named president and chief operating officer of Bombardier

Aerospace. In late 1998, he was rewarded for his performance with a promotion to the president and chief executive officer positions of Bombardier.

Born in 1945, Brown was the son of a Canadian soldier stationed in Britain and his British wife. When the war ended, the Brown family left Britain and settled in Ottawa, where young Robert emerged as a solid student and athlete at Nepean High School. After high school, he attended the Royal Military College (RMC) in Kingston. The purpose of the college was to train individuals to be officers in the Canadian military, but Brown was also interested in getting a tuition-free university education. While at RMC, the six foot, two inch (1.88 meter) cadet was the captain and high scorer of the basketball team, the Redmen. In 1967, he graduated with a Bachelor of Science degree. A fellow member of the Class of '67 recalled that Brown "was the quiet, intellectual type.... You could tell he was destined for great things."[1] His caption in the yearbook described him as "serious and reserved."[2]

Following military college, Brown went to Germany to serve in the Canadian Forces for a few years. In 1971, he returned to Ottawa for a job in the federal civil service, getting a big break there when he was hired in 1974 as executive assistant to Gordon Osbaldeston, then deputy minister of the Treasury Board. Afterward, he rose rapidly through the ranks, and in 1983, he completed the Advanced Management Program at Harvard Business School. By the age of 40, he was an associate deputy minister in the Department of Regional Industrial Expansion (DRIE), the department administering over $1 billion in financial assistance to industry. Brown was head of the branch covering capital-intensive sectors of economy, such as aerospace, petrochemicals, telecommunications, and Crown corporations such as Canadair.

As the environment for DRIE grew less favorable under the newly elected Progressive Conservative Party, Brown commenced a search for employment elsewhere. He had been thinking of pursuing a career in business and now seemed to be the time to do it. A former Liberal Cabinet minister under whom Brown had worked, Ed Lumley, spoke to Laurent, who called Brown and arranged a meeting weeks after the purchase of Canadair was closed. Brown had not been directly involved in the negotiations, which were handled by another government agency under Minister of State for Privatization Barbara McDougall.

"We met and I found Bob and I had personalities that went well together," recalled Laurent. "The chemistry worked."[3] Brown accepted Laurent's offer of employment and in February 1987, he joined Bombardier as vice president of corporate development. (He was promoted two years later to senior vice president of corporate development and strategic planning.) Of course, Laurent understood how Brown's ties to the federal government could come in handy. Brown had spent his last 10 years there in senior positions responsible for implementing industrial strategies, so he would be an important conduit. "He has been at high levels within the federal government. He understands how it functions, and you need someone with those sorts of skills to run a global company," said brokerage analyst Benoît Chotard.[4]

In the early stages of Brown's employment, Laurent discovered not only a worthy gin rummy opponent on long flights to distant meetings, but also a very effective negotiator in several key deals. The "best kept secret in Canada,"[5] Lumley called Brown. He credited his former mandarin with playing an important role in negotiating several billion dollars worth of investment in Canada by US automobile companies in the early 1980s. Brown was to put this kind of experience to good use at Bombardier, playing an important role in several key negotiations. Laurent first noticed Brown's performance in the negotiations to acquire Short Brothers. "That's where I saw Bob's talent as a negotiator," he said. "He has a way of getting people to accept his ideas."[6]

Brown's negotiating forte was grounded in a very clear vision and set of values. Before starting anything, he said, one needed to decide who they were and what they were trying to do. In the case of Bombardier, it boiled down to: 1) ensuring a superior return to shareholders, 2) controlling one's destiny, and 3) cultivating entrepreneurialism. These were the values that set the context for Brown's negotiation style at Bombardier. Once this framework was in place, one had "to try and figure out what the other side wishes to accomplish."[7] It was not necessarily just a matter of the return on investment to the other side. In fact, more often that not as in the case of Bombardier's many acquisitions of government-owned corporations, there were a broad range of concerns and stakeholders to address, as Brown himself knew so well from his previous years on the other side of the fence in government.

So, rather than offer a solution that did little to allay suspicions of a dismantling of parts, as other bidders did in the 1989 auctioning off of Shorts, Bombardier offered a proposal outlining what it would need to promote the interests of the various stakeholders. Specifically, in return for adequate levels of government support and a consolidation of the seven unions into one unit, Bombardier would commit to capital investment plans and subcontracts relating to the regional jet program.

A critical period in those negotiations was the final two days. Brown, along with Laurent and Barry Olivella (then vice president of acquisitions), had laid their final numbers on the table and were told that it was not good enough. So the two sides agreed to part, but to think about their positions overnight before calling it quits. The Bombardier team stayed up far into the wee hours of the morning poring over balance sheets and financial statements, trying to find an angle to save what was looking like a lost cause. But then the other side phoned early the next day. Brown and Olivella went back to meetings and sat tight while the other side put forward a series of positions. Finally, they got to a set of numbers satisfactory to Bombardier. A deal was struck.

"So you have to have the courage to stop and wait for the other side to respond," explains Brown. "This was one of those cases where we had to let it come back. Many times, you have to let things go in life and negotiations. If it makes sense, the other side will come back in time." An important element in that approach was learning to "keep my mouth shut...the biggest discipline here is to make sure your people do not start to talk before the other side when the discussions get to a difficult point." It was not always an easy thing to do. Brown chuckles at his attempts to instruct his children on the value of silence: "I've done this with my children just for fun. We'll sit around the dinner table and see how long we can go without someone speaking."[8]

Appointed to the presidency of Canadair in early 1990, Brown was responsible for overseeing the transfer of the Bombardier Manufacturing System (BMS) from the rail transportation group. Spearheading this multiyear initiative was one of the creators of the BMS, Roland Gagnon. Brown also presided over a multiyear enhancement of the productivity of the engineering force. In this regard, the chance to work on a $1.7 billion subcontract to make fuselage components and wing assemblies for the Airbus consortium was a help. It gave Canadair engineers access to Aerospatiale's techniques and processes, showing them the full potential of software tools when used properly.

An example of the operational efficiencies realized was the use of a new tooling scheme and a modularized design to reduce by 30 percent the hours required for final assembly of the CL-415 water bomber. These new techniques resulted from having design and manufacturing engineers work more closely together and

new technologies that improved precision in the cutting and joining of parts. In turn, the time and space savings allowed Canadair
to assemble the CL-415 alongside the Challenger and Canadair
Regional Jet in the same building at Montreal's Dorval Airport.
The building was made for only one line, but Bombardier was
able fit in three, thus avoiding the cost of leasing other buildings.

To get the regional jet into regular production mode, the
Regional Jet Division was created within Canadair just before
Brown's arrival. Put in charge as president of that division was Bob
Wohl, who had been the executive vice president in charge of the
regional jet development phase (of which McConachie had been
a key member). Wohl was a lawyer by profession, but he had
acquired considerable experience in program management and
engineering development over the years with Canadair and previous employers. And as a veteran from Canadair, he was someone who knew all the faces and could provide a vital link between
Canadair staff and Bombardier executives. The first cutting of
metal parts for the regional jet commenced in November 1989.

A few months into his new job at Canadair, Brown got additional product lines to look after: the line of Learjet business jets
that would give Bombardier a complete family of products in this
niche. Learjet executives would be allowed a free hand to run
their operations, but they would have to report to Brown. Some
two years later, Brown got yet more product lines to manage
when the purchase of de Havilland brought a family of propeller-
driven regional airplanes into the fold. A major exercise in connection with this acquisition was the integration of marketing
departments and production operations.

Within this somewhat topsy-turvy environment, the ramping
up of production processes for the regional jet went ahead
smoothly. The first prototype was rolled out and flown in May
1991, virtually on schedule and within budget. Following the

testing and certification process, Canadair was able to deliver the first regional jet to its initial customer, Lufthansa, in late 1992 as promised. The latter had been demanding during the development phase, but Lufthansa was quite satisfied after taking delivery, publicly acknowledging that their jets were flying relatively free of the bugs that usually are found in new designs.

No rival manufacturers were ready to make deliveries at this time. The challenge from Shorts had of course been neutralized when Bombardier purchased it, while Embraer, then still under government ownership, was falling far behind in its announced plans to release a product at the same time as Bombardier. Setting back its efforts was the failure to fit jet engines onto its existing 45-seat turboprop model.

However, things were not going as smoothly for Bombardier on the marketing side. Following a preliminary burst of interest, orders for the regional jet trailed off after 1989 as a recession settled in, the Gulf War flared up, and energy prices spiked. The first year of Brown's tenure at the helm yielded few encouraging signs in market acceptance. Of the letters of intent previously obtained from more than 100 potential customers, only about a dozen had sealed their commitments by making the $150,000 deposit. One customer, Ansett Worldwide Aviation, actually canceled its order for 10 jets.

Around this time, Bombardier's Olivella lashed out at the Bank of Canada's monetary policy, which was pushing up interest rates and the exchange rate for the Canadian dollar. "It is uneconomic for most of us to invest in Canada or export from Canada," he said, because the Bank of Canada's high interest rates and high dollar make Canadian production uncompetitive.[9]

By the middle of 1991, the marketing team under Wohl was in transition. McConachie had been assigned to do market research for a 70-seat jet (and would soon leave Bombardier to return to his consultancy). Tom Appleton, a marketing veteran from de Havilland was brought in as executive vice president of marketing for the Regional Jet Division. A new marketing strategy was developed, which de-emphasized the rivalry between turboprops and jets and portrayed the regional jet as a hub-extender—that is, as an alternative to the major airlines' big jets on thinly traveled long routes.

Over a 29-day period in the fall of 1991, the calm was interrupted by a flurry of deals worth almost $1 billion in total. One was the official signing of a 20-plane order (with options on 20 more) by Comair Inc. (a feeder airline for Delta Air Lines Inc. of Atlanta), the company that would be the launch customer for North America. Government officials in attendance at the announcement mentioned that the Export Development Corp. (EDC) would be guaranteeing 90 percent of the $395 million financing provided to Comair by an international banking consortium. Bombardier also closed a contract with the French government for 12 new Canadair water bombers as well as a contract with the Canadian Department of National Defence for training Canadian Forces student pilots.

The unnerving quiet returned afterward, however. For most of 1992 and nearly three-quarters of 1993, there were no new orders. The absence of demand over this 20-month period was increasingly a worry for Bombardier staff. The company had bet half its market capitalization on the new product, and now the gamble was starting to look like a considerable risk. Talk of rolling back elements of the regional jet program began to surface. In combination with the Chunnel contract troubles, the lack of market interest in regional jets induced a period of weakness in Bombardier shares.

In the middle of this anxious period, Brown gave a speech calling for government aerospace programs to become more efficient in the distribution of benefits to aerospace firms. "Government policies requiring regional economic spin-offs from major contracts create overcapacity and weaken existing centres of excellence," he told a chamber of commerce audience. Subsidies offered to foreign firms to locate in Canada often had the same effect. Instead, Canada's centers of aerospace excellence in Montreal, Winnipeg, Vancouver, Calgary, Edmonton, and Halifax needed buying policies that would intensify their R&D and build a capacity to compete globally. "We must create a long-term, industry-government partnership like the Europeans if we are to gain from globalization," Brown concluded.[10]

Finally, the dark cloud lifted in August 1993 with two megadeals for Canadair Regional Jets. SkyWest Airlines Inc. a Utah-based feeder for Delta Air Lines, bought 10 jets and optioned 10 more. The second customer was Air Canada, which had signed a letter of intent for 24 aircraft and options on 24 more. Helping to finance the Air Canada order was a joint financing arrangement between Bombardier and the EDC. The mandate of the latter had recently been expanded to permit, among other things, the granting of credits to domestic customers if the sale in some way promoted exports. In the case of the Air Canada purchase of Canadair jets, the rationale was that the planes would help Bombardier become stronger as an exporter while allowing Air Canada to generate passenger traffic on point-to-point routes across the US border once the Open Skies agreement went into effect between Canada and the United States.

On August 30, 1993, Wohl retired from Bombardier, and his position (converted to president of Bombardier Regional Aircraft Division after the amalgamation with de Havilland) was assumed by Pierre Lortie, a high-energy and ultra-ambitious individual. He had university degrees in engineering, business, and economics. He was also author of a prize-winning book, *Economic Integration and the Law of GATT*,[11] and had served in a variety of executive positions: chief executive officer of the Montreal Exchange from 1981 to 1985, chief executive officer and president of grocery chain Provigo Inc. from 1985 to 1989, and chairman of Canada's Royal Commission on Electoral Reform and Party Financing from 1989 to 1992. In 1990, he joined Bombardier as president of Bombardier Capital Group.

This dynamo was to guide the regional aircraft division over the next four years before moving on to his next challenge (Bombardier International Group and later, Bombardier Transportation). During those four years, his stewardship and an improving economy combined to fuel momentum within the division. New orders for regional jets poured in. Sales of de Havilland's Dash 8 series of airplanes picked up as well. The full order book brought successive increases in rates of production. Hikes in the autumn of 1995 from four to five Canadair Regional Jets per month and from three to four Dash 8 turboprops per month were just steps in a series. By 1996, Bombardier had emerged as a new force in regional airplanes. Its share of the world market had rocketed to 42 percent, up from 10 percent in 1992.

The Lortie era also saw the launch of several new airplane models. The Dash 8 Q400 included a noise and vibration suppression system that made the model the quietest and smoothest ride in the turboprop class, very nearly equal to the regional jet. Several years in the making, it was an advanced system based on 72 microphones placed inside the skin of the fuselage. Their job was to pick up the noise and vibrations produced by the propellers beating air against the body of the plane, and then pass that information onto a computer that would instruct 40 metallic devices inside the fuselage to vibrate in an offsetting way.

Also, toward the end of Lortie's term, the 70-seat Canadair Regional Jet (CRJ-700), costing $645 million to develop, was launched into production with a price tag of $23 million a piece.

The CRJ-700 would offer a more user-friendly cabin than the 50-seat model in that the seats would be lower and the windows higher, thus making it more comfortable for most passengers to look outside. Analysts said the timing of the new model was good since the demise of one of the largest makers of turboprops, Fokker, in 1996, had left a gap in the 70-seat market.

Laurent was a fan of Brown's managerial skills. "I am basically the entrepreneur," he said. "Bob is a more professional administrator. He is more organized than I am."[12] Brokerage analysts are fans too. "Look at what he did in aerospace," said John Reider of RBC Dominion Securities. "The thing that strikes you the most is that he did so much so successfully in such a short period of time."[13] "One of Bob's great qualities is that he not only surrounds himself with the right people but also takes the tough decision if somebody is not performing," said Paul Tellier, president of Canadian National Railways.[14]

"To be happy with myself, I *have* to get things done," Brown suggested as an answer to why he had gained a reputation for getting things done. Before he acted, he would sit down and think things through, scoping out the context and itemizing the pieces of the puzzle. Then he would write it down to keep track of it all. Working his way through the list of things to do was a source of satisfaction. "If I can't do my list of things every day, cross them off, then I'm not a happy camper,"[15] he said.

But there was more to it than that—a lot more. Sometimes the scoping of scenarios and itemizing of actions were to no avail. Reality intervened and the plan did not unfold as expected. "So, you've got to be able to react, and many times it just takes an absolute sense of determination to make things happen," declared

Brown. To be avoided at all costs was a paralysis in decision making. When Brown saw executives "torturing themselves looking for perfect information," he moved them. The organization had to stay in motion, and executives needed to make good choices with imperfect information. They "must not be afraid to make decisions... and have to accept they sometimes are going to be wrong." It was all right to make the wrong call on occasion as long as the individual learned from the experience and did not repeat it.[16]

In addition to good decision-making skills, executives needed to get into the thick of things, to be at risk. It was like an entrepreneur living on the edge, figuring out what had to happen and then making it happen. This called for getting out to where the action was to make sure that the troops had bought into the action plan. As Brown described it: "I'm a strong believer that you've got to be there. You've got to see people, their body language, to make sure everybody's embracing the values of the company. And when you ask for something to be done, you've got to go back to make sure its been done."[17]

Leading through personal example was an integral part of the process. Brown's shoes were always polished to a bright shine. He worked 12-hour days, six days a week, following a schedule that at times was quite grinding (going through monthly and quarterly reviews of operations) and time-consuming (traveling to various locations to get in touch with things). Harkening back to lessons learned at military college, Brown declared: "I believe that in order to have discipline in an organization, you have to show you have discipline yourself. The way you present yourself is extremely important."[18]

The people element was very important to Brown. In essence, his job was not to get results himself but to select and nurture the people who did. "You can have corporate governance and other structures in place, but what it really, really comes down to is people," he emphasized. One of his biggest challenges over the next five years would be addressing the need to keep pace with Bombardier's growth through a doubling of the top-management cadre to 350 people. "There is an absolute requirement to grow leaders," to identify individuals from the various cultures within Bombardier, whether existing or newly acquired.[19] They would be people who identify with Bombardier values such as the importance of shareholder value, controlling one's destiny, and an entrepreneurial approach to getting results. Several formal mechanisms were in place within the corporation for the purpose of finding and cultivating new leadership, including the Six Sigma program and annual getaways to Florida for general managers. Once identified, leadership candidates were groomed by moving them through a series of increasingly challenging positions throughout the corporation.

Beyond having "a good selection process in place and a good nose for appointing people," Brown believed executives had to be optimistic about the people working for them. Once the best available people were in place, they would be given space to make things happen. Bombardier was "geared for having the person run the company almost as if they owned it...people are expected to take the initiative, to define responsibility, and to take charge,"[20] Brown commented. And, from his experience, Brown had found that he was not often disappointed. He tended to find that people performed better in an environment of trust and confidence; they might do things differently and make the occasional wrong turn, but, in the end, they often finished up with good results.

Brown participated in many turnarounds of troubled operations. The key again was the people element. It might be tough at first dealing with bad morale and other problems, but the job of the executive was to demonstrate to people that they could do more than they thought they could. His task was to break through the mood of resignation and opposition by having the operation achieve a success in some endeavor. "Once people have done that, they want to do it again. It's a rush," explained Brown. After a success, people "are going to start feeling good about themselves, more confident. Once that happens, its a snowball."[21]

Building Bombardier Aerospace over the 1990s had been demanding work. In his spare time, Brown liked to relax at his two-storey log house, which he built by hand near Perth, Ontario. Like all good Bombardier executives, he had a variety of Bombardier recreational vehicles on hand to enjoy at his vacation home, including a Ski-Doo, Sea-Doo, and Bombardier-made leisure boat for cruising the canals and rivers south of Ottawa.

12 CHAPTER

Dogfight in the Clouds

In the middle of 1996, Bombardier got a big jolt. It lost its status as the only supplier of regional jets when Embraer announced the sale of 25 units of its new 50-seat jet, the ERJ 145, to regional carrier Continental Express of Houston. Bombardier appeared to have the better airplane overall—it climbed faster, was more durable, and had a longer range and more efficient engine—but Embraer's list price was $15 million US, while Bombardier's was $18 million US.

The competition for the contract was a no-holds-barred affair. Bombardier accused the Brazilian government of giving Embraer illegal subsidies to reduce the list price of its jets effectively to $12.5 million US each. Robert Brown also acidly noted: "Before the deal with Embraer, Continental had no flying rights to Brazil. After the deal, Continental suddenly acquired Brazilian rights. You figure it out."[1] Embraer countered with accusations that Bombardier was benefiting from Canadian government support

as well. Both combatants appealed to their respective governments to lodge formal complaints to the World Trade Organization (WTO) in Geneva.

In June 1997, Brown got a telephone call from the president
of American Eagle, a regional airline affiliated with American Airlines. He offered to buy over 40 of Bombardier's 50-seat jets if
their prices were reduced to be in line with what Embraer was
offering. Brown considered the request but he could not find a
way that made sense for Bombardier yet still matched the price
offered by their new competitor. Fighting to the last, he had to
concede the contract, worth nearly $1 billion. American Eagle
did sign an order for 25 of Bombardier's new 70-seat jets
(Embraer had no models in this category), but still, Embraer had
achieved a major breakthrough, winning a deal with the largest
regional airline system in the world.

In early 1998, some rumblings were heard from another
front: the ranks of the aerospace giants. Boeing announced plans
to increase production of its new 717 jetliner, a 100 seater aimed
at the top end of the regional market. The Airbus consortium also
announced plans to shrink its A319 jetliner to a size comparable
to Boeing's entry. With their size and resources, these two firms
could become formidable competitors.

Meanwhile, at the low end of the market, there were more
models appearing. Embraer announced a 37-seat version of a
regional jet, which would be a threat to the Dash-8 turboprop
line. This new development served only to intensify Bombardier's
motivation to bring the export-subsidy program of the Brazilian
government before world trade tribunals. As Brown claimed:
"Embraer is eating into our market share on the basis of a subsidy .... Airplane products should be judged on...performance,
operating cost and reliability—financing should not be a factor."[2]
Or more precisely, below-market financing rates should not be
a factor.

Soon after, yet another competitive threat arrived on the scene. Fairchild Dornier Corp., an amalgamation of a former state-owned German company and US Fairchild Aerospace Corp., announced at the 1998 Paris Air Show that it was going to develop a complete family of regional jets. It would do this by adding to its recently introduced 32-seat jet several new models with capacity for 44, 50, 70, 90, and 105 passengers. The 70 seater would be brought to market first, in late 2001, and the 50 seater would come last, in early 2004. Supporting its gamble were letters of intent from Lufthansa and Swiss regional airline Cross-Air to buy 120 planes and take options for another 120. Loan guarantees from the German government, backing up at least $300 million US in development costs, would also help.

Chairman and chief executive officer of Fairchild Dornier, James Robinson, was complimentary to Bombardier, but he declared the next decade would see some stiff competition. "We are going to hammer each other," said Robinson, who two years earlier had been president of Bombardier's Learjet division. He predicted a big shakeout coming in the regional jet market sometime in the 2000s, similar to what happened in the turboprop market during the 1990s. "You had a bunch of companies like Fokker, Saab, and BAE, all of which are now out of the business," he said. They went down because, with so many manufacturers, the carriers "played them all like a stringed instrument....There's room for us all [in the regional jet market] now, but when the pipeline is filled up, that'll change."[3]

About a year later, Fairchild Dornier's weak financial position was bolstered by $1.2 billion US in equity and debt financing from German insurance company Allianz Group and US investment firm Clayton, Dubilier and Rice Inc. The two institutional investors were willing to put up the money because they believed Fairchild Dornier's models would bring state-of-the-art technology and comfort standards associated with long-haul traveling to the fast-growing regional jet market.

Embraer, for its part, also announced intentions to develop a family of regional jets, adding to its existing 37- and 50-seat versions new varieties with 70, 98, and 108 seating arrangements (the earliest of which would be out in 2002). The company also had decided to enter the business jet market, preselling 50 of its Legacy models at prices averaging 15 percent less than comparable models on the market. Moreover, it had adopted a strategy of building up its military business, proceeding with investments in new designs for its Tucano trainer and a fighter aircraft (that was sold to price-conscious Third World countries in the 1970s and 1980s).

Company officials predicted that the growth to come from military aircraft would outpace even the stellar growth of its regional jets. Belgium, Greece, Mexico, and Venezuela were on the customer list, and many Third World countries would soon need to replace aging F-5, MIG-21, and Mirage 3 fleets. The Brazilian Air Force itself had embarked upon a multiyear modernization project that required the purchase or refurbishment of over 100 fighters and transports. Furthermore, Embraer had formed an alliance with four French aerospace companies: Dassault Aviation, Aerospatiale Matra, Thales (formerly Thompson-CSF), and Snecma. They had purchased a 20 percent stake in Embraer and would likely transfer under licensing agreements advanced technology from the French Mirage jet.

By 2000, Boeing and the Airbus consortium were displaying increased interest in the regional jet market. Boeing was investigating a downsizing of its 717 model to 70 and 90 seats, even going so far as to conduct wind tunnel tests on scale models. However, analysts believed that it would be difficult for the aerospace powerhouse to come down to the level of the regional airplane manufacturers as it was technically more difficult to shrink a larger airplane to a smaller size than to stretch a smaller airplane to a larger size. The latter requires mainly inserting extra plugs into the fuselage and wings, while the former requires more radical changes—almost like designing a new plane from scratch.

For these reasons, Boeing was also considering the alternative of a partnership with a regional jet maker. Boeing publicly stated it was open to an alliance with either Bombardier, Embraer, or Fairchild Dornier. In response to this statement, Bombardier spokesperson Michel Lord said: "If they wanted to see us and talk to us about this, we could be open for discussions."[4] The other aerospace giant, the Airbus consortium, was also interested in forming a partnership. Given that one of its main members, Aerospatiale, was already part of the four-country team with an investment stake in Embraer, analysts speculated that the Airbus group would likely side with the Brazilian manufacturer.

Despite all the gathering forces in the marketplace, Bombardier was still doing very well because demand for regional jets was exploding faster than supply. In the spring of 2000, the company announced its largest deal to date: a $3 billion order for 94 regional jets from Comair and Atlantic Southeast Airlines, two Delta feeder airlines that already were flying 125 of Bombardier's jets. Part of the order was for 40- and 44-seat formats, which Bombardier was going to supply by tailoring its 50-seat model. The order also included options on 406 more jets, worth $9 billion, for delivery over the decade.

Bombardier was also ahead in the introduction of 70- and 90-seat models (based on stretches of the 50-seat jet). First deliveries of the 70-seater occurred in early 2001; the 90-seater is expected in late 2002. Both were at least a year ahead of nearest alternatives. Being first to market was an important part of Bombardier's strategy. It created a significant barrier to entry for competitors because once a carrier has signed up with a given manufacturer, it is costly for them to switch. Pilots had to be retrained and servicing requirements had to be reorganized.

Bombardier's aerospace group was putting in a good showing, but the regional jet market was at risk of reaching a mature stage at some point. Just like the snowmobile market in the 1970s and the personal watercraft market in the 1990s, the specter of a glut loomed, whether due to supply accelerating too quickly, demand leveling off as consumers got their fill, or a combination of both. The end result would be an erosion in profits and an exodus of firms from the industry or into the arms of larger brethren.

But Bombardier was preparing for the shakeout scenario. Pursuing its goal of becoming number one in its industries, Bombardier had purchased Adtranz and Outboard Marine Corp in 2001. There remained much work to do to improve profitability for both acquisitions, but given success with the usual turnaround formula, the rail and recreational groups would provide more of a counterbalance to the aerospace group.

Shortly after taking over as chief executive of Embraer in the fall of 1995, Maurico Botelho placed a picture of the company's CBA-123 turboprop airplane in the lobby of the corporate headquarters situated in Brazil's Silicon Valley—the bucolic São Jose dos Campos some 80 kilometers (50 miles) away from São Paulo. While it is not unusual for an aerospace manufacturing company to have a picture of one of its airplanes on the wall, in this case, it was. The CBA-123 model was one of Embraer's biggest flops.

Why put an embarrassing failure on display so that employees would see it every day? "That picture is there to remind us of our mistakes," explained Botelho. "The CBA-123 was developed by the company in 1990 to include all the good tricks that a pilot would want to have in an aircraft. It was very fast, very silent, low vibration—a fantastic aircraft—but it cost 50 percent more than the market was prepared to pay for it. We didn't sell one."[5]

This change in focus toward greater market sensitivity was one reason for Embraer's dramatic turnaround that started with the 1996 entry into the regional jet market. The company was three years behind Bombardier, but it quickly made up for lost time. By 2000, meteoric sales growth placed Embraer in a neck and neck race for market share. A high point in the chase was the announcement of $6.6 billion US worth of orders at the 1999 Paris Air Show, a major step toward becoming Brazil's largest exporter and a national icon.

The Embraer story has its roots in World War II, when the importance of air power to national security became widely recognized. In the late 1940s, the Brazilian government picked São Jose dos Campos as a site for a military complex with technical institutes for research and training in aeronautical engineering. Graduates of the institutes were hired when the Brazilian Air Force created Embraer in 1969. Over the next two decades, the company designed and manufactured military trainers, patrol planes, and basic fighter jets. (The AMX fighter, developed in partnership with Italian aerospace companies, was flown by the Brazilian and Italian air forces in the Kosovo war.)

Originally designed to serve the transportation needs of the Brazilian Air Force, Embraer built the 19-seat, propeller-driven Bandeirante aircraft that became one of the first widely used commuter planes. It won international accolades, flying with lower noise levels and at faster speeds. Next came the EMB-120 Brasilia, a turboprop commercial aircraft capable of carrying 30 passengers over longer routes. Over 350 were sold in more than a dozen countries. The EMB-120 design and the jet technology acquired in the development of the AMX fighter were brought together to create Embraer's first jets for civilian use: the ERJ-135 and ERJ-145 regional jets now filling the skies in Europe and the Americas.

The transition from turboprops to regional jets was not an easy one. By the early 1990s, Embraer was in deep financial trouble, having accumulated losses of $1 billion US and a debt burden equivalent to 400 percent of equity. The winding down of the Cold War reduced the need for military aircraft, cutting into a main source of revenues. Embraer tried to diversify into commercial markets, but it was still encumbered by political appointees and a bureaucratic management style. Also, its engineering culture, bred from decades of responding to the military's preference for the best in technology regardless of the cost, led to commercial fiascoes such as the CBA-123.

A recession, exchange crises, and a passage to civilian rule were the final factors that led to a decision in 1992 to privatize Embraer, a process that dragged on and delayed the refinancing of development projects for regional jets. To spruce it up for the privatization, the Brazilian government reportedly assumed about $700 million US of Embraer's debt and invested another $350 million US. The auction finally took place in December of 1994. The buyers of 85 percent of the company at a price of $125 million US were a Brazilian investment bank, the Bozano Simonsen Group, and two Brazilian pension funds. Shares in Embraer were listed on the Brazilian stock exchange and later on the New York Stock Exchange.

The new owners did a top-to-bottom revamping. They slashed costs, cut the workforce of 6,000 nearly in half, and pumped over $500 million US into a capitalization program. Professional management was installed headed by Botelho, a mechanical engineer then in his early fifties with no aviation experience but a reputation for being more of a strategic thinker than the average Brazilian executive. Under the Redemption Project, he reorganized along lines of a partnership between shareholders, executives, and employees. Anticipating the potential of the regional jet, he concentrated developmental resources on new products for that market.

Supporting Embraer's recovery was financial assistance from the National Development Bank (BNDES). Embraer's regional jet, the ERJ 145, was rescued from the drawing board with the help of a $120 million US loan from BNDES. After development, exports of the ERJ 145 and ERJ 135 were promoted by BNDES's Pro-ex export financing program, a subsidy that paid down interest rates on private sector financing to customers. Another BNDES program, Finamex, provided credit lines at rates lower than domestic interest rates in Brazil. The impact of these BNDES programs were augmented in 1999 by a 39 percent devaluation in the real, the Brazilian currency. (Because Embraer receives most of its revenues in US dollars, a lower real reduces the cost of its domestic inputs.)

The Pro-ex program was to become the focus of a lengthy and bitter trade dispute between Brazil and Canada. Its official purpose was to offset the so-called "country risk premium" in making loans to Embraer's foreign customers. Because of Brazil's history of hyperinflation and currency depreciation, the Brazilian government and banks could only borrow at rates higher—as much as 4 to 6 percentage points—than their counterparts in North America and Europe. This risk premium put Brazilian companies such as Embraer at a disadvantage in winning large export orders since they could only offer to finance them at higher lending rates. To give Brazil and other developing countries a chance, therefore, the WTO allowed governments in these countries to legally buy down (subsidize) lending rates to levels where the country risk premium was erased.

An example illustrates. Say that a Brazilian financial institution can borrow at 6 percentage points above the rate the US Government pays on its Treasury bonds (debt), whereas a typical regional airline can borrow at 2.5 percentage points above US

Treasuries. Under WTO regulations, it is legal for the Brazilian government to provide an interest rate subsidy of 3.5 percentage points to enable Embraer to offer a loan at the same rate that the regional airline faces in the market.

However, Pro-ex was not implemented in this way. Instead of providing a buy down on the borrowing rates of a Brazilian lender, it was provided directly to Embraer's client. This pushed their cost of borrowing below US Treasuries. In its first application, to the Continental Express sale in 1996, the actual amount of the subsidy was 3.8 percentage points, which drove the airliner's borrowing rate to almost 1.5 percentage points below US Treasuries. The second application, to American Airlines in 1997, provided a buy down of 2.5 percent.

In early 1997, Canadian Prime Minister Jean Chrétien met with Brazilian President Fernado Henrique Cardoso, and both agreed to appoint independent mediators in an attempt to resolve the trade dispute quietly. The mediators submitted their report five months later. They concluded that Pro-ex was a legitimate program but recommended measures to guard against abuse in application; as for Canada, the mediators disapproved of joint ventures between Bombardier and the Government of Canada, deeming them import substitution. The mediators also urged both sides to uphold the rules of the WTO and the Organization for Economic Cooperation and Development (OECD).

Canada was prepared to concede on the joint venture issue (which was interpreted as pertaining to the joint financing facility used only once for the sale to Air Canada) and was ready to sign a treaty as long as Brazil would adjust its Pro-ex to adhere to WTO and OECD rules and accept a third-party monitoring mechanism. Brazilian authorities refused. They felt Brazil was exempt from the WTO's prohibition against export subsidies because of Article 27 of the 1995 Subsidy Agreement, which gave developing countries until 2002 to comply.

Making the dispute even more rancorous at this time was a side issue. In late 1997, Bombardier won a contract to train NATO pilots. Embraer 's Tucano planes were in line to be used as trainers for the pilots, but Bombardier switched instead to another supplier that they believed would more likely deliver in time for tight NATO deadlines. Embraer saw it differently. "That hurt," said an Embraer spokesperson. "It was a big loss and...a big part of the bitterness of this dispute. It was a done deal and a political move took us off that deal."[6]

The acrimony spilled into the public arena in July 1998 when the two countries filed formal complaints against each other at the WTO. Brazil looked like it had a chance to eke out a win using the developing country defense. It was, after all, receiving a $41 billion US rescue package from the International Monetary Fund and others, surely a sign of a country in a development phase.

But the WTO adjudication panel found that Brazil had violated conditions for qualifying under the Article 27 clause. Among other things, it had hiked subsidies subsequent to the writing of the Article 27 clause and had made commitments to provide financial assistance past 2002. Canada did not escape either. Its Technology Partnerships Canada program was judged illegal. Following unsuccessful appeals, Brazil finally responded by reducing the Pro-ex interest rate subsidy to 2.5 percentage points, and Canada amended its technology program.

In late 1999, Canada returned to the WTO again, seeking authorization to levy trade sanctions against Brazil for failure to comply with the WTO's earlier decisions. Two main points of contention were that the interest equalization payments knocking 2.5 percent off commercial financing arrangements were still reducing rates below sanctioned levels, and that Brazil had no intention, as required by the WTO, of canceling over $3 billion US of prohibited subsidies embedded in contracts for aircraft not yet delivered by Embraer.

The WTO agreed that the Pro-ex interest rate subsidy was still too high. In response, the Pro-ex subsidy was subsequently reduced so that interest rates were paid down just to the level of the Commercial Interest Reference Rate (the CIRR is set 1 percent above the rate on specified US government bonds). In parallel judgments, the WTO panel ruled that Canada's Technology Partnerships Canada program was now compliant, but that the Canada Account might not be. They could not say for sure because the WTO needed to see minutes of Cabinet meetings, and the Canadian government was not willing to release them on the grounds they were not relevant to the case under investigation. Spokespersons claimed that the only time the Canada Account had been used in an aerospace transaction during the specified period was for a turboprop sale to a South African regional airline shortly after the end of apartheid.

Nevertheless, Brazil still refused to cancel the billions in subsidies on contracts for undelivered aircraft as that action would entail breaking contractual agreements. This left Canada free to pursue two options: to enter into direct negotiations with Brazil for compensation or to proceed with the final steps for imposing WTO-sanctioned tariffs on Brazilian exports. The negotiation route was chosen. At one point, Brazil had agreed to compensate the Canadian economy for losses inflicted, bring Pro-ex into full compliance with international standards, and discuss a bilateral monitoring mechanism. But just hours after officials expressed optimism about reaching an agreement in the summer of 2000, the talks broke off. Near the end of 2000, the Canadian government went back to the WTO and obtained final authorization from the WTO to impose $1.4 billion in retaliatory tariffs on Brazilian exports.

However, it held off and ultimately opted for another approach. In the spring of 2001, the Canada Account was activated to make a $1.7 billion loan at special terms to Air Wisconsin for the purchase of 75 regional planes from Bombardier. The Canadian government claimed it was just offsetting Brazilian credit terms, which reportedly was not a market rate in this instance since it did not take into account the credit worthiness of the client.

But that explanation was not good enough to prevent Brazil from going back to the WTO to register a complaint against the Canada Account. Canada filed a complaint as well in connection with Pro-ex offering terms without regard to the riskiness of a borrower. Hostilities were further fanned by another side issue: a Canadian-led ban on Brazilian exports of beef to North America. Canadian authorities said the ban was just related to concerns over mad-cow disease, but protests in Brazil suggested otherwise. The ban was rescinded a few weeks later, following verification of the safety of Brazilian beef.

A WTO ruling on Canada's use of the Canada Account in the Air Wisconsin deal (and more in the subsequent Northwest Airlines case too) could provide an outcome on which the two sides could base an agreement. But emotions are riding high, and it might be some time before both sides see the logic of sharing the huge potential of the regional jet market. The WTO route may not hold the answer, but perhaps a privately negotiated bilateral agreement does—either at the company or country level. According to forecasts from several market research firms, there is plenty of room for both Embraer and Bombardier to enjoy rapid growth in the same market for many more years.

13

A Jet Takes Off From the Drawing Board

The telephone rang, and John Holding picked it up. Laurent Beaudoin was calling from his car phone. The two men had just left a company meeting where the topic of discussion had been what kind of airplane Bombardier should next develop in the executive jet class. Should it be an upgrade of the Challenger or a completely new model? Laurent left the meeting somewhat unsure, but riding later in his car, he came to a resolution.

He suggested that Holding should start thinking about leapfrogging the competition with a clean-sheet design that would fly faster, farther, and more comfortably than any other model on the market. He did not want just an improvement on the Challenger. He wanted something that was brand new, designed virtually from scratch. He asked Holding to put forward a proposal. That was how the Global Express got started.

It was 1991. Bombardier had the Challenger product line and had just acquired the Learjet family. But Laurent and Robert Brown saw the need for another model. Noting the trend toward globalization, both men believed there was a need for a business jet with more range and speed to fit the needs of the rising number of business people running worldwide operations. Market intelligence was also telling them that corporate executives liked to trade up to larger business jets as their businesses grew, often keeping their smaller jets in order to have a diversified fleet.

Holding was certainly the person to call about designing a new airplane. A native of northern England, he got his master's degree in aerospace engineering at the University of Manchester and had worked at British Aerospace for 17 years, where his duties included design work for the Concorde supersonic airliner. In the late 1970s, Canadair offered him a job, and he decided to take his young family to Montreal. When he showed up at work, he found things so chaotic that he told his wife not to unpack until he got a handle on what was going on. He stayed on, however, excited by the concept of the Challenger business jet, which for its time was cutting edge in many respects. And he felt at home. The multicultural atmosphere of Montreal and the presence of many other British engineers at Canadair reminded him of Europe.

He started out as a design engineer and got a chance to distinguish himself when the Challenger was put into service and some teething problems had to be ironed out. He was put in charge of the team set up to improve the aircraft's reliability and performance. He turned in a good enough performance to be asked to step in and salvage the Aerospatiale subcontract when it hit the skids. He found the problem to be management related. There was a lack of focus and discipline. Once this deficiency was corrected, the subcontract work proceeded smoothly, and Aerospatiale ended up "a very pleased customer."[1]

With this kind of performance record, Holding was "in the right place at the right time,"[2] just when Bombardier was looking for a vice president of engineering to head the design team at Canadair. Recognizing Holding's expertise, knowledge of procedures, and familiarity with people, Bombardier awarded him the job over several candidates. And as the aerospace operations expanded at Bombardier, Holding's vice presidential duties expanded along with them. A full schedule it was. Over the 1990s, Bombardier Aerospace originated one new airplane model every year, mainly extensions to its stable of Learjet, de Havilland, and Canadair airplanes. The exception would be the Global Express, the first plane that would carry Bombardier's own livery.

Holding and Bryan Moss, president of the business jet division, eagerly took up Laurent's challenge. Holding put a team of engineers to work on a conceptual design. Moss brought in marketing personnel to collaborate with Holding's engineering team, passing on feedback from potential customers. From that market research, they learned the importance of linking city-pairs (establishing an air route between two prominent cities). This research, along with a general awareness of the growing importance of Asia to world business, led to a focus on the New York City and Tokyo connection.

"We realized that a lot of business is done out of the eastern US and that New York-Tokyo was the key. That is the driving city-pair behind the Global Express,"[3] said Holding. So Bombardier was going to provide the first jet capable of a fast, nonstop service between these points. But it would be useable on other routes, too. The Rome to Beijing trip, for example, would be reduced to a nonstop trip of less than 10 hours.

Laurent was very much involved in the design of the Global Express. As someone who logged several hours each week on business jets, he relished the chance to provide input from the user point of view. "He challenged me and was involved in the configuration," Holding revealed. "Laurent is not one to sit in his office. He's passionate about new products. I think secretly he is a repressed engineer," Holding added with a smile. Yet, this kind of close interaction was welcomed; in fact, it has been one of the things that has kept his chief aerospace engineer at Bombardier. "Laurent is very hands-on, but in a supportive way. When you have that sort of enthusiasm at the top, that love of the product, it's hugely rewarding—a real motivator. Bombardier is not just numbers-driven, it's also product-driven."[4]

Perhaps the greatest challenge Laurent laid in front of the design team was to be as creative with the business plan as with the engineering plan. The development team had come up with a design concept that they believed was technically feasible, had no commonality with previous airplanes, and would offer world-beating features. But it would require $1 billion to develop. That was too much to spend on a new design with no guarantee of succeeding, Laurent told them. They would have to apply their inventiveness to find a more economical way.

The solution came fairly quickly. While managing the Airbus subcontract, Holding saw firsthand how his client spread the risks of developing new products across joint ventures. The Global Express could be made a less risky endeavor by doing the same—by finding other aerospace companies willing to partici-pate in the development process in return for a percentage of the proceeds. Instead of contracting part of the work out at a fixed price, Bombardier would remunerate contractors at a rate tied to the success of the venture.

By mid-1993, major risk-sharing partners were lined up. The engines would be supplied by Frankfurt-based BMW-Rolls Royce GmbH. The forward fuselage and tail would be built at Bombardier subsidiary Short Brothers. The center fuselage and wings would come from Mitsubishi Heavy Industries Ltd. of Japan. The wings were the key breakthrough feature, a new design that distributed pressure across the surface more efficiently, allowing the Global Express to go faster and farther than any other business jet then in existence. Canadair engineers would play the role of system integrators, making sure all the parts were designed to fit together and then assembling them.

By this time, the leading manufacturer of business jets, Gulfstream Aerospace of Georgia, had stirred into action. It had announced plans of its own to launch an alternative to the Global Express by 1996, two years ahead of Bombardier's delivery date. They would get to market first by extending their largest model, whereas Bombardier would use a new design.

So, while Bombardier was attempting to sign up enough customers to reach a threshold for production, Gulfstream was promoting their version to the same people. The competition was fierce. Harassed business executives joked that as a sales rep from one company was going out the back door, a rep from the other company was coming in the front. Even after they signed up with one of the manufacturers, that still did not stop the other side from knocking on their door, urging them to switch.

Bombardier ran a two-page centerfold advertisement in the *Wall Street Journal* to point out that the Global Express, although coming to market later, would offer a roomier cabin and more range at greater speeds than the Gulfstream V. Gulfstream countered with *Wall Street Journal* ads showing Global Express as a crumpled paper plane, with a caption stating that Canadair would still be making promises when Gulfstream was making airplanes. The ad also promised $250,000 US to any Global Express customers who canceled their contract and signed with Gulfstream. No Bombardier customers bolted, and shortly afterward, Bombardier announced that it had secured 30 firm orders at a price of $30 million each, a large enough commitment to go into full-scale production.

The preliminary task at hand was a joint definition phase wherein all the engineers from the different suppliers were brought together in one spot to hammer out specifications. The chosen location was a football-field-size room in Bombardier's main manufacturing facilities near the Dorval airport in Montreal. Over 500 engineering staff sat in front of computer screens to map out their respective bits and pieces. The floor plan showed the Mitsubishi people in one section, the BMW Rolls-Royce people in another, and Shorts, de Havilland, and Canadair staff in others.

A system based on milestones and exit interviews was put in place to make sure that the work progressed at a reasonable pace and came together as a seamless whole. The work was divided into stages with gates in between that would not allow work to pass unless it met requirements. When suppliers thought they were ready to go back home to start building components, they would have to do a presentation describing their deliverables. If the promised results were not up to grade or failed to dovetail with the other components, the groups were not allowed to leave until they did. The interfaces between their packages and the others had to be particularly well defined.

The Global Express was the first of Bombardier's new aerospace models to be designed and put into production almost entirely as a virtual plane. Gone were most of the old drawings and physical mock-ups. Instead, a digital prototype was created in a 3-D format on a computer network comprised of hundreds of UNIX workstations, two supercomputers, and a state-of-the-art CAD/CAM software suite called CATIA.

Automating much of the design process generated new economies of scale. Whereas most other aerospace companies were still struggling to exploit the full potential of new computer technology—often times using it as no more than a glorified digital drafting board—Bombardier was able to advance application of the tool. CATIA software evolved into a controlling authority for every step of the design and production process, keeping every one on the same page and abreast of the latest changes. As such, the team was able to work concurrently rather than sequentially (as had been the case in the old days of handing off constantly altered blueprints down the chain of participants).

Other gains were the elimination of much of the wind tunnel testing through simulations on the Cray supercomputer, which, despite being the most powerful of computers, still required a day of processing to run the code for some of the exercises. Another gain was achieved by having CATIA as a common interface across the teams, while allowing each of them to use their own systems for designing their components.

"Its how you apply the tools that's the real secret," explained Holding. Any company could buy the tools and hire the people. Thinking the purchase of advanced gadgetry bestowed immediate productive gains "is like saying a paintbrush turns the owner into a painter." Holding liked to say that aerospace "was a high-tech industry with low-tech processes," a reflection of the era of regulation, subsidies, and military spending. Companies "always had been able to price their way out of a problem." So, struggling during the transition to more competitive markets, many companies ended up buying new tools that amounted to no more than $30,000 pencils, Holding stated.[5]

Perhaps because Bombardier lacked a heritage in the older era, it emerged as a recognized leader in the application of advanced tools. "Its just not training employees in their use, but a focus on how systems and processes are designed," stated Holding. "We spend a lot of time on processes; it's systems development as well as technical development." And "a lot of it is people …developing them, getting the right ones…the right attitude and spirit." Holding concludes the point with: "Technology and tools are there for everybody—the only thing you have to play with are the people…encourage them to use those tools in creative ways, and investing in people…it's the core values, everything else can be purchased."[6]

Meanwhile, the rivalry between Bombardier and Gulfstream was escalating. On one front, Gulfstream ran ads that portrayed itself as an American icon doing battle against government-subsidized foreign entities. On another, Gulfstream tried to throw Bombardier's campaign into disarray by hiring away their top business jet executive, Bryan Moss, who left without giving notice. Bombardier's going-away present was a lawsuit filed to prevent him from taking confidential information to their foe. The suit was eventually withdrawn, but the bitterness lingered. "They made it very unpleasant for me," Moss said. Privately, the reaction of Bombardier executives to Moss's departure is summarized up in a single epithet: traitor.[7]

As the Global Express development project moved along, Gulfstream and other competitors took their best shots. They said Bombardier could never get all its international partners moving in the same direction, the plane would miss delivery dates, and performance guarantees would not be met. But the Global Express had its maiden flight in 1996 and received its type certificate from Transport Canada in 1998, all according to schedule. At the certification ceremony, Holding proudly proclaimed: "The fact that this has been accomplished in accordance with a schedule established five years ago is a tribute to the skill, dedication, and hard work of all Bombardier employees and our partners involved in their visionary program."[8]

The airplane had many best-in-its-class attributes. It could fly eight passengers and a four-person crew 12,000 kilometers (6,500 nautical miles) nonstop and could cruise at nearly the speed of sound (0.88 Mach). The cabin was at least 20 percent roomier than rival aircraft and could be divided into three sections: boardroom, office in the sky, and living quarters. Because of the specially designed wing, the Global Express could land on the shortest of runways for business jets, making it handy for visiting smaller airports around the world. It was designed with the intent of meeting ETOPS (extended twin-engine operations) requirements for long, over water flights. Flexibility and reliability were enhanced by the independent electrical and hydraulics systems with multiple power sources. At the time of its certification, the Global Express had 80 firm orders.

As Bombardier worked on its backlog, more orders came in. Demand remained vigorous due to long-term trends such as the increasing globalization of business and also cyclical factors such as an expanding economy. An additional factor was new customers from the military: at the 1999 Paris Air Show, Bombardier announced that the Global Express would serve as the airborne platform for Britain's battlefield surveillance radar system..

As a consequence of the success of its business jets, Bombardier had supplanted Gulfstream as the leading firm by the end of the 1990s. But Gulfstream was still doing well, and in 1999 became a more formidable opponent when owners Forstmann and Little (a leveraged buyout firm) sold the company to defense contractor, General Dynamics Corp. Now Gulfstream would be backed by deeper pockets, have access to advanced aerospace technologies, and no longer be a David to the diversified Bombardier Goliath.

Nevertheless, a market research firm predicted the "Bombardier gorilla"[9] would remain as the leader in business aircraft. In the summer of 2000, the Teal Group projected that Bombardier would claim more than one-quarter of the market over the next decade, with Gulfstream in second place at a market share of 20 percent. The Falcon line of France's Dassault group would occupy third place with a 17 percent slice of the market.

They might not be immediate threats, but wild cards in the scenario were Embraer's new business jet, the Legacy, and a proposal from Eclipse Aviation Corp. to build an entry-level business jet priced at less than $900,000 US. This price was so much lower than anything available that it would be a major disruptive force. But many industry veterans did not believe that it was possible. A price that low was simply unheard of, and such a cheap jet was deemed to have virtually no chance of appearing. Still, Eclipse spokespersons said they had collected more than $30 million US in deposits from 160 customers and planned certification of the airplane by June 2003. They intended to radically lower the costs of production by using a new technique—friction stir welding—in place of the traditional riveting and bonding process. The cost of the engine would be reduced by using the Williams EJ22 turbofan engine, which was in test trials.

For its part, Bombardier, with so many new models launched to market over the past decade, was becoming quite efficient in the process. Successive introductions built on lessons learned earlier and consequently, the company experienced faster development cycles and improved quality levels. The system of risk-sharing partners was fine-tuned even more with commonality among suppliers ensured by the use of the CATIA software as a common interface. Digital modeling experienced refinements as well. Overall, the "company has a very disciplined approach to product innovation," said an industry consultant.[10]

"We're not into technology for technology's sake, and we will not embark on any sort of 'blue sky' program such as a supersonic business jet," said Holding. "R&D has got to buy its way onto our aircraft. If we don't think a technology will reduce an aircraft's life-cycle costs or benefit the customer in some other way, we won't pursue it. At the end of the day, the measure of whether we have succeeded is profitability."[11] Holding added: "Some people say, why develop so many new aircraft models? I tell them it's not my choice, it's the market's. If we want to be No. 1, we have to listen to the market. It's not an engineering imperative, it's responding to what customers want."[12]

As part of that listening process, Bombardier is now looking at reconfiguring the Global Express as a regional jet to be operated by airlines on long, thinly traveled routes where larger jets cannot make money. The Global Express, which can fly over twice the distance of current regional jets without refueling, would be stretched to seat 30 to 50. The appeal of having such an airplane would be to cut out several hours of travel time in the air (Global Express is faster than a Boeing 747) and on the ground (no stopovers required at hubs). Some observers are skeptical about its feasibility, but one aerospace analyst at a brokerage firm is a supporter. "People pooh-poohed the 50-seat regional jet when it was first floated...and its become really quite something," he said.[13]

14 New Generations

C H A P T E R

Over the late 1970s and early 1980s, the condition of the snowmobile industry went from bad to worse. A second energy crisis and sky-high interest rates hit hard. Bombardier got through it fine, mainly because of its diversification into mass transit. Yamaha and Polaris scraped by. John Deere, Kawasaki, and Arctic Cat did not. That left only three suppliers standing in 1983, a year in which annual sales totaled 87,000 (quite a contrast to a dozen years before when nearly 500,000 units were sold by over 100 snowmobile makers).

Bombardier was still the leader during those tough times, supplying over half the market. In fact, it was on track to move toward a monopolistic position. In 1980, Textron Inc., the parent corporation of Polaris, declared its intention to sell or shutter its subsidiary. Bombardier's bid was accepted by Textron but not by the antitrust division of the US Department of Justice. The following year, with the employment roll pared down to 50 persons, Polaris was finally rescued by a group of former managers who arranged a leveraged buyout.

In 1984, Bombardier got some more competition when a fourth company joined the industry: Arctico Inc. It rose out of the ashes of Arctic Cat, the assets and trademarks of which had been picked up by a Wisconsin dealer during the bankruptcy proceedings. The plant and tools remained idle until a group of former Arctic Cat managers came along and bought out the dealer.

All four manufacturers experienced growth over the 1980s as inventories were worked off and snowmobile sales revived in tandem with the economy. Also, enhancements to the machines lured more people to the sport, as did greater organization among snowmobile enthusiasts, and a vast extension to the system of groomed trails throughout North America. Bombardier maintained its dominant position during this recovery phase, but competitors began to chip away at its lead. Much of the erosion was linked to forces beyond the control of the company. From 1986 to 1990, the Canadian dollar rose almost uninterruptedly from $0.72 US to $0.90 US, putting upward pressure on the prices of Ski-Doos in the US market. Other causes, according to brokerage analysts, were quality problems and a misreading of the market that left Bombardier without high-performance models then gaining popularity.

In 1990, Polaris jumped ahead with a 30 percent share of the market, while Arctico and Yamaha climbed to just a hair behind Bombardier's 25 percent share. A further sign of trouble for Bombardier was a startling loss of $30 million in the recreational products group during fiscal 1991. Once dominant, the Ski-Doo line was now locked in a fight for survival against brands that a few years earlier had been almost eradicated.

Bombardier responded by increasing the automation of factory operations, adding high-performance models to the snowmobile line, and focusing on quality control. These measures, along with a partial unwinding of the appreciation in the Canadian dollar, helped the recreational products group return to profitability over the first half of the 1990s and narrow the Polaris market lead.

But the most important factor in the turnaround was the launch of a new product: a redesigned Sea-Doo. Annual sales soared from zero in the late 1980s to more than 100,000 units in fiscal 1995, claiming 50 percent of the market for personal watercraft (PWC). The profits from this product line accounted for the majority of the earnings of the recreational products group between fiscal 1992 and 1997. The high point came in fiscal 1997 when net income reached $212 million.

Instrumental in the turnaround was Laurent Beaudoin's son, Pierre Beaudoin, a reluctant recruit to the company in the beginning. "I didn't really want to start working for Bombardier," Pierre revealed.[1] But just as his father had found himself working unexpectedly for the company, so did Pierre. In 1985, at the age of 23, he accepted his father's invitation to work on a redesign of the Sea-Doo. "I more or less took on the Sea-Doo to keep myself busy until I found something else to do,"[2] explained Pierre.

Pierre was the youngest and only son of Laurent's four children. As a teenager, Pierre got an informal training in business by accompanying his father on business trips to witness the negotiation of multimillion-dollar sales agreements and the acquisition of other companies. His formal training included business administration studies at Brébeuf College and industrial relations at McGill University. Afterward, Pierre worked for a year as a customer service manager at a Toronto-based sporting goods manufacturer, BIC Sport Inc., before accepting his father's invitation to lead the redesign of the Sea-Doo.

Pierre's initial reluctance to join Bombardier may be attributed to the fear of not measuring up to the challenge of being his father's son. Nor did he like the idea of having a position in the company merely because he was the boss's kid. He had to be deserving in his own right. So, he was thinking of setting out on a path of his own, if only to gather experience before coming back to the family firm. But that all changed with the Sea-Doo. About six months into his assignment, he discovered it was quite interesting and decided to stay.

During his childhood, Pierre had enjoyed many hours of fun scooting around on the recreational vehicles made by the family firm, including prototypes of the Sea-Doos stockpiled after the false start in 1968. As a result of this experience, Pierre was convinced of the appeal of the product and felt he had a good idea of what would make it even more enjoyable to users. So he was quite eager to get on with the challenge.

What helped lure the son even more into the company fold was his father's suggestion that the project be started outside the organization as a separate company. That way, employees would not have to be convinced of its value for it to work within Bombardier (it was later brought in-house when functional prototypes were ready to be mass produced). And, as was typical at Bombardier, Pierre and his coworkers would be given a free hand. They would have the flexibility to write their own rules and plenty of chances for trial and error without recrimination.

They ended up working on the Sea-Doo for several years, developing prototypes, manufacturing processes, marketing campaigns, and distribution channels. As new versions of the Sea-Doo came out of the lab, Pierre spent time testing them, further refining his ideas of what would appeal to the customer. This experience left him with the conviction that intensive use of company products by managers was crucial to the design process: "If I think about what created our success, it is simply that our managers are users of our product," Pierre told a reporter in 1995. "By experiencing it for themselves, they understand what customers want."[3]

Getting the Sea-Doo into production mode involved signing up 60 partners to provide various components. Bombardier's strategy was to become a systems integrator, to maintain control over design and set up an assembly line that would fit all the parts together. (Bombardier staff would spend only four hours working on each Sea-Doo.) This high degree of outsourcing allowed the Sea-Doo group to ramp up production quicker. And in keeping processes simple, it allowed Bombardier to better understand its costs while bestowing a greater degree of flexibility in responding to business fluctuations.

Another challenge was building awareness. This was accomplished with a classical marketing campaign consisting of several million dollars worth of television and magazine advertising. A policy of limited production runs protected price levels and dealer markups (although a cut in list prices in one year angered dealers who still had unsold inventories of the prior year's models). In any event, as a result of its marketing and pricing stance, Bombardier was able to win market share without having to discount or rebate its products.

When Bombardier launched the Sea-Doo in 1988, it was taking on an entrenched rival: Kawasaki Heavy Industries Ltd. The latter had launched its PWC model, the Jet Ski, way back in 1973. It was a stand-up version: riders stood or knelt on the craft and gripped a set of handlebars for steering. For the first 10 years, sales were lackluster. But the cadre of enthusiasts grew over time, and Jet Ski races began to pop up in the early 1980s. Some new Kawasaki models, more nimble and easier to maintain, were also sparking interest.

Just before Bombardier released its Sea-Doo, a second company entered the PWC market: Yamaha Motor Corp. In 1987, it introduced a sit-down model: riders sat on the craft in a fashion similar to a motorcycle. This was a more comfortable position in that riders got less wet and did not need to perform an athletic balancing act while in motion. In the same year, PWC magazines, such as *Splash* and *Personal Watercraft Illustrated* began to appear, creating even more interest.

When Bombardier's sit-down model came onto the scene shortly after, it took the PWC riding experience to new heights. With its V-hull design, the handling was a whole lot better, slicing through waves with ease. The Yamaha model, fitted with a flat hull, slapped across the surface, making it uncomfortable at high speeds. Pierre's market research and testing had got the Sea-Doo off to a good start.

Witnessing the erosion of its market share to the two new challengers, Kawasaki responded with a sit-down model of its own in 1989. Its extra-wide hull made it more stable and a favorite with PWC rental operators—for a brief time. Bombardier quickly followed suit with more stable models and fielded the Sea-Doo XP, which was able to go 80 kilometers per hour (50 mph) out of the box. Being the fastest on the water, it wrestled away racing crowns from Kawasaki and kept winning them for several years afterward, giving Bombardier a huge lift in sales.

Bombardier's two main rivals in snowmobile manufacturing, Polaris Industries and Arctico Inc., both decided to get into the PWC market, but their models did not appear until 1992 and failed to have much of an impact. Bombardier kept upgrading its models to ensure they were the highest performing and the first to incorporate new advances, such as digitally encoded, theft-deterrent systems, shock absorbers in the seat, and a tunable hull (that is, customizable to the rider's weight and riding style).

A key feature in terms of product design was Bombardier's use of specially engineered fiberglass material for the body shell, as opposed to the sheet metal compounds used on competing models. This differentiation made the Sea-Doo lighter compared to rival models, allowing it to go faster. It also allowed

Bombardier to do faster turnarounds on model changes since it was easier to create dies for fiberglass than for metal parts.

Another Sea-Doo advantage was its cost. Despite many enhancements to models each year, Bombardier held the line on pricing. A key reason was volume production, which lowered Bombardier's unit production costs dramatically. Another factor was the decline of the Canadian dollar against the US dollar in conjunction with an appreciation of the yen against the US dollar. So while Bombardier was finding it easier to keep prices down in the US market, Kawasaki and Yamaha were finding it more difficult. Polaris and Arctico were in the same boat as the Japanese companies because PWC engines and other components were imported from Japan (while Bombardier's were mostly made or purchased within Canada).

As the Sea-Doo product line blossomed, so did Pierre's position in the company. He was named vice president of product development for Sea-Doo/Ski-Doo in October 1990, president of the Sea-Doo/Ski-Doo division in June 1992, and president and chief operating officer of Bombardier Recreational Products on April 1, 1996. The last promotion was no April Fools' Day joke. In fact, with the spectacular turnaround of the recreational products group, there was serious talk that Pierre had emerged as the natural successor to his father .

Unfortunately, fiscal 1996 was the peak year for the group and Pierre's turnaround magic. Profits slipped to break even the next year and to losses of $45 million and $17 million in fiscal 1999 and 2000. The main problem was a collapse in Sea-Doo sales, resulting from a saturation in demand and restrictions imposed by local and regional governments concerned about noise, pollution, and safety. With inventories piling up, Bombardier announced a 50 percent cut in production for the 1998 season. It was like a replay of the snowmobile bust of the 1970s.

Attempts to create a new growth dynamic with new products did not pan out. The Neighbourhood Electric Vehicle,
essentially a golf-cart-like vehicle for seniors to ride in retirement communities, had production runs halted several times
pending signs of a pick up in demand. In 1998, Bombardier
launched the Traxter, an entry into the four-wheel, all-terrain
vehicle (ATV) market. The ATV was a larger and faster growing
market, which Bombardier was able to approach through its Ski-
Doo and Sea-Doo dealerships. But standing in the way of a fast
ramp up in sales were six other established players, including
Polaris and Honda.

As the recreational products group faded in the late 1990s, so
did talk of Pierre's prospects. In 1999, Robert Brown, the president of the highly successful Bombardier Aerospace group, was
appointed Bombardier's chief executive officer and president.
Pierre, still in his thirties, would have to spend more time prov-
ing himself. Hugo Uyterhoeven, a Harvard Business School professor and member of the Bombardier board of directors, noted
at the time that Bombardier might be a family company, but "it
is also a meritocracy."[4] In early 2001, there was a reshuffling of
responsibilities at the senior executive level. Pierre's new assignment was president of the business aircraft division within the
aerospace group.

Over the 1990s, the development of high-performance snowmobiles had produced some machines with startling capabilities.
The experience of riding these "muscle sleds" had "about as much
to do with traditional snowmobiling as a Formula One racecar
has to do with a John Deere tractor,"[5] declared one observer. For
example, Ski-Doo's flagship 1997 model, the 800-cc Mach Z,
could accelerate from zero to 95 kilometers per hour (60 mph)

in less than three seconds. Professional racers said of the beast: "It's not fast, it's too *#@%ing fast."[6] Other manufacturers, like Arctico, had some monsters, too. Compare the 172 horsepower generated by its 590 pound (270 kilogram) Mountain Cat 1000 model to the 136 horsepower generated by a four-cylinder Toyota Camry weighing over four times as much.

Sleds (snowmobile enthusiasts called their machines sleds) have come a long way since the days of Joseph-Armand Bombardier. They are so much lighter and loaded with horsepower that they can race up nearly vertical hills and glide through powder that would absorb people up to their armpits. The high-end models have helped popularize several new pastimes—one being mountain snowmobiling. Samples of this sport can be seen on sports television channels. Viewers can watch contestants race up, for example, the 85 degree slope of Snow King Mountain in Wyoming. The goal is to reach the top in less than two minutes, but if a snowmobile flips en route, as many do, it just keeps tumbling down to the bottom until a net catches it before reaching the audience.

Off television, one can find many other manifestations of extreme snowmobiling. Attempts to establish the record for the fastest snowmobile have set the mark at 305 kilometers (190 mph). Then there are the pulling contests featuring heavy cargo loads such as elephants. Or the "water cross" competitions in which snowmobilers plane across open water. Jumping contests in which snowmobiles shoot off ramps into the air have established a world record of 33 meters (108.2 feet). Could Armand have ever imagined it all?

Water skimming is perhaps one of the trickier and least-advised categories of extreme snowmobiling. Nevertheless, for those crazy enough to give it a try, guidelines are offered by veteran Urban Öhman. He writes on his Web site: "I prefer a classic drivers' position; feet in front, back in the middle of the seat.

Make efforts to find the absolute center balance in your position. Hold the grips firmly…. Any attempts to turn during the crossing are banned!"[7]

Öhman adds a useful footnote: "I also recommend tying a (heavy) rope from the frame to an old bleach bottle…so if you do sink, you can come along with a (large) boat and winch to pull it back up. If not, you may not be able to get the sled back after it sinks."[8] And if one grows weary of water crossings, one can review Öhman's tips on his version of winter skiing—that is, skimming across open winter water on a snowmobile towing a parka-clad person on skis.

At the other end of snowmobile users are the novices who sign up for snowmobile tours offered by vacation and travel agencies. They usually come back invigorated by the experience. One captured some of the thrill with the following description of a particularly exciting moment: "I looked over the hood of my snowmobile and gasped. The souped-up sled's skis were sticking straight out over an abyss with nothing but air and a 60-degree slope between them and the valley floor 45 meters (150 feet) below… I gunned the 120-horsepower engine…and went airborne…This is the closest I'd ever come to feeling like…Evel Knieval."[9]

Not surprisingly, novices are also likely to report a few harrowing experiences. A common mishap is running into trees. Traditionally, steering a snowmobile requires more than turning the handlebar; the rider usually has to lean into the turn, much like a motorcycle rider does. A first-time rider recounted her encounter with a trunk: "…the sweeping uphill turn seemed rather benign. As I entered it, I dutifully leaned into the corner …Nope—my flimsy arc was taking me straight into a fir tree. With a crack, the left ski kissed the trunk, and I bounced neatly onto the trail…I wanted to yell, 'Why didn't you just say that I had to actually hang my butt completely off the seat?'"[10]

Another snowmobiler experienced the usual tree mishap and then some. He summed up his track record as follows: "In two days of touring I was thrown off twice, had a head-on collision with the bottom of a hill, cracked the windshield with my noggin, got stuck seven times, front-ended a stump, did an unintentional 360-degree roll, was airborne, and had the unfortunate experience of hitting a tree (aim for evergreens, they're softer)."[11] Nonetheless, he concluded, it was an exhilarating experience.

15

Lessons in Strategic Governance

Until his retirement in the summer of 2001, he was the *éminence grise* at Bombardier, the person who had Laurent Beaudoin's ear when it came to matters of governance, strategy, and diversification. In the later stages, he was also active in helping to run the corporation. Various groups reported to him in areas such as corporate strategy, financing, and acquisitions. And at key crossroads, such as the decision to develop the Canadair Regional Jet, he was on the spot performing assessments and passing judgment back to Laurent.

Just into his sixties and wearing wired-rimmed glasses, his grayish-white hair was combed neatly to touch the top of his ears. He was a bit short and a bit chubby. Nevertheless, he had a youthful air. In photographs, he looked almost cherubic. But in person, he had a dynamic and forceful quality, an impression furthered by his articulate speech and clarity of expression. Listening to him speak about management topics, one nearly always came away with a penetrating insight or two.

Former associates from his pre-Bombardier days describe him as an ambitious individual who found in Bombardier a challenge on a par with the scope of his aspirations. He had a serious manner, and, like many persons of towering intellect, he did not suffer fools gladly. Sloppy thinking was corrected whenever it surfaced.[1] Yet, he and Laurent functioned smoothly as a team, mutually appreciative of each other's talents. The long-running dialogue between the two men had been a key dynamic in the success of Bombardier.

Dr. Yvan Allaire was the *éminence grise*. His mind was well honed from decades of study. Following completion of Bachelor of Science (summa cum laude) and Master of Business Administration degrees at the University of Sherbrooke (Laurent's alma mater), he attended the Massachusetts Institute of Technology (MIT), and graduated with a doctorate in management science in the early 1970s. He was then at various times a professor of business strategy at the University of Sherbrooke, University of Ottawa, and University of Quebec, as well as a visiting professor at MIT and other foreign universities. The years of study and teaching were supplemented with practical experience: he cofounded and was chairman of an influential management consulting firm, Groupe Secor Inc.

While in academia, Allaire met a Romanian émigré and German citizen who was to become his wife and career partner. Her name was Mihaela Firsirotu. She and Allaire shared a deep interest in business and management topics. Her doctoral thesis, entitled "Strategic Turnaround as Cultural Revolution: The Case of Canadian National Express," won the *A. T. Kearney Award* in 1985 for the best thesis on management issues in North America. The pair were engaged in their own long-standing dialogue and had jointly authored several articles and books in the field of strategy. Their 620-page tome published in 1993, *L'entreprise Stratégique: Penser la Stratégie* (The Making of Strategy), was considered a leading text in the French language.[2] Today, Firsirotu is a professor at the University of Quebec at Montreal, where she holds the Bombardier Chair in the Management of Multinational Enterprises.

Allaire's involvement with Bombardier commenced in April 1985 when Laurent extended an invitation to lunch. Laurent was thinking about diversifying Bombardier, of adding a third product group to counterbalance snowmobiles and mass transit. And he wanted to deal with the challenge of managing the growing size and complexity of his company. He wanted advice on these matters from Allaire.

By this stage, Allaire had reflected at length and advised many companies on management issues, particularly strategic planning. In a 1988 paper,[3] he summarized some of his views. He agreed there was no future for strategic planning if it was based on predicting the future. Predictions were invariably off the mark and planning based on them usually led to a dead end. As an alternative to the predict and prepare model, Allaire proposed two alternatives. The first was the "power response," which called for proactive actions to shape or control external environments. Examples included lobbying regulators for changes to legislation, passing risk to others through measures such as fixed-price contracts, disciplining competition through the courts, cooperative market sharing, and other approaches. The second alternative was "developing a capacity for flexible response," which entailed (among other things) diversifying the product portfolio to provide more staying power to develop big-hit products.

Following the 1985 lunch with Laurent, Allaire began his involvement with Bombardier as an outside consultant, meeting with Laurent to carry on an intense dialogue on how to avoid the pitfalls of diversification. As the pace picked up with Bombardier's entry into the aerospace industry, Laurent tried to get Allaire to join Bombardier as a full-time executive. But he was attached to his career as a university professor, so he chose to remain apart, even though by 1992 he was working so much at Bombardier that he was compelled to cut back on his university duties to part-time. In 1996, he finally accepted a post when Laurent reorganized Bombardier and created a new executive position, executive vice president of strategy and corporate affairs. This position put Allaire in charge of key corporate functions including strategic initiatives, structured finance, treasury operations, and organizational development.

It would be an interesting real-world case study for the professor. "Why not try it for a few years as field work?" he mused to himself.[4] And what field work it was to be: among his specific responsibilities would be the handling of the dispute over Pro-ex financing and participation in the negotiations to acquire Adtranz.

As Bombardier diversified and increased in size, Laurent found it difficult to adjust at first. Just as some people are fanatics about sports, the arts, or some other subject, Laurent was passionate about the world of business. When he ran Bombardier in the 1960s and early 1970s, he loved to immerse himself in the details of engineering, production, marketing, and sales. Not surprisingly, the early Bombardier was a centralized company in which the head executive had a hand in nearly all decisions.

As the organization started to expand in the early stages, Laurent's reluctance to delegate led one observer to comment: "Mr. Beaudoin is an autocrat and does not share power easily."[5] There was the friction with Claude Hébert when the latter was CEO during the 1970s. And in 1982, there was the sudden and unannounced departure of president and chief operating officer Louis Hollander. When news of the resignation filtered out a couple of months later, neither side would provide an explanation, leading to suspicions of a less than amicable parting. Laurent took over

Hollander's duties, and it was not until Raymond Royer was promoted to president in February 1986 that any of the top executive posts were handed out again.

Laurent readily admits that as Bombardier sprawled, his approach was becoming less appropriate. The company was just getting to be too big for one person to stay on top of things. Yet, it was hard for him to change his style. As he remarked: "When you are so intimate with a business, it is not easy to hand it over to someone else. It was difficult not to be hands-on, to try to do it through another individual. It took me quite a number of years to change."[6]

But change he did, accomplishing a transformation that was instrumental to Bombardier's ascendancy. Behind that evolution was the ongoing dialogue between Allaire and Laurent. It began with the question "Why have most companies failed in their attempts to diversify?"[7] and culminated in a 1992 document prepared by Allaire (with some assistance from Firsirotu) that outlined four pillars for a strategic governance system: 1) architecture and leadership, 2) strategic management and planning, 3) information systems, and 4) incentive and reward systems. This document was to become a blueprint for Bombardier and the integration of acquired companies. The underlying theme was that senior management could not sit back and be a passive observer in a decentralized and entrepreneurial organization; it had to be actively involved in maintaining a system of checks and balances as well as an ongoing dialogue with the operating groups.

Within this framework, there was a realization of the need for Laurent to change his leadership style—to go from managing to governing. Instead of making the calls on everything, Laurent needed to have his vice presidents, officers, and managers make the calls. As Allaire stated:

The first step in achieving effective governance rests with the leader, who must change his leadership style and mindset—always a difficult trick—as he brings more diversity and complexity under the corporate umbrella. He must resist the impulse, often born of years as a line manager, to make decisions that would be the responsibility of operating groups. Bombardier is fortunate in that respect. Laurent Beaudoin...has grown as a leader more quickly than the corporation has grown...he has imposed on himself and Bombardier the exacting discipline of a first-rate governance system.[8]

But a key reason why Bombardier has been one of the few companies to avoid the pitfalls of diversification, said Allaire, is the fact that the "increase in the sophistication in management was achieved in parallel with corporate growth." The mistake of most entrepreneurs was to try to bring in governance systems after a period of rapid growth. "By then," said Allaire, "it is too late. The company outgrows their management systems and either implodes or stagnates."[9] Laurent did not wait until Bombardier was a $20 billion company to change styles; he began working on it with advisers beforehand.

Under the strategic governance system put in place, decision making was decentralized downward to the five (as of 2001) operating groups: aerospace, rail transportation, recreational products, financial services, and international markets. Each group was led by a president with considerable latitude over fabrication, marketing, product development, and other matters. In essence, Bombardier was made up of profit centers that were judged more by their initiatives and bottom line results. "I see myself as the conductor of an orchestra," Laurent liked to say. "I don't play all the instruments, but I can tell you when they are playing in tune."[10]

An indication of Bombardier's commitment to decentralization was the small size of its corporate office. Along with expanding scale came complexity; many large corporations responded in kind by designing complex systems and structures that required more staff at the top to coordinate and monitor everything. Not Bombardier. With approximately 150 staff at corporate headquarters in Montreal overseeing an organization of approximately 77,000 employees around the world, the center was lean.

With a decentralized format in place, Bombardier's core values stressed entrepreneurship at different ranks. "We judge managers on their ability to come to us and tell us where their business has gone, where it's going, and where it should go. It's up to them. If you let them know they are expected to be entrepreneurial, it shows up very quickly."[11] Reward systems were designed to reinforce this *modus operandi*. Promotions to and within management were based on entrepreneurial traits; incentive schemes rewarded growth, which invited people to take the initiative and embrace risks.

To ensure that the entrepreneurial spirit thrived, it was important to remove people's fear of taking risks, said Laurent. "People should not be afraid of making a mistake. We all make mistakes—that's OK as long as we learn from them and don't repeat them. Otherwise, people freeze up and do not initiate things or make decisions. Then you have an organization that is stagnant. Staff wait for what their boss is going to say.[12]

There were some trade-offs in having a decentralized design. Bombardier might have been described as having a "stove pipe" organizational design, in which information flowed mostly up and down within separate groups and less so across the groups. Opportunities to share knowledge, coordinate policies, and achieve economies of scale might not always have been acted upon. But that was all right with the corporate office. It was the price of keeping bureaucracy at bay. Bombardier would rather have gone with what might have been a suboptimal allocation of resources as long if it preserved the ability of line managers to act freely on their projects. As Laurent declared: "We would rather lose some synergy across the groups than hamper decision making and entrepreneurialism within them."[13]

Thus, Bombardier remained a firm adherent to decentralization. The corporate office, for example, did not formulate central plans to pass down to the operating groups. Instead, strategic planning was a bottom-up process centered around two meetings that took place each year. The first occurred half way through the fiscal year when management teams from the groups and divisions met with executives at the corporate office to discuss challenges, opportunities, competitive pressures, strategic direction, and proposals for new products. The second meeting happened near the end of the fiscal year and was focused on a review of performance goals, including those outlined in the action plans formulated at the first meeting, the three-year performance commitment, and the five-year financial projection.

The second meeting was also the time when budgets and operational plans were presented. They were reviewed quarterly, top to bottom within the company. The process was exacting, but it brought a discipline. Regular review of financial budgets and reports at most employee levels had always been an important part of Bombardier, right from the start. Laurent, with his background as a chartered accountant, made sure of that. It was a tool for determining what was going on in his company. "I wanted to know where the hell I was going. You have to be sure people at the top are getting the right information, and that everyone participates and knows what they are responsible for…it's a lot of work every cycle. But you cannot make decisions without it. You cannot respond to requests for support because you are not really aware of what's going on."[14]

Over the years, the financial reporting system has been tweaked and nudged, but today, it remains basically the same one from Laurent's early days. "There is no miracle about it," said Laurent. "I am always surprised when we acquire a company and find out the business plan is made by the accountants. The staff did not seem to participate, it was there basically to satisfy the accountants and was not really a tool to work with.... They had no budget, and the business plan was done at the top. There was no regular review, and they did not know if they were behind or ahead of budget. Then at the end, they got a big surprise."[15]

Supplementing this process of strategic plans and budgets, now overseen by president and chief executive officer Robert Brown, was an informal, ongoing dialogue between the corporate office and the operating groups. Prior to Brown's promotion, Laurent used to spend about half of his time in daily contact with top-level persons in the groups, discussing their major concerns one-on-one. They explored opportunities and assessed what could be done better. And each month, they looked at operations and did some forward planning. "It's very intense, it's very unbureaucratic..." stated Allaire in 1997.[16] No doubt, this continuous communication, now under the aegis of Brown, kept the focus on performance issues very tight within the corporation.

One of Laurent's (and now increasingly Brown's) predominant preoccupations in these communications with the field offices was product development. A key role of the chief executive, as Laurent saw it, was to push the field continually for more innovation. At strategy sessions, he would ask what they are coming up with. "My job is to challenge management, to ensure they are thinking about the future and making the right decisions," stated Laurent in 1997. "They have to manage their operations and deal with today's problems, but at the same time they must look forward and plan for the future."[17] Through this intense and continuous focus on product development, cascading down from the seat of authority, Bombardier was successful in maintaining the small-firm qualities of innovation and sensitivity to markets.

In his formal and informal meetings over the years, Laurent has encouraged the open exchange of ideas prior to taking decisions. But it was always clear who was in charge. "People do not want to displease him," stated Allaire. "He is a real authority figure within the corporation."[18] He realized people needed to be given some rope in order to give their best, even though some might have ended up hanging themselves. That is, in cases of incompetence, he could act decisively. It was not something he relished or did callously; loyal and sincere employees were usually given the benefit of the doubt. Not surprisingly, Laurent had garnered a reputation for being firm but fair. Thus, Laurent allowed freedom of expression and action but remained a disciplinarian.

Both Laurent's management style and the organizational framework appeared to be interesting blends of seemingly opposite characteristics. He was open to guidance yet was still in charge. The corporation also exhibited simultaneous loose-tight properties. On the one hand, autonomy, entrepreneurship, and innovation flourished at different levels. On the other hand, the corporate office maintained a capacity for orientation, monitoring, and control. It seemed like a paradox in concept and action, but upon such dualities rested, as management gurus Peters and Waterman claimed, excellence in the corporate realm.[19]

One of Allaire's specific interests at the corporate office was keeping abreast of the latest developments in management practices. To weed out fad from substance, he, along with other senior staff, subjected whatever came along to an analysis. If it was found to be conceptually sound and appropriate to Bombardier's situation, it was swiftly implemented. Consequently, Bombardier was usually at the forefront of adopting new business practices in North America. This was particularly true of the economic value added (EVA) concept for allocating capital funds and Six Sigma techniques for assessing quality in manufacturing processes.

Put simply, EVA was defined as net operating profit less the true cost of capital. The true cost included interest payments on debt plus the opportunity cost of equity capital (which was defined as the return on government treasury bonds). EVA was positive if net operating profit was higher than the true cost of capital. Proponents of EVA said it was a better alternative to assess performance than using only operating profits.

Under conventional accounting rules, a firm might demonstrate growth in profit but still not be a good investment because its EVA could be negative. The growth would yield a return below the return on alternative assets with equal or less risk. If a firm would therefore be better off putting its capital into these alternative investments, so would investors. In effect, the company would not be a viable operation over the long term because investors would not continue to put up financing when they could earn a better return on assets of equal or lesser risk. They might for a time be induced to invest on the promise of better returns in the future, but eventually, failure to deliver would erode investor support.

Bombardier employed EVA to measure its performance throughout the corporation. Use of EVA sought to improve the allocation of resources by giving managers rewards for keeping capital out of projects that were not profitable enough to cover the true financing costs. So, instead of investing $100 million in a project with a projected return of 4 percent, the funds were free to be invested in a government bond paying 6 percent until a better in-house project came along. The end result was a more efficient use of capital and the creation of sustainable share-holder value.

Use of the EVA measure helped align employee interests with those of the shareholder (and in doing so, improved the flow of capital to the corporation). It generated more incentives to root out wasteful operations (for example, the product line that brought in some profits but not enough to cover the capital costs associated with carrying inventories). And with managers focused on using capital resources more effectively, there was less scope for empire-building behavior, of expansion for expansion's sake.

According to Stern Stewart & Co., the consulting company that originated the EVA concept in the 1980s, Bombardier's EVA was found to be significantly positive in their 1999 survey. The company earned 14.2 percent on its operating capital, which was 4.7 percentage points better than its capital cost of 9.5 percent. This made Bombardier one of the best performing firms in North America.

Another company-wide program was the Six Sigma method for improving quality in manufacturing. It was very rigorous and statistics driven. The phrase Six Sigma was itself a statistical one, indicating a very low likelihood that a manufacturing process would produce a defective output: just 3.4 tries in one million would be off. The Six Sigma objective was thus very lofty. Good manufacturing companies operated at less than four sigma, or 6,210 defects every one million iterations. That might not seem too bad, but costs could be considerably reduced by getting to six sigma. In the case of an automobile manufacturer, it meant repairing only 3.4 cars per million versus 6,210. But not only were costs reduced by doing things right the first time, customer satisfaction levels improved and company managers spent less time handling consumer complaints.

Since 1997, Bombardier had pulled groups of people off its production lines for training at the Sigma Academy in Arizona. After several weeks of classroom instruction and subsequent months of on-the-job training, they became full-time Sigma masters who helped guide, under a vice president at corporate headquarters, the training and efforts of line staff. To encourage implementation, managers got bonuses for successfully implementing Six Sigma practices.

Six Sigma shaved $242 million off costs in fiscal 2001. One example of the successful application of Six Sigma techniques involved the paint shop in the aerospace group. After five years of trying to solve a problem with paint peeling off freshly minted regional jets, a Six Sigma team was asked to take a look. It was a knotty conundrum because there were at least 10 possible causes, all interacting with each other. Within five months, however, the group discovered that the solution laid in changing the thickness of the undercoat.

Describing how General Electric had organized to sustain growth under his leadership, Jack Welch once said: "We set out to shape a global enterprise that preserved the classic big-company advantages, while eliminating the classic big-company drawbacks. What we wanted to build was a hybrid, an enterprise with the reach and resources of a big company—the body of a big company—but the thirst to learn, the compulsion to share, and the bias for action—the soul—of a small company."[20]

One way Bombardier attempted to realize this goal was through a commitment to maintaining a continuous pipeline of business-building initiatives. Management consultants Baghai et al.[21] cited Bombardier as a prime example of a company that had mastered their concept of the "alchemy of growth," which they said involved a program of product development simultaneously focused on "three horizons." These horizons were distinguished by the timing of their contribution to the bottom line: 1) core market products, 2) new businesses just coming to market, and 3) businesses still in the concept or prototype stage. Many other large companies, entangled in various imperatives, tended to neglect the early stages development until core product lines reached a mature phase, when it was often too late.

Another way in which Bombardier tried to combine the properties of small and large businesses was through a continuous reshaping of the organizational structure. The process involved hiving off units from broader groupings in order to assign specific accountability for tasks or growth opportunities that might have been falling between the cracks. The objective was to spur results in these niches by placing them clearly under one command post, with a higher profile and an unfettered environment for taking action. "Recreating and reshaping Bombardier is a continuous process,"[22] Allaire said. Management specialists Brown and Eisenhardt[23] concurred. They viewed this tendency at Bombardier as an example of their concept of "patching"— that is, the use of small and frequent reorganizations to keep a corporation flexible and adaptive under evolving conditions.

An illustration was the 1997 reorganization of the recreational product group. It split off the Sea-Doo and other marine products from the Ski-Doo operations to form a separate division under a new president. This move to raise the profile of the marine operations was made necessary by the growing popularity of the Sea-Doo. Rival Kawasaki undertook a similar reorganization shortly afterward. An observer explained the changes as follows: "Before, mistakes were easy to explain away because you could always say you were working on something in another market. Now, people are going to be responsible for one market. They're going to have to know what's going on in that market. There won't be any excuses anymore."[24]

A second illustration of corporate reshaping was the creation in 1998 of a fifth operating group, Bombardier International. The primary objective of this new entity was to accelerate expansion into markets outside North America and Western Europe through market research, pursue foreign alliances/acquisitions, serve as the key interface with foreign authorities, and coordinate strategies among the four other groups. By grouping these activities under one president and chief operating officer and allocating more resources to them, Bombardier had signaled a determination to make geographic expansion a priority.

In December 1998, the head of Bombardier Aerospace, Robert Brown, was elevated to the positions of president and chief executive officer of Bombardier. Laurent remained as chairman and Allaire reported directly to Laurent as executive vice president and as chairman of Bombardier Capital. Thus, after 1998, a somewhat curious situation existed at the top echelons. Brown was responsible for the day-to-day operations except for the capital group, while Allaire was responsible for acquisitions, strategy, and the capital group.

This split in authority might have raised concerns among some, but it was actually welcomed by analysts as putting a succession plan in place. With Laurent's heart condition and his approaching retirement, there was trepidation over how the company would fare when he left. By phasing in new leadership in stages, Laurent was reassuring analysts and investors that the organization would have a foundation for flourishing in his absence.

It was thought to be wise to ease the new leader in gradually as a way to give him time to learn the ropes in all the operating groups. If Laurent were to wait until his retirement to dump onto his successor all his responsibilities of running such a large, diversified corporation, it might be too overwhelming. After all, Joseph-Armand Bombardier's tight grip on all the reins right up until his sudden departure contributed to the difficulties his son experienced back in the 1960s.

Allaire's depiction of the troika at the top was: "we have a three-way dialogue that is quite intense."[25] That such a sharing of power could be put in place without fear of a turf war had a lot to do with the makeup of the men involved. All were dedicated to the task of running Bombardier. Laurent still held sway through his presence and knowledge of Bombardier and its markets. Brown was a team player glad to have the help of some of the best minds in the business. And Allaire did not have long-term ambitions at Bombardier. He had signed on with Laurent for a five-year mandate that ended in the summer of 2001, and he was looking forward to new endeavors afterward.

With his duties less onerous, Laurent was looking forward to an easier work pace, just coming into the office three days a week. But his keenness for strategy and acquisitions was as intense as ever. And soon enough, he became fully engaged on that front, as highlighted by the bid for Adtranz. This acquisition was motivated by Bombardier's drive to be number one in the industry as well as by its guiding principle of diversification and balanced growth. With the overwhelming success of the aerospace division, Bombardier was turning once again into a one-product firm. The purchase of Adtranz would rebalance the product portfolio, giving rail and aerospace groups nearly equivalent shares in corporate revenues. Because of low margins in rail transport, corporate profits would not be balanced out as nicely as revenues, but a restructuring plan would be put in place to improve rail profits over time.

While the Adtranz bid awaited regulatory approval, Laurent was busy on another acquisition that would add mass to the recreational products group and promote balanced growth at Bombardier. It was a vintage Bombardier deal involving a bankrupt company with a troubled balance sheet that was interfering with the potential of a promising new technology. It was a company Bombardier had its eye on for years but refused to buy at the asking prices demanded in the past.

In February 2001, the assets of recreational boat maker, Outboard Marine Corp. (OMC), were auctioned off in US Bankruptcy Court. Bombardier put in a bid of $42.7 million US for OMC's engine business, which included the Johnson and Evinrude brands, FICHT fuel-injection technology, and production facilities. The dominant US maker of recreational boat engines, Brunswick Corp., countered with a $46 million US offer.

Bombardier responded by teaming up with another boat maker, Genmar Holdings Ltd., to jointly bid $95 million US for all the assets of OMC, which included boatbuilding companies such as Chris Craft, Four Winns, Hydra-Sports, Seaswirl, and Stratos (the boating products to all be claimed by Genmar). Brunswick was mulling over its next step when OMC creditors and bankers asked them to post a nonrefundable $25 million bond in order to continue bidding. Unwilling to do so, Brunswick withdrew.

The OMC's creditors threw Brunswick a monkey wrench because they were concerned that the Federal Trade Commission (FTC) would disallow the Brunswick takeover on antitrust grounds given the latter's 50 percent share of the US outboard engine market (which would be greatly augmented by OMC's 28 percent share). As the value of OMC's assets could deteriorate while government lawyers studied the matter, the creditors wanted protection against the downside risk.

Moreover, they were suspicious that Brunswick's true motives were to shut down most of the engine business. In the likely event the FTC would not issue an approval, Brunswick would be in a position to liquidate (the fact that a liquidation specialist had been retained was a hint). The benefit to Brunswick in shutting down OMC, of course, would be to keep it out of the hands of a viable competitor. The $50 million US or so lost was simply the price paid to secure the market.

Following the exclusion of Brunswick, OMC's engine divisions fell into the hands of Bombardier. Michel Baril, president and chief operating officer of Bombardier Recreational Products, said the purchase of Evinrude, Johnson, and the FICHT direct fuel-injection technology was an ideal fit for Bombardier. "We think at this stage, we have a great opportunity to improve on the operation that existed," he said.[26]

The FICHT fuel injection reduces gas consumption by one-third and oil consumption by one-half on two-stroke engines. This would be appealing to consumers in itself, but the economies would also reduce emissions by about 75 percent. This kind of improvement would allow Bombardier to make products that would comply with new environmental regulations in the United States and elsewhere.

16

A Prototype for the Twenty-First Century?

Noted business journalist Peter C. Newman wrote in 1989 that Bombardier was "a prototype of the kind of company Canada needs for the 21st century."[1] He applauded its foray into global markets—the 1982 contract won in New York City, the expansion into the European railway industry, and the acquisition of Short Brothers in Northern Ireland. By 1990, over 75 percent of Bombardier's sales were to export markets. Newman also applauded Laurent Beaudoin's "secret" for competing worldwide, which he was quoted as saying consisted of a strategy of targeting niche markets and building a highly decentralized structure capable of motivating staff.

Supporters of Bombardier take particular note of its role in the creation of a thriving aerospace industry in Canada. This had been a long-cherished goal of provincial and federal governments ever since Allied countries had used Canada during World War II as a haven to build airplanes and train pilots. When the war ended, the foreign aerospace companies were persuaded to stay in Canada with government loans and subsidies, but results were mixed. One of the more famous disappointments was the cancellation of Hawker Siddeley's Avro Arrow project, seen by many as a missed opportunity for Canada to develop a jet fighter.

As the Vietnam War wound down in the 1970s, most foreign aerospace companies wanted to dump their Canadian subsidiaries, particularly Canadair and de Havilland. To save the accumulated base of skills and technologies, the federal government bought both with the intention of redirecting production toward civilian aircraft. These corporations struggled under state ownership until the mid-1980s, when they were both sold off as part of a privatization drive.

This gave Bombardier a chance to enter the Canadian aerospace industry and perform a turnaround. While nearly all other countries were experiencing difficulties in their aerospace sectors during the 1990s, Canada's effort was roaring ahead. The phenomenal success of Bombardier's airplanes would set the company on a course to repay most of the government aid received under technology development programs while generating profits that provided ever-rising tax revenues to the federal treasury. In fiscal 2001, for example, Bombardier paid close to $500 million in corporate income taxes. Assistance to Bombardier therefore appeared to be paying off quite well as evaluated by the return on invested public monies, not to mention the socioeconomic benefits generated in the areas of employment, national income, and national unity. Over the seven years to 1997, Bombardier led all other corporations in the number of persons hired in Canada—over 9,000.

As such, Bombardier's aerospace business provided a case study in successful private-public sector partnership, one in which a profit-seeking enterprise and public assistance to level the playing field proved to be a winning formula. The lesson seemed to be to forget about bailing out losers and funneling money to bureaucrat-picked sectors and, instead, to ensure that Canadian companies were not disadvantaged when competing against government-supported rivals in foreign markets. On the one hand, this might mean providing assistance to a large and successful company, but on the other hand, it increased the odds that government money would be effective in generating a net benefit overall.

The diversification into aerospace brought Laurent and Bombardier considerable praise. The acknowledgments included:

1991
"CEO of the Year"—*The Financial Post* survey
"Canadian Business Leader of the Year"—University of Alberta

1992
"International Executive of the Year"—International Chamber of Commerce

1993
"Personality of the Year"—*Flight International* magazine
"Aerospace Laureate"—*Aviation Week* and *Space Technology*

1995
"Canada's Most Respected Corporation"—*Globe and Mail* survey
"C.D. Howe Award"—Canadian Aeronautics and Space Institute

1996
"Canada's Most Respected Corporation"—*Globe and Mail* survey
"Canadian Business Leadership Award"—Harvard Business Club (Toronto)

1997

"Canadian Business Hall of Fame"—Junior Achievement of Canada
"Prix de Carrière"—Conseil du patronat du Québec [Employers Council of Quebec]

1998

"Distinguished Entrepreneur Award"—University of Manitoba
"Entreprise du siècle au Québec"—*Revue Commerce*
"Personality of the Year"—Gala Excellence, *La Presse*

As the main engine of growth during the 1990s, the venture into aerospace brought wealth to Bombardier shareholders. Investors who purchased 1,000 shares in December 1989 at $15.75 saw their $15,750 investment rise to $233,600 by December 1999 (following several splits of the steadily appreciating shares). That worked out to an annual rate of return of more than 30 percent over the decade. Laurent's personal gains were substantial too. For example, in December 1999, he exercised stock options worth $94 million.

While Bombardier had handsomely rewarded shareholders, it had not neglected its role as a corporate citizen. Each year, approximately 3 percent of its pretax income was allocated to the J. Armand Bombardier Foundation, the purpose of which was to contribute to organizations active in education, health, culture, and social services. In education, funding was provided to the University of British Columbia, University of Quebec, University of Alberta, and other educational institutions for chairs and professorships in transportation studies. In health, donations have been made to Granby Hospital, Jewish General Hospital, La Providence Hospital, and other health care centers. In the cultural field, the foundation provided support to the J. Armand Bombardier Museum, the McCord Museum at McGill University, and similar organizations. In social services, the foundation assisted the Fondation québécoise pour l'alphabétisation (Quebec Literacy Foundation), the St. John Ambulance organization and many other community associations.

However, there was by no means universal agreement that Bombardier was the kind of company Canada needed for the twenty-first century. In fact, as one of the more visible beneficiaries of government assistance programs, Bombardier had been a lightning rod for protests of various sorts over the years. The furies ebbed and flowed, cresting whenever the headlines revealed another fillip from the government sector.

Early complaints came on the heels of the 1982 interest rate subsidy to New York City, the awarding of the CF-18 maintenance contract, and the assistance received from the federal government and the province of Quebec to develop the 50-seat regional jet. One of the most intense episodes, however, occurred in the fall of 1996 when Bombardier received an $86 million interest-free loan from the Technology Partnerships Canada program to develop the 70-seat Canadair Regional Jet.

The financial assistance moved Ralph Klein, the premier of Alberta, to complain: "I'm really, really annoyed and upset that the feds would give [this money to] Bombardier, one of the most successful aerospace companies in the world."[2] The previous fiscal year, Bombardier had recorded net income of $158 million on revenues of $7.1 billion. Given this financial strength, it did not seem necessary to hand out the government money. Moreover, with the Canadian dollar trading at $0.74 US following a substantial depreciation, it hardly seemed necessary to deliver any more of a boost. "The devalued dollar...is already providing Canadian exporters with enough of an advantage that they shouldn't need more support."[3]

Bill Gilmour, a member of the Reform Party (now the Canadian Alliance Party), declared that Bombardier could have raised its own money from the banks or debt markets. If no private financing were available, it would be a sign that the 70-seat jet was not an economical project and should not proceed. If the private sector deemed the expected return insufficient to cover the cost of capital, then the government would likely end up pouring money into a losing proposition. The Reform critic believed that the real motivation was political, coming as it did on the eve of an economic summit in Quebec, where the unemployment rate was 13 percent. "There is an agenda on the federalist side," said Gilmour. "They shovel money into Quebec and hope Quebeckers see what good guys we are, and they'll stay part of the country."[4]

Lastly, the terms of repayment for the $86 million disbursed under the Technology Partnerships Canada program seemed to suggest the monies were more in the nature of a grant than an interest-free loan (or "royalty-based investment," as government officials called it). The terms stipulated that the government would be paid back out of royalties once certain sales milestones were achieved. In the case of the 70-seat jet, the royalties would come due after 200 of the airplanes had been delivered; once deliveries reached 400 units, the royalties would be sufficient to cover the amount distributed.

Another furor erupted in the middle of 1998 when news spread that Bombardier had won a 20-year federal government contract worth $2.85 billion for the training of NATO military pilots in Canada. The government was to defray about 80 percent of the annual training costs and give Bombardier scope to attract business from other NATO countries to cover the remaining 20 percent of costs and hopefully earn a profit besides. In addition, the $600 million cost of purchasing several dozen training aircraft would be kept off the government books by having Bombardier arrange the purchase. The planes would be financed by government-guaranteed bonds issued by a shell company jointly owned by Bombardier and the federal government.

What drew fire was the "special federal Cabinet exemption from normal tendering and notification procedures."[5] As Art Hanger, a member of the Reform Party, commented: "There was no tender process. That's the shameful thing. I call it the great Ski-Doo heist."[6] Defence Minister Art Eggleton said the Cabinet did not see how any other group in Canada could render the service, and they were under pressure to meet a deadline in the bidding for the training NATO contract. Detractors were not mollified and alleged that political connections may have played a role. Some even went so far as to draw attention to the presence of Prime Minister Jean Chrétien's son-in-law, Power Corp. executive Andre Desmarais, on the Bombardier board of directors.

Other flare-ups have periodically surrounded Bombardier in the ongoing rivalry with Embraer. On balance, WTO rulings have favored Canada in the debate over export subsidies, bestowing the right to impose sanctions on exports of Brazilian products. The federal government, however, was reluctant to use this weapon because of the costs it would impose on Canadian consumers, innocent Brazilian firms, and Canadian exporters doing business in Brazil. Instead, the preferred strategy was to fight fire with fire, as signaled in early 2001 by the announcement of a $1.7 billion loan from the Canada Account at low rates to Air Wisconsin Airlines Corp. (later followed by another cut-rate loan to help finance the purchase by Northwest Airlines Corp. of $2.6 billion worth of aircraft from Bombardier).

Some commentators claimed that this policy of engaging in tit for tat was a form of brinkmanship that risked sparking a competition in export subsidies. As such, there could be rising costs to taxpayers on both sides of the fence. This worry over the potential for a subsidy war led some journalists to think the unthinkable: that companies like Bombardier should be set free to find their own way. As one columnist asked: "What price are Canadians willing to pay for corporate nationalism?"[7]

Bombardier had not taken the attacks lying down. Allaire pointed out[8] that no taxpayer funds were used to lower interest rates on the loans to Air Wisconsin and Northwest Airlines. The Canada Account obtained the funds at Government of Canada rates, which were below the lending rate set at CIRR (about 1 percentage point over US Treasury rates). So there was no need for subsidies.

Admittedly, there was the possibility that Canadian taxpayers would be on the hook in the event of a default on a Canada Account loan. However, this risk was reduced by the fact that the airline companies shared some of the risk too. In order to get the Canada Account loan, they had to obtain nearly 25 percent of the borrowing requirement through their own commercial lenders. To walk away from the Canada Account loan would therefore require the customer to declare bankruptcy with its commercial lenders. And even if this were to occur, the residual value of the regional jets would help recoup the value of the loans.

As for other issues raised by Bombardier critics, Laurent provided a response in a 1996 speech. He expressed concern that media coverage of government intervention in the aerospace sector may have created the false impression that Bombardier's success was due to government largesse. Actually, as he said, only 25 percent of Bombardier's annual revenue (at the time) was in the sector in which the government offered support. The remaining 75 percent of Bombardier's revenue was in sectors—recreational vehicles, mass transit, and business jets—that did not receive such support. And in those sectors, Bombardier was performing very well against fierce competition, maintaining dominant positions.

Furthermore, in the product areas receiving assistance from Technology Partnerships Canada and other programs, the amounts provided were only a modest offset to the levels of government support provided in other countries. "Almost all commercial plane manufacturers in other countries are funded through military aircraft programs. In the United States, $12 billion US a year in aerospace research and development is funded by the federal government, mostly through military contracts. Military aircraft programs are also key to the commercial aerospace sector in France, Great Britain, Italy, Brazil, and even in relatively small countries like Holland and Sweden."[9]

The military funding not only provided a stable source of revenues and earnings, but allowed the companies to develop new technologies that they could later commercialize. In effect, foreign governments provided the funding to develop the technology for military purposes. But once government requirements were met, the aerospace contractor was at liberty to market the new technology in different forms to other customers. Bombardier, receiving only 4 percent of its revenues from defense spending, was disadvantaged in that regard. By comparison, the proportions were 27 percent for Aerospatiale, 40 percent for Boeing, and 71 percent for British Aerospace. Embraer's proportion was slated to rise from under 5 percent to over 20 percent. Other major competitors in France and Italy not only received large military orders, but were owned in whole or in part by their national governments, opening up other channels of assistance for them.

In this kind of environment, the support given by foreign governments for developing aerospace products typically reached

60 to 90 percent of costs. Assistance from the Technology Partnerships Canada program was therefore moderate by comparison. Moreover, there were strings attached. For every $1 provided by the Canadian government, recipients had to invest at least $3 of their own capital in the project. Even then, the $1 obtained from the government was not a gift; it was an investment, which the government expected to be repaid through a stream of royalties.

"Eliminating all government support in one fell swoop before our competitors' governments do the same would stall our industry's growth in Canada and channel our aerospace investments to other countries," said Laurent. "Canadian government leadership in this area should not mean that we naively expect other countries to stop overnight supporting their aerospace industry just because Canada would have chosen to do so."[10]

Instead, the effective solution would be for aerospace countries to work together to bring down and eventually eliminate subsidies. Efforts, in fact, were already under way toward banning state interference with market forces, something Bombardier fully endorsed. As Laurent said in his speech: "Canada, with the full support of Bombardier and other members of the aerospace industry, is working actively in bilateral and multilateral discussions at the WTO and OECD to reduce the support provided by other governments. We fully back these initiatives because we believe that, on a strictly commercial basis, Bombardier and the rest of the Canadian aerospace industry could take on the world. Indeed, Canada has a number of important comparative advantages in the aerospace sector. We have a critical mass of excellent companies in Quebec, Ontario, and increasingly BC with many years of experience and global credibility."[11]

In June 1998, Bombardier released a document responding to claims made by the Reform Party that Bombardier had received

$1.2 billion in aerospace handouts over the 15 years to 1996. This figure was "either a misreading of data or a misunderstanding of commercial business."[12] Nearly half of the amount, $536 million, was not government support at all but EDC loans and contracts at commercial rates to customers of Bombardier. As such, they were fully repayable on commercial terms, meaning that the EDC, as a financial intermediary, had provided the credit for the purposes of making a profit from the principal and interest payments. Another $180 million of payments, bringing the total to $715 million, were mistakenly attributed to Bombardier, representing either money never spent or provided to Canadair and de Havilland before Bombardier took over.

In sum, the $1.2 billion figure was overstated by $715 million and some other miscellaneous items, leaving $399 million of assistance to Bombardier. This amount was applied toward developing a variety of airplanes, including the Canadair 415 water bomber, the Dash 8-400 turboprop, the 50-seat regional jet, and the 70-seat regional jet. This assistance might still seem to be on the high side to some, but it is easily dwarfed by the $5.2 billion Bombardier invested of its own capital.

Sensitive to criticism over government support, Bombardier executives have stopped applying to government technology development programs in recent years. The development of new airplanes, such as the 90-seat regional jet, is thus being financed from Bombardier's own coffers and those of its partners. In addition, until recently, Bombardier rejected federal cabinet offers of low-interest loans to fight subsidized competition from Embraer.[13] Bombardier only relented recently in the Air Wisconsin and Northwest Airlines cases because of the prolonged ineffectiveness of formal channels in halting breeches of world trade rules.

The opposition Bombardier experiences at intervals is somewhat reminiscent of the story of another Canadian global giant: Nortel Networks Corp. As described in Chapter 6 of *Nortel Networks: How Innovation and Vision Created a Network Giant*,[14] Nortel built up a formidable research and development capability in the 1960s and 1970s thanks to help from its parent corporation, Bell Canada Enterprises (BCE) Inc., which enjoyed considerable financial strength as a regulated monopoly in telephone services.

Critics alleged that BCE was exploiting telephone subscribers to cross-subsidize the building up of Nortel. As a consequence, BCE and Nortel were under investigation by regulatory authorities for most of the 1970s to see if Nortel should be brought under regulatory purview or else severed from BCE—both courses of action that could have endangered Nortel's growth potential.

The evidence was pointing to one of these two options being selected. But, in the early 1980s, the investigations were called off, and Nortel was set loose to break into the US market and challenge AT&T and its manufacturing arm, Western Electric, for dominance in the manufacturing of telephone switches. Then, in the 1990s, Nortel became a leading supplier of wireless networks and infrastructure equipment for the Internet.

Therefore, the issue of government support for Bombardier perhaps boils down to whether or not the Canadian public, as represented by their provincial and federal governments, want winners on the world stage and the resulting socioeconomic benefits. If so, they would not begrudge the cost and trade-offs with other priorities. Of course, the best solution is for all countries to get together and jointly reduce subsidies to allow comparative advantages and free markets to determine the optimal allocation of resources. But with the world as imperfect as it is presently, the Bombardier model may be worth retaining. It appears to be the kind of company needed for the realities of the twenty-first century.

17

The Challenges Ahead

Tom Mann once dreaded Thursdays. That was the day he had to fly from his home in Santa Barbara to Phoenix, where he was supervising the construction of a residential complex. There were no direct flights between the two cities, so Mann had to take a small turboprop to Los Angeles and transfer to a second flight going to Phoenix. Then Mesa Air Group bought some regional jets and put in a direct connection between Santa Barbara and Phoenix. Mann was ecstatic with the change. The jets were more comfortable and turned what had been a half-day excursion into an hour-long trip. Now he could work a full day at the construction site and still get home in time to sleep in his own bed.

Mann's experience illustrates part of the dynamic driving demand for regional jets, which are "proliferating faster than aluminum scooters on city sidewalks."[1] They spare travelers many of the inconveniences of the hub-and-spoke system, as well as the noisy, rough ride of the "puddle-jumpers." And they also allow regional airlines to garner more revenues through service enhancements, new point-to-point connections, more off-peak service, and extensions in the number and length of spokes into the hubs.

In 2000, the annual output of regional jet manufacturers increased 40 percent, bringing the total number of jets in operation to over 600 (compared to 78 in 1995). Delta Airlines and its regional affiliates were the biggest customers, with over 150 regional jets in service. And it had orders for hundreds more, which would be put into service at a rate of about one a week for the next 10 years. Other airlines in North America and Europe had similar plans for expansion, while those in Latin America and Asia were just getting started with their regional jet orders.

A leading aerospace consulting firm, Forecast International/DMS Inc., predicts that deliveries of regional jets in the 30- to 110-seat category will total 5,000 between 2000 and 2010, a market that would be worth over $95 billion US. The consultants expect Bombardier to be the top supplier in 2010, with a market share of 30 percent compared to Embraer's 21 percent and Fairchild Dornier's 13 percent. Beyond 2010, there still appears to be potential for many more sales. Figures from Fairchild Dornier Corp., for example, imply that 3,000 more aircraft will be made during the 2010 to 2020 period, for a total of 8,000 over the coming two decades.

Bombardier, therefore, appears to be well placed to enjoy growth over the long term. However, there are a few risks to this rosy scenario above and beyond the usual culprit of downturns in the economy. These noncyclical factors could slow the pace of growth at times or perhaps even lead to lower forecasts of the overall market potential and Bombardier's share.

One wild card relates to "scope clauses" in the union contracts that pilots at the major US airline carriers have signed with their employers. These clauses, won through actual and threatened strikes, typically limit the size of regional jets to less than 70 seats and place restrictions on how large regional jet fleets can become. In controlling the spread of regional jets, the pilots at the major carriers hope to protect their jobs and salaries. In Europe, scope clauses are not as extensive, so 70-seat-plus regional jets are likely to enjoy greater penetration there in the near term.

Nevertheless, the scope clauses in the United States complicate the outlook for manufacturers such as Bombardier. Over time, the clauses may be weakened or strengthened depending on the outcome of collective bargaining sessions, which could alter the timing and extent of orders for regional jets. In addition, future alterations to scope clauses may impact Bombardier's customer base differently than Embraer's or Fairchild Dornier's, in turn altering Bombardier's relative position within its industry. For example, if one of Bombardier's customers were to win concessions from its union on the scope clause, it could raise demand for Bombardier's jets while demand for Embraer's and Fairchild Dornier's jets remained unaltered.

A second risk pertains to infrastructure constraints. Shortages of pilots and maintenance workers could pose limitations at times. But the more serious bottleneck in this regard could be the air traffic control system. With many more smaller jets in operation, there are fears that air traffic controllers may become overloaded and unable to cope. One aerospace executive says: "I don't think we'll be able to use the full capacity of this wonderful tool because the Federal Aviation Administration has failed to invest in the air traffic control system."[2]

A third risk factor, and perhaps most serious, is the influx of new suppliers into the regional jet market. So far, just Bombardier and Embraer are battling it out, but a third manufacturer, Fairchild Dornier is developing a product line for release starting in 2002. In addition, the two giants in aerospace manufacturing, Boeing and Aerospatiale, have expressed interest either as producers or in alliance with others. Others are interested too. For example, a Chinese group, China Aviation Industry Corp., is planning to introduce its own regional jet within the next five to seven years.

The potential therefore exists, despite the strong demand, for a supply glut to appear at some point. Indeed, the chairman and chief executive officer of Fairchild Dornier warned a few years back that the whole regional jet market would eventually be flooded, leading to a general shakeout sometime in the 2000s. During this phase, several suppliers will disappear from the market. Those surviving the consolidation phase may maintain their sales volumes but during the adjustment period, would face sustained pressure to discount prices, which could lead to thin margins and even losses. Bombardier's profit momentum may thus be dealt a blow, although its focus on operational efficiency through programs such as Six Sigma will lower the corporation's break-even point and help contain the damage.

There is always the possibility that the industry could avoid the trauma of a shakeout. Given the small number of suppliers operating in an international market, arrangements could be negotiated to share the market in an orderly fashion. But rivalry is presently very bitter between the two leaders: Embraer and Bombardier. A sticking point, export credits, appears to be a very difficult issue to resolve. And it may remain a difficult issue as companies from other countries join the market.

The potential for overcrowding is even more real in the business jet market given the existence of over 30 airplane models from 10 manufacturers in 2001. If and when a shakeout period comes to business jets, Bombardier's profit margins could again be adversely affected. What might soften the blow is the ongoing expansion in Bombardier's Flexjet program, which, similar to time-sharing of vacation properties, allows customers to own a piece (as little as one-eighth) of a Bombardier business jet. This initiative, introduced in the mid-1990s, is bringing a whole new class of smaller corporations and less wealthy individuals into the business jet market. As the popularity of fractional ownership increases, so does the fleet of Bombardier aircraft used in the Flexjet program.

A large proportion of Bombardier profits come from its aerospace group. In fiscal 2001, 85 percent of Bombardier's $1 billion in profits were derived from this source. This means that a period of oversupply or downturn in Bombardier's aerospace markets could have a major impact on the stock price. For now, Bombardier appears to be protected by its immense backlog of orders. As of January 31, 2001, the regional jet backlog consisted of firm orders for 574 aircraft and options for another 1,047 units. Including business aircraft, the total value of the aerospace backlog was $23 billion. Therefore, in the short term, Bombardier appears to have a reasonable prospect of meeting its profit targets of 30 to 40 percent growth in fiscal 2002.

After that, it seems to be a question of how fast Bombardier can improve its recreational, capital, and rail transportation groups to raise profitability enough to provide an offset to a loss of momentum in the aerospace group. If the backlog of orders in the aerospace group begins to fall off more quickly than the rate of turnaround in the other groups, there could be a period of uncertainty among investors. In short, Bombardier, presently more of a one-product company than a diversified entity, faces the specter of a replay of the 1970s snowmobile era, depending on how the timing plays out in its aerospace and nonaerospace groups. An important question, therefore, is whether or not the latter groups can be brought around in time.

The recreational group has several motorized products for personal amusement and utilitarian uses. The two main categories —snowmobiles (Ski-Doo) and personal watercraft (Sea-Doo)— address mature, largely commoditized markets capable of providing steady but unspectacular growth. Another legacy product line is the Rotax engine series made for Bombardier's recreational vehicles and other manufacturers' motorcycles, scooters, go-carts, and ultra-light aircraft. New generations of Rotax engines, as well as the newly acquired Evinrude and Johnson engine brands, represent interesting growth opportunities. So does the opportunity to move to new environmental standards in small-engine technology. Bombardier is working on developing environmentally cleaner versions of its engines, and has also assumed control of the revolutionary FICHT fuel-injection technology.

A newer recreational product line for Bombardier is all-terrain vehicles. The market here is large and growing strongly, but Bombardier is a Johnny-come-lately and is up against several entrenched contenders, including leaders Honda, Polaris, and Yamaha. Still, Bombardier's innovative Traxter models have given the company a toehold, a market share presently estimated at less than 5 percent. Current and future innovations to the Traxter line may wrest away more market share, but competition is stiff, and the going will be tough.

The capital group, which offers inventory financing, leasing, commercial lending, and other financial services, is expected to become a key growth area in the future. In 2000, management continued with the implementation of a restructuring plan to refocus Bombardier Capital on areas where it has demonstrated know-how. In addition, there are opportunities to grow by acquisition. The industry has been going through a consolidation phase, and Bombardier, committed to being number one in its various industries, may at some point see a chance to take over other players.

While Bombardier's recreational and capital groups have several interesting growth opportunities, the fact remains that their products presently target relatively small markets. As such, even if a number of the commercial opportunities manage to yield rapid growth simultaneously, they are not likely to match the contribution of the aerospace group to profits. The better hope of doing so, in the absence of major acquisitions in the recreational or capital groups (or perhaps even in a completely new industry), rests with the rail group. It has several large product lines with sales nearly equaling those of the aerospace group.

Over the past few decades, markets for railway equipment have provided only single-digit rates of growth. So, on the face of it, the prospects for the rail group to provide a counterbalance do not seem all that great. But, as Laurent Beaudoin likes to say, with rising energy costs, pollution concerns, and congestion on other transportation modes, rail may enjoy something of an upturn in the 2000s and beyond.

Moreover, some niches in the railway industry are expected to experience strong demand as aging equipment is replaced. For example, transit authorities in the United States "are expected to announce major investment programs which should create additional demand for rapid transit and commuter vehicles. According to the American Public Transit Association, the year 2000 represented the highest peak in transit ridership in four decades."[3]

The niche of maintenance and service shops has some lucrative growth possibilities. A global trend toward privatization in railway services has increased the number of privately owned railway operators. Lacking established repair and service yards, they tend to contract the work out to companies like Bombardier. Such service contracts provide a rising inflow of stable revenues and magnify the countercyclical attributes of the railway manufacturing industry.

There is also a potential to improve earnings in the rail divisions by realizing greater operating efficiencies. In fiscal 2001, margins in rail operations were 4 percent; in aerospace, they were 11 percent. Now that Bombardier has taken over Adtranz, it should be able to address situations of overcapacity and excessive competition, providing a foundation for rationalizing prices and margins.

There is also scope to improve profit margins by shifting production to the more efficient plants and applying Bombardier's strengths in financial controls, entrepreneurial culture, and capital resources. The inefficient distribution of production over too many small plants, particularly in Europe, was a vestige of the era when local content rules required manufacturers to set up plants in individual countries. With the creation of the European Community in 1992 and the drive toward a common market, these preferential purchasing policies are no longer acceptable. It is taking some time to dismantle these market distortions, but as they come down, they will allow companies like Bombardier to consolidate their production and become more efficient.

New technologies in rail transportation are emerging that offer exciting growth opportunities too. High-speed trains are a case in point. The European Community, as part of its plan to create a common market, has drawn up a blueprint for a 30,000-kilometer (19,000 mile), high-speed train network over the next two decades. The Chunnel link, which Bombardier worked on in the early 1990s, was a preliminary step in that direction. The purchase of Adtranz was advantageous in this regard, giving Bombardier a shot at winning more high-speed train contracts, thanks to the addition of Adtranz's high-speed technology and expertise in electrical and propulsion systems.

High-speed rail service is not as developed in the United States because of low levels of public funding. But there could be some catch up over the 2000s, given healthier government finances. Amtrak faces a Congressional challenge to become profitable by 2002 or die, but it appears that the US national railway has enough political support to avoid that fate regardless of its financial position. Profitable or not, it thus appears Amtrak will be able to proceed with its plans for high-speed rail service on 22 corridors within the United States (beside the existing Acela service connecting Boston, New York, and Washington). The *High-Speed Rail Investment Act*, which is expected to pass through the US Senate sometime later in 2001, will authorize Amtrak to issue $12 billion US in tax-exempt bonds to pay for such projects.

Another new technology is automated metros, an alternative to conventional subways. As the Union Internationale des Transports Publics noted in a 1997 study, "totally automated metro is less expensive in both investment and ongoing maintenance costs than a metro system with a driver."[4] Bombardier, the supplier of the Vancouver Skytrain and a similar elevated track service in Kuala Lumpur, is the leader in this new niche. From its plant in British Columbia, the company hopes to leverage its experience and skills to supply advanced systems around the Pacific Rim. "There are 13 cities in Southeast Asia with more than 10 million people each—and no mass transit system," revealed a Bombardier project manager. "That is our market for the future."[5]

A third new technology in rail transportation are people movers, the monorail systems now in operation at over 80 locations around the world for short-haul ferrying of pedestrians at airports, leisure parks, and casinos. Adtranz, once a major player in the niche, has passed on a dominant position to Bombardier. Forecasts call for about $10 billion to be spent on new projects over the next decade. As Bombardier's 1994 contract win in Jacksonville, Florida shows, monorail technology has further potential to be incorporated into full-fledged public transit systems. People movers at Newark and O'Hare airports now reach out to remote parking lots, and they connect JFK Airport to New York City's rail networks. Other people mover schemes include links to off-airport hotels, office parks, car rental facilities, and intermodal stations.

The creation of Bombardier International highlights the company's determination to pursue geographic expansion around the world. The proportion of company revenues derived from markets outside North America and Europe was only 10 percent in 2001. Thus, there is considerable growth potential for Bombardier in meeting the transportation needs of the emerging economies of China, Latin America, India, the former states of the USSR, and other countries. These are huge markets that should become more accessible as the trend toward economic liberalization progresses.

Of these emerging markets, China appears to hold the most promise. In 1997, Bombardier teamed up with Power Corp. and Sifang Locomotive and Rolling Stock Works in a joint venture to manufacture railcars. The three partners have built a plant near Qingdao in Northern China and are working on a big order from the Chinese national railway for 300 intercity railcars. Bombardier is also hoping China will be a significant market for its aircraft. A study released by a Chinese research group predicts that nearly 500 regional jets will be purchased over the next two decades. (And there should be new opportunities in the infrastructure investments China is planning to undertake in preparation for the 2008 Olympics in Beijing.)

In 1992, Bombardier acquired a railway equipment manufacturer in Mexico, Constructora Nacional de Carros de Ferrocarril (Concarril), for the purpose of expanding into Mexico and
eventually, South America. Some contract wins have kept the
facilities operating over the 1990s, but there has been no dramatic ramp up just yet. Nevertheless, Bombardier still believes
in the long-term potential of the region and is hanging in. A sign
of its commitment was the joint venture arranged in 1998 with
a US company, The Greenbrier Companies, to make railroad
freight cars at the Concarril plant.

There are several background factors to take into consideration
in the outlook for Bombardier. One is Bombardier's growing size.
The bigger a company gets, the more challenging it is to maintain
high growth rates. In the first place, when a company emerges as
a leader in a given market, it increasingly runs up against the constraint of antitrust legislation. Regulatory authorities are more
likely to block acquisitions and penalize undue influence over
the market. Second, the problem of size surfaces in the context
of government relationships. Ever larger levels of assistance may
be required as a highly successful public-private sector partnership increases in size, risking at some point a diminishing in public support. Third, size complicates the issues of control,
execution, and innovation within a corporation.

Another assumption underlying the outlook for Bombardier
involves the political environment. Over the 1990s, the Liberal
Party of Canada, under Prime Minister Jean Chrétien, has held
power at the federal level and has provided a supportive environment for public-private sector initiatives. In the case of Bombardier,

the Liberals may feel a special relationship because of Bombardier's successful track record in turning around floundering operations and capitalizing on commercial opportunities. And as the federal official who gave the go-ahead to the Challenger jet in the mid-1970s, Chrétien may take pride in the fact that he is, in a sense, the grandfather of two major aerospace triumphs: the Challenger and the Canadair Regional Jet. Hence, a change in power at the federal level may alter the environment for public-private sector partnerships.

Lastly, Bombardier faces succession risk. The triumvirate at the top—Laurent, Brown, and Allaire—key to Bombardier's past success, will not be around forever. Indeed, Allaire has already left. Laurent, who will be 65 in 2003, began pulling back on his involvement in 1999 and may be seeking further disengagement. Brown, in his mid-fifties, has a few more years before retirement.

Will successors be able to fill the shoes of the triumvirate's members as they leave? It will be a challenge. Maintaining momentum at a large and diversified organization requires an uncommon level of skill and knowledge. But Bombardier is working on enhancing the probabilities with extensive succession planning, which shows up in programs to identify and challenge leaders, as well as the rotation in 2001 of senior executives across operating groups to increase the breadth of their operational knowledge.

Laurent's son Pierre may ultimately prove himself deserving of the top job, but it does not appear to be a foregone conclusion. Given that Bombardier is a meritocracy as much as a family firm, he will have to prove himself. Until then, the door could be open to other persons. Leading candidates would be the current heads of the operating groups: Michael Graff in Aerospace, Pierre Lortie in Rail Transportation, Michel Baril in Recreational Products, Robert Gillespie in Capital, and Robert Greenhill in International.

These background factors, along with other elements discussed, are important variables to consider in an assessment of the outlook for Bombardier. Clearly, they point to a future containing some challenges. Missteps may occur along the way and periods of retrenchment might ensue. During these times, it might be difficult for investors to maintain confidence, especially after getting used to seeing Bombardier put up strong growth figures nearly every quarter over the 1990s.

However, Bombardier is a corporation that has been built to last. The diversification into aerospace has been so successful that Bombardier once again is dependent on one main product line, but it is taking measures to return to a path of balanced growth. There may be bumps in the road, but if any company has accumulated staying power, it is Bombardier. Building an organization to last has been the goal of its chief architect, Laurent Beaudoin.

18 Bombardier Encounters Turbulence

CHAPTER

O**n** September 11, 2001, the thunderbolt struck. Terrorists hijacked four passenger jets and smashed two of them into the towers of the World Trade Center, a third into the Pentagon, and a fourth into a field in Pennsylvania.

Bombardier was jolted. Its shares, already weak as the recession cut into the demand for business jets, plunged over the following days. By the end of the month, they were down to $12, less than half the 52-week high established in mid-August.

Bombardier had felt *forces majeures* before. A 1939 expansion in plant capacity collided with war-time rationing. Half of company sales evaporated in 1947 when legislation mandated snow removal on public roads. A quadrupling of oil prices in the 1970s turned the Ski-Doo boom into a bust.

From such shocks originated the strategy of diversification, of creating a portfolio of product lines to spread the risks of unforeseen events. The products would be extensions of core competencies but chosen for their ability to offset each other through various conditions.

But as the case of Bombardier illustrates, one challenge with diversification is that product lines tend to grow at different rates. In particular, the foray into aerospace manufacturing had been so successful that it accounted for over three-quarters of profits by the fall of 2001. Bombardier was virtually a one-product firm once again.

The acquisition of Adtranz, which doubled revenues in the railway group to near parity with the aerospace group, was a step toward restoring diversification. But since profit margins were less than half those in aerospace, some time and effort would be required to turn around railway operations to the point where they would provide a balance on the basis of earnings.

The terrorist attack, therefore, came at an inopportune time. Bombardier was still dependent on its customer base within the airline industry for the majority of its profits, yet many of those customers, already in loss positions, were now experiencing a free fall in passenger traffic. Looming was the specter of bankruptcies as carriers defaulted on their high debt loads.

Analysts revised their forecasts downwards. One, Marko Pencak of Credit Suisse First Boston Securities Canada Inc., lowered his recommendation to "hold," offering the rationale: "We think the order drop-off will be precipitous. There is a very significant risk of material order cancellations ...." [1]

On September 27, Bombardier announced that it was going to slow down aircraft production and lay off 3,800 aerospace workers. Over a third would occur in the business-jet and turboprop operations, where orders were clearly on the wane. The rest would come out of the regional-jet operations in anticipation of order cancellations.

Growth targets were trimmed back. Bombardier President and CEO Robert Brown said that he expected earnings per share to grow 15 percent in fiscal 2002 instead of the previously expected 30 to 40 percent. For fiscal 2003, the growth rate would be lowered to 15 percent as well.

Several hefty special charges were announced. They consisted of $663 million to pull out of manufactured-housing financing, $264 million to write off development costs associated with the Q-400 turboprop, $180 million for the integration of Adtranz, and $45 million for aerospace layoffs.

In early fall, the US government came to the rescue of the US airline industry. Direct grants of $5 billion US and loan-guarantees of $10 billion US were made available for transitional relief. Bombardier, for its part, worked on arranging public and private sources of financing to shore up its backlog of orders for 550 regional jets and options for 1,100.

These actions helped stabilize the situation. For the fiscal year ended on January 31, 2002, there were no cancellations of orders for Bombardier's regional jets. In fact, production returned to nearly the same rates as before September 11, and 800 laid-off workers were called back to work.

Regional jets indeed had held up quite well. In response to dwindling passenger traffic, airliners had parked jumbo jets in the desert and replaced them with Bombardier's jets. Moreover, although sales of 50-seat jets were leveling off, sales in the new 70-seater category, of which Bombardier was the only producer, were still advancing.

Thus, much of the 60-percent drop in fiscal 2001 profits to $391 million ($0.31 per share) had little to due with the terrorist incident. It reflected the special charges mostly pertaining to other matters. Excluding these one-time items, profits actually exceeded $1 billion.

But a red light was flashing on the dashboard: a fourth-quarter tumble in aerospace margins to 8 percent, down from 12 percent in the same quarter the year before. Some analysts suspected price discounting. "I think they're giving the planes away to make the numbers," said one. [2]

Another warning signal was a rise in vendor financing. In the third quarter ended October 31, 2001, for example, Bombardier's loan portfolio on continuing operations stood at $7.1 billion, 22 percent higher than the beginning of the year. The majority of the increase was related to credit provided to aerospace customers. [3]

In fact, outside of the accrual-accounting framework, things did look not as rosy. Bombardier ended the year with a $2-billion shortfall in cash compared to the previous year. [4] Cash burn had more than doubled.

To shore up its cash position, Bombardier issued additional preferred shares and unsecured notes in the first half of 2002. Nevertheless, Standard & Poors still went ahead with a downgrade of Bombardier's long-term debt rating to triple-B plus.

Meanwhile a number of analysts at brokerage houses remained concerned that the full brunt of recession and terrorism was yet to be felt as of mid-2002, especially considering ongoing warnings over further terrorist attacks. With air travel remaining at depressed levels, air carriers could be pushed into reductions in capital spending as a way to conserve cash.

They also worried that spending sprees of the late 1990s and early 2000s had fulfilled nearly all requirements for regional jets. The economics of the small jets were attractive, but most US carriers had run up against union "scope clauses," which ruled out further expansions.

Finally, a few analysts drew attention to the danger of shrinkage in the customer base, particularly in the US carrier segment where eight major carriers were scrambling for pieces of a smaller pie. Barely profitable in the best of times because of high labor costs and debt levels, a consolidation of the industry was seen as a distinct possibility.

Yet, Bombardier appeared to be on the verge of tightening its grip on the regional-jet market. The same forces that were buffeting Bombardier had accelerated the financial troubles of rivals and pushed a couple to the sidelines. The first collapse came in November 2001 when BAE Systems, maker of the Avro RJX, pulled the plug on its small program.

The second came in April 2002 when Fairchild Dornier AG filed for bankruptcy protection. Its order backlog was comprised of 61 commitments to buy its 30-seat jets and 122 orders for its larger regional jets under development.

As for the intense rivalry with Embraer SA of Brazil, observers had become more optimistic for a resolution to the long-standing dispute over government subsidies. Discussions had resumed in January 2002 between Canadian and Brazilian trade delegations, and both sides were expressing a higher level of seriousness this time around. "My sense is it is going to be more fulsome than the last time," said one Canadian official. [5]

Indeed, two Brazilian newspapers in May leaked rumors that Bombardier and Embraer were studying a joint bid for a $1.4-billion US order from US Airways Group Inc. If true, the rumors would signal a new, co-operative approach to the global marketplace.

In 2002, that market still faced a dearth of new orders and potential disruption to the backlog of orders. Longer term, however, there was the prospect for an easing of scope clauses, which would provide a windfall for Bombardier. Forecasts from market researchers for 8,000 regional jets by 2020 (compared to just over 1,300 in service in 2002), would not look so fanciful after all.

In mid-October 2001, Bombardier Inc. issued a press release announcing the "appointment of Mr. Pierre Beaudoin as president and chief operating officer of Bombardier Aerospace." He was replacing Michael Graff, the McKinsey consultant who joined Bombardier in 1996.

Graff had resigned to "pursue other interests in the United States," according to the release. A Bombardier spokesperson added that Graff had informed Bombardier a few months earlier that he wanted to step down and rejoin his family in New York, but that he had stayed on the job to oversee completion of a number of milestones.

The announcement surprised some observers. The aerospace group was doing well under Graff. And Pierre Beaudoin, 39, had only nine months experience as president of the business-jet division. "I honestly don't know if he's ready to run the aerospace business. It would seem to be quite a step up in responsibility," BMO Nesbitt Burns analyst Andreas Hoppe said to a reporter.

Being the son of chairman Laurent Beaudoin and grandson of founder Joseph-Armand Bombardier, Pierre's appointment invariably raised questions about nepotism. "He's obviously being groomed to be CEO. There's no question about it. There's a lot of people who could do the job and they're giving it to him," one unnamed analyst said. [6]

The high-profile promotion prompted a discussion within the media and academic circles on succession issues within family firms. *Toronto Star* columnist David Olive raised a concern about the risk of scaring away non-family executives. Promoting a family member to the top "... tends to discourage talented managers from joining or staying long at such firms," he wrote. [7]

Yet, Olive noted that family favoritism is just a fact of life in corporate Canada, where 22 of the top 100 companies, accounting for $184 billion in annual sales, are family owned or controlled. Sons and daughters at the top include Pierre Péladeau at Quebecor Inc., Desmarais brothers at Power Corp. of Canada, Belinda Stronach at Magna International Inc., Linda Hasendratz at Linamar Corp., Jim Shaw at Shaw Communications Inc., David Thomson at Thomson Corp., and Michael McCain at Maple Leaf Foods Inc.

It is a fact of life around the world, too. About three-quarters of registered companies in industrialized countries are family controlled, and they employ about half of the workforce. A third of the listed companies in the Fortune 500 have families at the helm. Forty-three of Italy's 100 biggest companies are family-owned. So are 26 of France's and 17 of Germany's top 100 companies. [8]

Family firms and succession are well-researched topics among business academics and consultants. The general message seems to be that family favoritism is not bad or good per se. As Drew Mendoza, managing principal of Family Business Consulting Group International, says, it is important "not to slide into the assumption a family connection is a hindrance. It can be an advantage as well, provided the right sets of talents and experiences are there." [9]

True, many family-controlled companies have floundered when the next generation took over. Eaton's of Canada Ltd. is perhaps one of the more notable cases in recent years. But many others have flourished. Firms such as IBM Corp. and Westons went on to bigger and better things under the next generation. Laurent Beaudoin, himself, is an example of a family member taking the family firm to new heights.

John Ward, Professor at the Kellogg Graduate School of Management, has studied family enterprises in depth. His thesis is that they have a longer-term view. "They are not living and dying by earnings per share ...," he said at the annual conference of the Family Business Network in the fall of 2001. [10] They are more likely to maintain research and development spending in tough times and have their eye not just on profits but also the long-run preservation of their firm.

In January, Laurent Beaudoin responded to questions about his son's appointment. "People feel he got the job only because he's my son," Laurent said. "I would say that's completely untrue . . . I think that he got there because he had respect from the people he is working for and he showed that he can do the job. But sure, the fact that he's got my name—that he's my son—didn't harm him." [11]

Despite his lack of experience in the aerospace group, Pierre did have 15 years experience working in the recreational-products group of Bombardier, where he earned stripes for developing the Sea-Doo product and taking it successfully to market. "He's proven he can run a large, complex organization, lead it through a difficult period and develop products that meet consumer demand," said one analyst. [12]

Pierre's passion for new-product development should come in handy within the aerospace group, which averaged about one new airplane per year during the 1990s. The trend looks set to continue into the 2000s: within days of Pierre's ascension, Bombardier Aerospace announced another new airplane: the Bombardier Global 5000. It will carry eight passengers, and will be capable of flying faster and further than other long-range business jets.

Another one of Pierre's qualifications, training in industrial relations, was put to the test within months. In the middle of April 2002, the 7,400 members of Local 712 of the International Association of Machinists and Aerospace Workers went on strike at Bombardier plants in Montreal. The union was seeking a 15 percent wage increase over three years and a lowering of the retirement age from 60 to 58. Bombardier had offered 9.75 percent over four years, with a $1,000 signing bonus.

Two weeks into the strike, talks broke off after Bombardier negotiators walked out of a conciliation meeting, claiming the union's demands were unrealistic. Analysts said Bombardier was hanging tough because its arch competitor, Embraer SA, had much lower labor costs. And US airlines were still hobbled by financing problems, so would not likely mind delays in deliveries.

In the third week, efforts at resolution went upstairs: the president of the Quebec Labor Federation called on Pierre Beaudoin with a request to intervene directly to get both parties back to the table. "Mr. Beaudoin's authority is needed to break the ice and get serious talks going," said a union spokesman.

The request was successful and the conciliation process resumed. By this time, Bombardier was estimated to be losing $100 million a week and analysts were beginning to revise downward their earnings projections. Several parts suppliers to Bombardier expressed surprise at how long the strike was taking.

Almost as soon as the conciliation talks resumed, the strike was over. On May 4, Local 712 announced that 70 percent of its members voted in favor of an enhanced offer from Bombardier. The offer provided for a 16 percent pay increase over four years, a $1,000 signing bonus, a reduction in the pension age to 58, and $15 million in other concessions.

A glitch arose soon after Bombardier acquired Berlin-based Adtranz from DaimlerChrysler AG for $1.1 billion on May 1, 2001. Company officials revealed that a dispute had arisen over the final purchase price. Nevertheless, Bombardier President and CEO, Robert Brown, sounded optimistic: "I think that we will be able to come to some kind of resolution hopefully before the end of the year...." [13]

However, the news at the end of 2001 and into early 2002 was not about a resolution. Instead, Bombardier's plan to close down three Adtranz plants attracted attention. Affected unions were expressing opposition, particularly at one site in eastern Germany where workers had raised a poster declaring: "Building the East, Canadian Wild West style."

Restructuring efforts were subsequently put on hold while alternatives were sought. Laurent Beaudoin flew to Germany to meet with Chancellor Gerhard Schroeder, after which a compromise was reached. One of the plants would stay open and fewer workers would be laid off than the 1,450 planned.

The labor dispute was shortly overshadowed by a flare-up in the dispute over the purchase price for Adtranz. Bombardier announced on February 14 that it was filing a $1.4-billion claim with the Paris-based International Chamber of Commerce to recover damages arising out of material misrepresentations by DaimlerChrysler.

As claimed in an evaluation by Bombardier's auditors, $600-million of costs on contracts with third parties had not been disclosed, and the value of Adtranz's assets had been overstated by several hundred million dollars. DaimlerChrysler rejected Bombardier's claim as "unfounded and unjustified in every respect."

Brokerage-house analysts were disappointed. "The size of the claim was a surprise," said Canaccord Capital analyst Robert Fay.[14] Banc of America analyst Ted Cho said, "For me, it's a bit of a surprise. The word out on Bombardier all along was the integration was on track ...." [15]

For other analysts, the claim sullied Bombardier's reputation. "We think investors will question closing a deal of this size without a more complete understanding of the assets being acquired," wrote J. P. Morgan analyst Don MacDougall in a research report. [16]

Bombardier explained that it was not able to perform a proper due diligence because of European antitrust regulations restricting access to information. It had chosen to deal with this constraint by making the sale conditional on a review by its auditors and by ensuring an arbitration process was in place to resolve disputes.

At least in terms of contract wins, the acquisition seemed to be a success. Multiyear orders in 12 months following the acquisition had been numerous. The deals included: $339-million for diesel trains in Australia, $222-million for subway cars to Shenzhen Metro Co. in China, $2.3-billion for high-capacity regional trains to a French railway operator, and $261-million for electric trains to Deutsche Bahn in Germany.

Still, analysts were left wondering just how bad business was at Adtranz when Bombardier was, in essence, claiming that DaimlerChrysler should pay it to take the division off its hands. According to Cho, it "raises questions whether or not Adtranz will be able to meet expectations."[17]

He and others thought Bombardier's timetable for boosting operating margins would now prove too optimistic. Furthermore, the undisclosed costs would be a drag on cash and operating margins while the International Chamber of Commerce deliberated, a process estimated to require two to ten years.

Despite the setbacks, Bombardier remained pleased with the Adtranz acquisition. Executives said it still had great strategic value, bringing complete solutions in passenger-rail transportation as well as a leading market position that would facilitate the process of winning contracts.

And Bombardier's track record indicated that, despite the concerns over due diligence and the cash drain, it should in time be able to successfully merge Adtranz with Bombardier Transportation. As Robert Brown commented: "People that question our ability to integrate companies should take a look at our history . . .We have experience with these sorts of things." [18]

꙳

It has long been an article of faith that most conglomerate corporations destroy value, as indicated by the tendency for their
share prices to trade below break-up values. There is simply more
value to selling off the separate parts than in keeping them
together.

But a few, such as General Electric Co., Tyco International
Ltd., and Bombardier Inc. were well-recognized exceptions. Studies by academics and consultants concluded that they added
value because of competencies in management, financial controls
and forms of corporate governance that de-emphasized central
control and bureaucracy in favor of autonomous units, lucrative
incentive systems, and unflinching culling of underperforming
managers.

Another explanation offered for their success was compe-
tency in the acquisition and integration of companies. Having
performed so many over the years, they had gained considerable
experience and ability in those functions. They had a workable
formula, one that involved the imposing of the conglomerate's
disciplined processes and unforgiving metrics on an underperforming business.

Over 2001 and 2002, however, skepticism about conglomerate corporations spread to even the exceptional cases
such as GE, Tyco, and Bombardier. They were now, like their
ordinary brethren, destroying value. In the eighteen months to
June 1, 2002, GE lost half its market capitalization, Tyco over
three-quarters, and Bombardier nearly half.

Contributing to the new skepticism was the accounting scan-
dal sparked by the collapse of Enron Corp. in the fall of 2001. It
brought a new focus on the pliability of generally accepted
accounting principles (GAAP) in the presentation of financial

results, as well as the apparent willingness of auditors to sign off on aggressive interpretations.

The overall effect was to cast doubt on the performance of large, diversified companies, where the complexity of operations and frequency of acquisitions provided fertile ground for creativity in the representation of earnings and balance sheets. Were their results merely a mirage stemming from accounting artistry and laxity in auditing? Some detractors argued yes to this question and offered several illustrations from the conglomerates' books.

Thus, it was no longer enough for conglomerates to manage their businesses well. Opacity in financial statements was now a problem, made all the more challenging by the fact that their diversity of operations almost necessarily implied a complexity to the accounts.

The year since the summer of 2001 has been full of trials and tribulations for Bombardier. As for Bombardier's rail-equipment line, it remained relatively immune from economic cycles, but troubles nonetheless surfaced with the Adtranz acquisition, Amtrak's complaints about the Acela high-speed trains, and the loss of a major subway contract in New York City. As for the aerospace line, the terrorist incident of September 11 and the downturn in the economy had an adverse impact on the demand for commercial air travel. The economic downturn also hit its customer base in business jets—to the extent that it was a major factor behind Bombardier's late-August profit warning, which knocked 22 percent off its market capitalization in one day. That brought the share price down to $7—about 70 percent below the high reached in the summer of 2001.

Analysts worried that more bad news was in store as the woes of Bombardier's aerospace customers mounted. Low-fare airliners continued to chip away at the business of Bombardier's customers. And all airliners were exposed to the risk of Middle East tensions boiling over and sparking even higher fuel prices. For US Airways Group, the accumulation of problems was too much: it filed for bankruptcy protection in the summer of 2002. And United Airlines parent UAL Corp. announced that it might have to file for protection in the fall of 2002. That was not good news for Bombardier since nearly one-third of its backlog of aerospace orders came from three of UAL's regional-airline subsidiaries.

Meanwhile, Anthony Scilipoti of Veritas Investment Research Corp. warned in his research reports that Bombardier's accounting was aggressive in areas such as pension-plan assumptions, and the Adtranz takeover. Rising vendor financing was another red flag in his opinion: as of April 30, 2002, Bombardier Capital's portfolio of loans showed financing of $3.7 billion extended to business-jet and commercial-aircraft customers. Also disconcerting was rising debt to finance Bombardier's own operations: as of April 30, 2002, liabilities on the balance sheet amounted to $24.6-billion, compared to assets of $29 billion. That left equity of $4.4-billion, or $3.20 a share. Stripping out goodwill, the book value per share was an even thinner margin of $1.20.

While questions surfaced in 2002 over whether or not Bombardier's golden era had passed, a number of analysts said it was a mistake to write off the company too quickly. Not all was doom and gloom. The storm clouds might linger into 2003, but there were a few silver linings.

In particular, the order backlog remained healthy. For aerospace products alone, it was $45-billion, double fiscal 2002 sales. No regional-jet contracts had been canceled, nor had Bombardier received any indications of cancellations. In fact, new orders were still coming, although they were in smaller bunches of four or five, versus the 50- to 100-jet deals of the previous years. Thus, as Richard Stoneman of Dundee Securities believed, the backlog appeared to be "adequate to bridge the uncertainty in the aerospace industry." [19]

Analysts acknowledged that the specter of a United Airlines bankruptcy threatened to take a sizable chunk out of Bombardier's backlog. But if United Airlines were actually to file, it would still be able to operate under bankruptcy protection laws—so its three feeder airlines need not shut down or cancel their regional-jet orders. And United Airlines still might be able to avoid going into protection if it managed to win aid from the U.S. government, a distinct possibility given the proximity of Congressional mid-term elections.

Indeed, the crisis situation in the airline industry was seen as positive by some because it would likely motivate the sweeping changes necessary to set things right all around. For example, concessions could be won from unions on wages and scope clauses. Success on these fronts would provide the financial wherewithal and freedom for airliners to continue substituting regional jets for less economical turboprops and jumbo jets.

As for rail-equipment product lines, there still remained long-term potential to improve operating margins and grow revenues. The acquisition of Adtranz brought greater dominance of key markets and provided the opportunity for more economies of scale. And Europe was progressing with its plans for continental high-speed rail service, while state governments in the United States were showing increasing interest in faster trains.

The elevation of Pierre Beaudoin to chief executive of the aerospace group was a reminder that Bombardier was a family firm. Pierre may or may not have been the best person to promote, but one saving characteristic of family firms was their focus on the long term. They tended to avoid the excesses of companies like Enron Corp., whose collapse resulted, as management consultants claim, from being managed by a collection of hot-shot executives focused on maximizing short-term performance in order to collect on performance bonuses and stock options.

Bombardier uses such incentive plans, but family ownership tempers the pursuit of short-term goals with long-term goals. The overall effect is more staying power. And so, Pierre Beaudoin's direct involvement in the management of Bombardier may be a way of ensuring that the company becomes a lasting monument to the Bombardier family, Quebec and Canada, as father Laurent has sought since the 1970s.

Endnotes

Preface
[1] John Kay, "Relativism Rules: No Single Perspective Will Give a Full Explanation of Business Behaviour," *Financial Times of London*, Feb. 21, 2001.

Introduction: The Rise of a Corporation
[1] Francois Shalom, "Adtranz Talks Tough," *Montreal Gazette*, May 26, 1999.

[2] R. Gibson, "Did Brunswick Want To Deep-Six Rival's Business?" *Dow Jones News*, Mar. 20, 2001.

[3] Brenda Daglish, "Tycoons in Progress," *Maclean's*, July 6, 1992.

[4] Matthew Fraser, *Quebec Inc: French-Canadian Entrepreneurs and the New Business Elite*, Toronto: Key Porter Books, 1987, p. 152.

[5] Ibid.

[6] Gordon Pitts, "CEO of the Year: Laurent Beaudoin," *Financial Post Magazine*, Dec. 1991.

[7] Christian Allard, "The Fast Track," *Canadian Business*, Jan. 1990.

[8] G. Goad & A. Freeman, "Bombardier Team is Making New Tracks," *Wall Street Journal*, June 9, 1989.

[9] R. Koselka, "Let's Make a Deal," *Forbes*, April 27, 1992.

[10] Edward Clifford, "More to Bombardier than Luck and Handouts," *Globe and Mail*, Aug. 25, 1990.

Chapter 1: Armand Starts a Company

[1] Roger Lacasse, *Joseph-Armand Bombardier: An Inventor's Dream Come True*, Libre Expression, 1988, p. 174.

[2] Ibid., p. 164.

[3] Ibid. p. 126.

Chapter 2: An Excellent Ski-Doo Adventure

[1] Matthew Fraser, *Quebec Inc: French-Canadian Entrepreneurs and the New Business Elite*, Toronto: Key Porter Books, 1987, p. 151.

[2] Kathryn Staley, *The Art of Short Selling*, New York: John Wiley and Sons, 1997.

[3] Roger Lacasse, *Joseph-Armand Bombardier: An Inventor's Dream Come True*, Libre Expression, 1988, p. 176.

[4] Bombardier [videorecording] / editor, Jean-Pierre Cereghetti; producers, Jacques Bonin, Claude Veillet; director, François Labonté Publisher [Toronto]: Astral Video, 1993 (156 min).

5 Matthew Fraser, op cit., p. 156.

6 Ibid.

7 Antonia Zerbisias, "How do You Make a Turkey Soar," *Report on Business Magazine*, October, 1987.

8 Anonymous, "The Ski-Dog Comes of Age," *Executive*, October 1970.

9 Interview with John Hethrington, former Bombardier executive, Dec. 13, 2000.

10 Carole Precious, *J. Armand Bombardier*, Markham, ON: Fitzhenry & Whiteside Ltd., 1984, p. 60.

11 C. J. Ramstad, *Legend: Arctic Cat's First Four Decades*, Deephaven, MN: PPM Books, 1999, p. 18.

12 Tom Williams, "Workhorse of Bush Comes to End of Trail," on Web site http://canadafarnorth.about.com/aboutcanada /canadafarnorth/cs/snowmobiles1/index.htm.

13 Ibid.

14 Steve Brearton, "Reality Check: Back to the Future," *Globe and Mail*, Nov. 24, 2000.

15 Anonymous, "The Ski-Dog Comes of Age," *Executive*, October 1970.

Chapter 3: Diversify or Die

1 Anonymous, "For Bombardier, it's a Bleak Winter," *Financial Post*, June 1, 1974.

2 Brian Roger, "Can Ski-Doo Team get Off the Skids?" *Financial Post*, Oct. 6, 1973.

[3] F. Rose, "Bombardier Picks Up Speed on Downhill Run," *Financial Post*, Dec. 29, 1973.

[4] M. Baghai, S. Covey, R. Farmer, and H. Sarrazin, "The Growth Philosophy of Bombardier," *The McKinsey Quarterly*, Number 2, 1997, p. 11.

[5] Ibid. p. 6.

[6] Rob Givens, "Beaudoin Aims to Make Bombardier a Global Operation," *Financial Post*, June 12, 1989.

[7] Interview with Laurent Beaudoin, Chairman, Bombardier, April 25, 2001.

[8] A. Booth, "Bombardier's Role Emerging in Quebec," *Financial Post*, June 28, 1975.

[9] Jeffrey Simpson, "Ontario Playing into Separatist Hands," *Globe and Mail*, July 21, 1977.

[10] Matthew Fraser, *Quebec Inc: French-Canadian Entrepreneurs and the New Business Elite*, Toronto: Key Porter Books, 1987, p. 158.

Chapter 4: A Breakthrough Deal

[1] Gazette News Service, "Quebec Minister Has Praise for Feds," *Montreal Gazette*, May 20, 1982.

[2] L. Ian MacDonald, "Bombardier Deal Brings Out Landry's Mean-Minded Side," *Montreal Gazette*, May 21, 1982.

[3] Aileen McCabe, "Canada's Cold Shoulder Irks Bombardier," *Montreal Gazette*, Dec. 12, 1983.

[4] CP News, "Aid to Bombardier Unfair, CAE Boss Says," *Montreal Gazette*, June 17, 1982.

[5] John Saunders, "Bombardier: The Government Did Something Right," *Montreal Gazette*, June 22, 1982.

[6] CP Service, "Political Action Puts Subway Deal in Jeopardy," *Montreal Gazette*, May 28, 1982.

[7] John King, "Bombardier Loan a $67-million Waste, Study Says," *Globe and Mail*, July 17, 1982.

[8] Interview with Ed Lumley, former Liberal Cabinet minister, Jan. 13, 2001.

[9] Norman Provencher, "Bombardier's Careful Research Helps it Win Transit Contracts," *Globe and Mail*, November 19, 1982.

Chapter 5: Making Subway Cars the Bombardier Way

[1] G. Goad & A. Freeman, "Bombardier Team is Making New Tracks," *Wall Street Journal*, June 9, 1989.

[2] Raymond Royer, "Managing By Commitment," *Business Quarterly*, Spring, 1991.

[3] Robert Perry, "We Helped Each Other to Beat Some Very High Odds," *Financial Post*, March 22, 1986.

[4] Raymond Royer, op. cit.

[5] Robert Perry, op. cit.

[6] Ibid.

[7] Ibid.

[8] Graham Warwick, "Canadian Turnaround," *Flight International*, August 9, 1995.

[9] Ibid.

[10] Raymond Royer, op. cit.

[11] CP Service, "Bombardier Train Called Lemon," *Montreal Gazette*, April 12, 1985.

[12] CP Service, "Quebec-made Subway Trains Break Down in NY," *Montreal Gazette*, June 8, 1985.

[13] AP Service, "New York Senator Denounces Bombardier," *Montreal Gazette*, October 24, 1985.

[14] Alan Gray, "The Next Station on Bombardier's Route," *Financial Times of Canada*, July 18, 1988.

[15] J. Lancaster, "Young's Brother Paid to Lobby City," *Atlanta Journal and Constitution*, May 18, 1986.

[16] Ibid.

[17] Ibid.

[18] Tara Parker Hope, "Rail Team Partner Hiding No Skeletons," *Houston Chronicle*, May 4, 1991.

[19] Ibid.

[20] Bertrand Marcotte, "Bombardier Counts on 'D' to Succeed," *Globe and Mail*, Oct. 24, 1988.

[21] Aileen McCabe, "Canada's Cold Shoulder Irks Bombardier," *Financial Post*, Dec. 12, 1983.

[22] Peter, Menyasz, "Bombardier's Formula for Growth," *Financial Times of Canada*, Nov. 28, 1983.

[23] Antonia Zerbisias, "How Do You Make a Turkey Soar," *Report on Business Magazine*, October, 1987.

[24] Peter Cook, "Foreign Moves Convince Ottawa to Subsidize Exports," *Globe and Mail*, May 25, 1981.

[25] Ibid.

Chapter 6: Becoming Number One

[1] Gordon Pitts, "CEO of the Year: Laurent Beaudoin," *Financial Post Magazine*, December, 1991, p. 14.

[2] P. McRae, "Bombardier Has Ability to Turn Around Lame Ducks," *Montreal Gazette*, May 7, 1990.

[3] Peter Lynch with John Rothchild, *Beating the Street*, New York: Simon & Schuster, 1994.

[4] Christian Allard, "The Fast Track," *Canadian Business*, Jan. 30, 1990, p. 31.

[5] Matthew Horsman, "Bombardier a Hit in Europe," *Financial Post of Canada*, Oct. 25, 1989.

[6] Barrie McKenna, "Bombardier to Build Channel Tunnel Trains," *Globe and Mail*, July 27, 1989.

[7] Ann Gibson, "Global Strategies," *Globe and Mail*, Dec. 31, 1993.

[8] Ibid.

[9] Konrad Yakabuski, "Bombardier Sets Out on a European Odyssey," *Toronto Star*, Dec. 19, 1993.

[10] Francois Shalom, "Adtranz Talks Tough," *Montreal Gazette*, May 26, 1999.

[11] Alan Freeman, "Bombardier Target Eastern Europe," *Globe and Mail*, May 11, 1998.

Chapter 7: Gravy Trains on the Horizon

[1] Innovative Transportation Technologies Web site: http://faculty.washington.edu/~jbs/itrans.

[2] Wendie Kerr, "Bombardier Looks to Amtrak's LRC to Open Doors," *Globe and Mail*, June 7, 1980.

[3] Ibid.

[4] Stephen Brunt, "Via's LRC Train Chugging Behind Promises," *Globe and Mail*, March 12, 1984.

[5] Deirdre McMurdy, "High-Speed Rivals," *Maclean's*, June 3, 1991.

[6] Drew Fagan, "Bombardier Hits Rail Jackpot," *Globe and Mail*, March 16, 1996.

[7] Paul McKay, "Deadbeat Loans Cost Taxpayers Billions," *Winnipeg Free Press*, March 19, 2000.

[8] Anonymous, "Critics Question $1B in Canadian Loans to Amtrak," *Congress Daily*, April 4, 2000.

[9] William Middleton, "120 Years of Passengers By Rail," *Railway Age*, June 1, 1996.

[10] Lawrence Fabian, "Driverless Metros Are on a Roll," *Mass Transit*, Sept. 19, 1997.

Chapter 8: Turning into Aerospace
[1] Antonia Zerbisias, "How Do You Make a Turkey Soar?" *Report on Business Magazine*, Oct. 1987.

[2] William Symonds, "Bombardier's Blit," *Business Week*, Feb. 6, 1995.

[3] Robert W. Moorman, "The Deal Maker," *Air Transport World*, July 1, 1992.

[4] Gordon Pitts, "CEO of the Year: Laurent Beaudoin," *Financial Post Magazine*, Dec. 1991.

[5] Interview with Laurent Beaudoin, Chairman, Bombardier, April 25, 2001.

6 Christian Bellavance, "Trains, Planes, and Snowmobiles," *CA Magazine*, Nov. 1992.

7 Interview with Laurent Beaudoin, Chairman, Bombardier, April 25, 2001.

8 Amanda Lang, "Honour Thy Grandfather," *Report on Business Magazine*, June 1995.

9 C. Waddell, "Ottawa Pays Premium in Buying Iltis," *Globe and Mail*, Feb. 14, 1985.

10 Robert Gibbens, "Bombardier Plans Mini-Car," *Globe and Mail*, June 17, 1986.

11 Michael Valpy, "Project Venus Failed to Take Off," *Globe and Mail*, Feb. 22, 1988.

12 Alan Gray, "Bombardier Steps into the Billion-Dollar Class," *Financial Times of Canada*, Aug. 25, 1986.

13 Christian Bellavance, "Trains, Planes, and Snowmobiles," *CA Magazine*, Nov. 1992.

14 D. Stoffman and E. Gajdel, "Bombardier's Billion-Dollar Space Race," *Canadian Business*, June 1994.

15 Christian Allard, "The Fast Track," *Canadian Business*, Jan. 1990.

16 David Olive, *No Guts, No Glory: How Canada's Greatest CEOs Built their Empires*, Toronto: McGraw-Hill Ryerson Ltd., 2000, p. 209.

17 Ken Romain, "BA takes option on 20 Canadair jets," *Globe and Mail*, June 10, 1989

Chapter 9: Portrait of a Turnaround Artist

[1] G. Goad, "Salvage Strategy for Units Helps Bombardier Sell Jets," *Wall Street Journal*, March 26, 1990.

[2] David Estok, "Putting a Bloom on Intangibles," *The Financial Post 500*, Summer, 1990.

[3] Harvey Enchin, "Consensus Management? Not for Bombardier's CEO," *Globe and Mail*, April 16, 1990.

[4] Kenneth Kid, "Cleared for Takeoff," *Report on Business Magazine*, Nov. 1992.

[5] David Olive, "Bombardier Retains Good Name in the M&A Game," *Financial Post*, August 9, 2000.

[6] D. Stoffman and E. Gajdel, "Bombardier's Billion-Dollar Space Race," *Canadian Business*, June, 1994.

[7] Ibid.

Chapter 10: Revolution in the Sky

[1] Francois Shalom, "The Roads Ahead," *Montreal Gazette*, April 17, 1999.

[2] Interview with Eric McConachie, Chairman, AvPlan Inc., Nov. 22, 2000.

[3] Ibid.

[4] Ibid.

[5] Ibid.

[6] S. Logie, *Winging It: The Making of the Canadair Challenger*, Toronto, Macmillan Canada, 1992, p.191.

[7] Letter to Dick Richmond, from Aviation Planning Services (internal document), Sept. 23, 1986.

[8] Letter to Donald Lowe, from Aviation Planning Services (internal document), Oct. 31, 1986.

[9] Interview with Eric McConachie, Chairman, AvPlan Inc., Nov. 22, 2000.

[10] Ibid.

[11] Barry Came, "Sky King," *Maclean's*, August 11, 1997.

[12] M. Baghai, S. Covey, R. Farmer, and H. Sarrazin, "The Growth Philosophy of Bombardier," *The McKinsey Quarterly*, Number 2, 1997.

[13] Ibid.

Chapter 11: Bombardier Takes Wing

[1] Konrad Yakubuski, "Bob Brown in Command," *Report on Business Magazine*, Oct. 27, 2000.

[2] Ibid.

[3] Ibid.

[4] S. Bourette, "Bombardier Rewards Brown by Promoting Him to Top," *Globe and Mail*, Dec. 9, 1998.

[5] Konrad Yakubuski, op. cit.

[6] Ibid.

[7] Interview with Robert Brown, President and CEO, Bombardier, May 7, 2001.

[8] Ibid.

[9] David Crane, "Takeover Pace Forecast to Pick Up Again in '90s," *Toronto Star*, Nov. 30, 1990.

[10] Robert Gibbens, "Canadair Chief Calls for Aid to Aerospace Firms," *Financial Post*, Dec. 27, 1993.

[11] Pierre Lortie, *Economic Integration and the Law of GATT*, New York: Praeger Publishers, 1975.

[12] Ann Walmsley, "Meet the New Boss," *Report on Business Magazine*, April, 1999.

[13] William Miller, "Bombardier CEO Has Tough Act to Follow," *Industry Week*, July 5, 1999.

[14] Konrad Yakubuski, op. cit.

[15] Interview with Robert Brown, President and CEO, Bombardier, May 7, 2001.

[16] Ibid.

[17] Konrad Yakubuski, op.cit.

[18] Ibid.

[19] Interview with Robert Brown, President and CEO, Bombardier, May 7, 2001.

[20] Anonymous, "Intelligence Management Philosophy," *The Weekly of Business Aviation*, Nov. 11, 1991.

[21] Interview with Robert Brown, President and CEO, Bombardier, May 7, 2001.

Chapter 12: Dogfight in the Clouds

[1] Barry Came, "Sky King," *Maclean's*, August 11, 1997.

[2] Kathryn Leger, "Tough Guy on the Tarmac," *Financial Post*, Aug. 1, 1998.

[3] Francois Shalom, "Competitors Set to Fight Bombardier," *Montreal Gazette*, Sept. 10, 1998.

[4] Anonymous, "Bombardier Open to Talks with Boeing," *AFX Europe*, Nov. 3, 2000.

5 Jennifer Rich, "Fly, Fly Away," *Latin Finance*, March 1, 1999.

6 Francois Shalom, "Meet Bombardier's Challenger," *Montreal Gazette*, Feb. 3, 2001.

Chapter 13: A Jet Takes Off From the Drawing Board
1 Interview with John Holding, Vice President, Engineering, Bombardier Aerospace, April 11, 2001.

2 Ibid.

3 D. Stoffman and E. Gajdel, "Bombardier's Billion-Dollar Space Race," *Canadian Business*, June, 1994.

4 Interview with John Holding, Vice President, Engineering, Bombardier Aerospace, April 11, 2001.

5 Ibid.

6 Ibid.

7 Anthony Bianco and William Symonds, "Gulfstream's Pilot," *Business Week*, April 14, 1997.

8 M2 Presswire, "Bombardier Global Express Certified," *M2 Communications Ltd.*, Aug. 4, 1998.

9 Anonymous, "Teal Group Predicts Bombardier Will Be Business Jet Market Leader," *The Weekly of Business Aviation*, June 19, 2000.

10 Anthony Velocci Jr., "Bombardier Disciplined in Innovation Strategy," *Aviation Week and Space Technology*, Dec. 4, 2000.

11 Ibid.

12 Interview with John Holding, Vice President, Engineering, Bombardier Aerospace, April 11, 2001.

13 Peter Fitzpatrick, "Bombardier Considering Jet for Long Distances," *National Post*, Dec. 8, 2000.

Chapter 14: New Generations

[1] Amanda Lang, "Honour Thy Grandfather," *Report on Business Magazine*, June 1995.

[2] Ibid.

[3] M. Baghai, S. Covey, R. Farmer, and H. Sarrazin, "The Growth Philosophy of Bombardier," *The McKinsey Quarterly*, Number 2, 1997.

[4] Amanda Lang, op. cit.

[5] Morgan Murphy, "Abominable Snowmobile," *Forbes*, March 20, 2000.

[6] S. Zesiger, "The Big Ticket; Zero to 60 In Three Seconds," *Fortune*, March 31, 1997.

[7] Urban Ohman, "How to snowmobile open water," www.itv.se/~ohm/snowopen.

[8] Ibid.

[9] Morgan Murphy, op. cit.

[10] S. Zesiger, op. cit.

[11] Morgan Murphy, op. cit.

Chapter 15: Lessons in Corporate Strategy

[1] Francois Shalom, "The Road Ahead," *Montreal Gazette*, April 17, 1999.

[2] Yvan Allaire and Mihaela Firsirotu, *L'entreprise Stratégique: Penser la Stratégie*, Boucherville, Quebec: G. Morin, 1993.

[3] Yvan Allaire, "Is Strategic Planning an Oxymoron?," University of Quebec Research Papers, 1988.

4 Interview with Yvan Allaire, Executive Vice President, Bombardier, April 25, 2001.

5 Harvey Enchin, "Consensus Management? Not for Bombardier's CEO," *Globe and Mail*, April 16, 1990.

6 Gordon Pitts, "CEO of the Year: Laurent Beaudoin," *Financial Post Magazine*, December, 1991.

7 Interview with Yvan Allaire, Executive Vice President, Bombardier, April 25, 2001.

8 M. Baghai, S. Covey, R. Farmer, and H. Sarrazin, "The Growth Philosophy of Bombardier," *The McKinsey Quarterly*, Number 2, 1997.

9 Interview with Yvan Allaire, Executive Vice President, Bombardier, April 25, 2001.

10 Nigel Holloway, "Bombardier's Master Builder," *Forbes*, April 19, 1999.

11 Interview with Yvan Allaire, Executive Vice President, Bombardier, April 25, 2001.

12 Interview with Laurent Beaudoin, Chairman, Bombardier, April 25, 2001.

13 M. Baghai et al, op. cit.

14 Interview with Laurent Beaudoin, Chairman, Bombardier, April 25, 2001.

15 Ibid.

16 Bruce Livesay, "Ceiling Unlimited," *Globe and Mail*, March 28, 1997.

17 M. Baghai et al., op. cit.

18 Bruce Livesay, op. cit.

[19] Thomas Peters and Robert Waterman, *In Search of Excellence: Lessons From America's Best-Run Companies*, New York: Harper & Row, 1982, p. 318.

[20] General Electric, *Annual Report*, 1995.

[21] M. Baghai et al., op cit.

[22] Ibid.

[23] S. Brown and K. Eisenhardt. "Patching," *McKinsey Quarterly*, Number 3, 2000.

[24] Joel Johnson, "Sea-Doo and Kawasaki Reorganize," *Boating Industry*, Aug. 1, 1997.

[25] Francois Shalom. op . cit.

[26] Steve Waters, "New Wave Emerges in OMC's Wake," *South Florida Sun-Sentinel*, Feb. 16, 2001.

Chapter 16: A Prototype for the Twenty-First Century?

[1] Peter C. Newman, "Flying High with the Little Engine that Could," *Macleans*, March 27, 1989.

[2] Michael Jenkinson, "Ralph Bombs Bombardier Loan," *Alberta Report*, Nov. 11, 1996.

[3] Terence Corcoran, "How We Pay for Ford, Bombardier," *Globe and Mail*, Oct. 23, 1996.

[4] Michael Jenkinson, "Back to National Unity Through Spending," *Alberta Report*, Nov. 4, 1996.

[5] Derek Ferguson, "Military Deal Won Without Tender," *Toronto Star*, June 1, 1998.

[6] Ibid.

[7] Thomas Walkom, "Why the Lion Bombardier is Under Attack," *Toronto Star*, June 6, 1998.

8 Notes obtained from Yvan Allaire, July 19, 2001.

9 Laurent Beaudoin, "Bombardier Plans to Fly Without Government Help," *Canadian Speeches*, Jan. 1997.

10 Ibid.

11 Ibid.

12 Bombardier Corp. "Bombardier and the Canadian Government —Backgrounder," www.bombardier.com, June 26, 1998.

13 H. Scoffield, "Bombardier Turned Down Ottawa's Low-Interest Loans," *Globe and Mail*, June 18, 1999.

14 Larry MacDonald, *Nortel Networks: How Innovation and Vision Created a Network Giant*, Toronto: John Wiley & Sons, 2000, Chapter 6.

Chapter 17: The Challenges Ahead
1 Alex Taylor, "Little Jets are Huge," *Fortune*, Sept. 4, 2000.

2 Ibid.

3 Bombardier Inc. *Annual Report for Fiscal 2001*.

4 Lawrence Fabian, "Driverless Metros on a Roll," *Mass Transit*, Sept. 19, 1997.

5 Anonymous, "Bombardier Uses Vancouver Base as Staging Area for Pacific Rim Market," *Design-Build*, Dec. 1, 2000.

Chapter 18: Bombardier Encounters Turbulence
1 Bertrand Marcotte, "The Brink of War: Airlines in Crisis," *National Post*, Sept. 19, 2001.

2 Sean Silcoff, "Bombardier chief sees slow year," *National Post*, March 21, 2002.

[3] Fabrice Taylor, "Vendor financing," *Globe and Mail*, Feb. 22, 2002.

[4] Sean Silcoff, op. cit.

[5] Steven Chase, "Canada and Brazil set subsidy meeting," *Globe and Mail*, Jan. 19, 2002.

[6] Keith McArthur, "Beaudoin says son may one day run Bombardier," *Globe and Mail*, Jan. 22, 2002.

[7] David Olive, "All in the family at Bombardier—Transportation giant follows dubious Canadian tradition," *Toronto Star*, Oct. 26, 2001.

[8] Paul Betts, "Family companies are ready for the worst," *Financial Times of London*, Oct. 29 2001.

[9] Sean Silcoff, "Family Ties," *National Post*, Oct. 20, 2001.

[10] Paul Betts, op. cit.

[11] Keith McArthur, op. cit.

[12] Sean Silcoff, op. cit.

[13] Sean Silcoff, "Bombardier-DaimlerChrysler Dispute," *National Post*, Feb. 15, 2002.

[14] Caroline Alphonso, "Bombardier stock slides," *Globe and Mail*, Feb. 21, 2002.

[15] Sean Silcoff, "Bombardier sues Daimler for $1.4B," *National Post*, Feb. 15, 2002.

[16] Sean Silcoff, "Bombardier credibility under fire," *National Post*, Feb. 16, 2002.

[17] Sean Silcoff, "Bombardier sues Daimler for $1.4B," *National Post*, Feb. 15, 2002.

[18] Keith McArthur, "Bombardier blasts critics," Globe and Mail, March 20, 2002.

[19] Allan Dowd "Bombardier shares slip as Amtrak sidelines trains," Reuters News, Aug. 13, 2002.

Index

ABB, 116

Acela Express, 118, 120, 281

Acquisition strategy, 129, 130, 147-157, 277–279

Adtranz, 105-107, 126, 190, 238, 262, 263, 270-271, 277-279, 281-283

AEG Westinghouse Transportation, 124

Aerospace
  acquisitions, 127-145
  business jets, 199-209
  future prospects, 255-259, 272, 281-283
  regional jets, 159-197, 271-273

Aerospatiale, 189, 258

Air Canada, 179

Air Wisconsin Airlines Corp., 247

Airbus, 188, 189

Airline Deregulation Act, 160

Alcan Canada Products Ltd., 112

Alchemy of growth, 236

ALCO, 49

All-terrain vehicle (ATV), 218, 260

Alsthom Atlantique, 83

Alstom, 90, 104, 105, 111, 115, 119

Alta Velocidad Espanola, 110

American Eagle, 186

American Locomotive Company (ALCO), 49

Amtrak, 112, 113, 118, 119, 263, 281

AMX fighter, 191

ANF-Industrie, 100

Ansett Worldwide Aviation, 177

Appleton, Tom, 178

Art of Short Selling, The (Staley), 22

Artic Cat, 30

Artico Inc., 212, 216, 217, 219

Asset freeze, 20

Atlantic Southeast Airlines, 189

ATR, 143

ATV, 218, 260

Automated metros, 121-125, 263

Avions de Transport Regional (ATR), 143

AvPlan Inc., 160

Avro Arrow, 242

Awards/acknowledgement, 1

B5, 14
B7, 6, 7, 11
B12, 11-13
BAE Systems, 273
Bandeirante aircraft, 191
Barents, Brian, 148, 153, 155
Baril, Michel, 240, 266
BCE, 252
Beaudoin, Laurent, 19, 20, 22-2, 27, 34,
    35, 41, 43, 46-48, 51, 53, 54, 56, 58,
    60, 61, 68, 79, 81, 82, 93, 94, 96, 97,
    109, 112, 121, 125-130, 132, 133,
    135, 138, 149, 159, 164, 169, 173,
    174, 181, 200, 202, 225-227, 229-
    232, 237-239, 243, 244, 248, 250,
    261, 266, 267, 274-276, 278, 284
Beaudoin, Pierre, 35, 213, 214, 216-
    218, 266, 273-277, 283-284
Bélanger, Jacques, 8, 9
Bell Canada Enterprises (BCE), 252
Biron, Rodrigue, 60
Bissonnette, Gaston, 21
Blizzard, 31
BMS, 74, 75, 156, 157
BN Constructions Ferroviaires et
    Métalliques S.A., 99
BNDES, 193
Boeing, 150, 151, 186, 188, 189, 258
Bombardier (video movie), 23
Bombardier, Alphonse, 7, 12
Bombardier, André, 24
Bombardier, Claire, 20
Bombardier, Gérard, 12, 15
Bombardier, Germaine, 12, 16, 21-24
Bombardier, Huguette, 47
Bombardier, Jean-Luc, 26
Bombardier, Joseph-Armand, 1-17,
    20-23, 274
Bombardier, Léopold, 12
Bombardier, Théophile, 15
Bombardier Capital, 260
Bombardier Eurorail, 103
Bombardier Inc.
    accounting, 280-282
    acquisition strategy, 129, 130,
        147-157

awards/acknowledgements, 243, 244
corporate governance, 223-240.
    See also Strategic governance
corporate logo, 1
future prospects, 255-267, 270-273,
    281-284
    See also Future prospects
history, ix-xv
operating groups. *See* Operating
    groups
share price, 244, 269, 281
size, 265
social responsibility, 244, 245
Bombardier International, 237, 264
Bombardier Limitée, 25
Bombardier Manufacturing System
    (BMS), 74, 75, 156, 157
Bombardier-MLW, 50
Bombardier Prorail Limited, 100
Bombardier-Rotax GmbH, 32
Botelho, Mauricio, 190, 192
Bourassa, Robert, 48
Brock, William, 62
Brown, Robert E., 171-186, 200, 218,
    231, 237, 266, 270, 277, 279
Brown, S., 236
Brunswick Corp., 239, 240
BT, 15
Budd Co., 56, 57, 61-63, 87, 95
Budd designs, 96
Budget, 231
"Building Our Future", 156
Bullet train, 110
Bush, Jeb, 117
Business jets, 199-209, 258, 259, 276,
    281
Buy American rules, 76

C4, 14
C18, 13
Caisse de dépôt et placement du
    Québec, 45, 46
Camoplast Inc., 43
Canada Account, 197, 247, 248
Canada-Brazil trade dispute, 193-197,
    247, 273

Canadair, 133-138, 149, 150, 154, 156
Canadair Regional Jet, 157-197
Canadian Aerospace Technologies, 135
Cardoso, Fernado Henrique, 194
Carter, Jimmy, 90
CATIA software, 204, 205
CBA-123, 190
Centre for Advanced Transit Systems, 124
CF-18 fighter jets, 137
CF-18 maintenance contract, 150
Challenger, 133, 134, 159, 163, 167
Challenges ahead. See Future prospects
China, 264
China Aviation Industry Corp., 258
Cho, Ted, 278
Chotard, Benoît, 173
Chrétien, Jean, 133, 134, 194, 265, 266
Chunnel, 98, 101-103
CIMT, 90
CIMT-Lorraine, 47, 48
CIRR, 196
Citroën, André-Gustave, 2
CL-415, 175, 176
Clark, Glen, 124
Comair Inc., 178, 189
Commercial interest reference rate
    (CIRR), 196
Compagnie Industrielle de Materiel
    Transport (CIMT), 90
Company size, 265
Conglomerate corporations, 280-281
Constructora Nacional de Carros de Fer-
    rocarril (Concarril), 265
Coolidge, Calvin, 41
Corporate divisions. See Operating
    groups
Corporate governance. See Strategic gov-
    ernance
Corporate logo, 1
Corporate philanthropy, 244, 245
Corporate reshaping, 236, 237
CRJ-700, 180, 181
Culver, David, 133
Culver, Michael, 132, 164

Daihatsu Motor Co., 132

Dash 7, 142, 143
Dash 8, 143, 144, 150, 180
de Havilland, 142-144, 150, 153, 154
de Havilland, Geoffrey, 142
Decentralization, 228-230
Defence Industry Productivity Program,
    168
Delta Airlines, 256
Desmarais, Andre, 247
Deutsche Bahn AG, 104
Deutsche Waggonbau AG, 104, 105
Disneyland, 125
Diversification strategy, 41-43, 48, 51,
    130, 269-270, 280-281
Dominion Foundries and Steel Ltd., 112
Dornier, Justus, 135
Dotte, Christian, 103
Due diligence, 129, 148
Dupaul, Marie-Jeanne, 12

Eclipse Aviation Corp., 208
Economic Integration and the Law of GATT
    (Lortie), 179
Economic value added (EVA), 233, 234
EDC, 56, 60, 119, 120, 178
Eggleton, Art, 247
Eisenhardt, E., 236
Élan, 30
Eliason, Earl, 3
EMB-120, 191
Embraer, 143, 166, 177, 185, 188, 191-
    195, 207, 247, 256-258, 273, 277
Emerging economies, 264, 265
Employee relations, 155, 156
Endnotes, 269-285, 303
Enron Corp., 280, 283
Entrepreneurial spirit, 229
ERJ 135, 191, 193
ERJ 145, 185, 191, 193
Euripides, 38
European expansion, 96-107
Eurotunnel SA, 101-103
EVA, 233, 234
Executive class jets, 199-209, 258, 259
Export Development Corporation
    (EDC), 56, 60, 119, 120, 178

Extreme snowmobiling, 219, 220
Family Firm, 1-24, 213-221, 265-267,
    273-277, 283-284
Fairchild Dornier Corp., 187, 256, 257,
    273
Fay, Robert, 278
FICHT fuel injection, 240
Fifth Estate, The, 134
Finamex, 193
Financial reporting system, 231
Firsirotu, Mihaela, 224, 225, 227
Flexible manufacturing, 67
Flexjet program, 259
Fokker NV, 148
Fontaine, Jean-Louis, 22, 47
Francorail, 56, 57
Future prospects, 255-267
    business jets, 258, 259
    capital group, 260
    company size, 265
    emerging economies, 264, 265
    political environment, 265, 266
    rail transportation, 261-264
    recreational group, 260
    regional jets, 255-258
    succession risk, 266

Gagnon, Roland, 74, 75, 175
Garage Bombardier, 1, 2
Gates Rubber Co., 141
GEC-Alstom, 104
General Dynamics Corp., 133, 207
General Electric, 235, 280
General Motors, 52
Genmar Holdings Ltd., 239
Georgia 400 project, 84
Gillespie, Robert, 266
Gilmour, Bill, 246
Global Express, 199-209
Governance. *See* Strategic governance
Government assistance, 168, 242-253.
    See also Export Development
    Corporation (EDC)
Goyer, Jean-Pierre, 52
Graff, Michael, 266, 274
Greenhill, Robert, 266

Gulfstream Aerospace, 203, 206, 207
Hanger, Art, 247
Hargrove, Buzz, 155
Hébert, Claude, 226
Hébert, Jean-Claude, 50, 51
Hethrington, John, 25, 27
Hetteen, Edgar, 29
High-Speed Rail Investment Act, 263
High-speed trains, 110-121, 262, 263
History, ix-xv
Holding, John, 157, 199-202, 205, 208
Hollander, Louis, 226
Horace, 41
Horizontal integration, 154, 155
Hub-and-spoke system, 161, 162

ICE, 110
Iltis military jeeps, 131
Industry consolidation, 33
Integrated Resources Inc., 141
Inter-City Express (ICE), 110
International Association of Machinists
    and Aerospace Workers, 276
International Chamber of Commerce,
    279

J. Armand Bombardier Foundation, 244
Jet Ski, 215
Just-in-time (JIT) inventory control, 156

Kawasaki Heavy Industries, 56, 57, 59,
    78, 80, 215-217, 236
Kearns, Fred, 133, 134
Kégresse, Adolphe, 2
Kiewit Construction Group, 85
Klein, Ralph, 245

L'Auto-Neige Bombardier, 2, 11, 12
L'entreprise Stratégique: Penser la Stratégie
    (Allaire/Firsirotu), 224
La Société générale de financement du
    Québec (SGF), 45, 46, 50
Labour relations, 155, 276-277
Landry, Adalbert, 3
Landry, Bernard, 60
Langdon, Steven, 136

Lapointe, Anselme (Sam), 34, 35
Lapointe, Denys, 35
Lavalin Industries Inc., 123, 124
Leadership triumvirate, 237
Lear, William, 141
Learjet, 141, 142, 148, 153
Lefebvre, André, 5
Legacy, 207
Leichter, Franz, 81
Les Entreprises de J. Armand Bombardier
    Limitée, 20, 49, 50
Les Industries Bouchard Inc., 33
Les Plastiques LaSalle Inc., 32
Lesage, Jean, 45
Lévesque, René, 45
Logo, 1
Lohnerwerke GmbH, 32, 46
Long Island Railroad, 83
Lord, Michel, 189
Lortie, Pierre, 179, 180, 260
Lowe, Donald C., 149, 164-166
LRC trains, 112-114
Lufthansa CityLine, 166, 177
Lumley, Ed, 59, 62, 66, 90, 173
Lynch, Peter, 96

MacDonald, Pierre, 115, 116
MacDougall, Don, 278
Mach Z, 218
Maglev trains, 111
Magnetic levitation (Maglev) train, 111
Major, John, 140
Malthieu, Albert, 98
Management practices. *See* Strategic gov-
    ernance
Mann, Tom, 255
Marine Industries, 46, 50
Marshall, Sir Colin, 140
Mass transit contracts, 87
Matra, 126
Mawby, Carl, 58
McConachie, Eric, 159-168, 177
McDougall, Barbara, 137, 173
McNulty, Roy, 151
Mendoza, Drew, 275
Mesa Air Group, 255

Methods department, 157
Metropolitan Transit Authority (MTA) of
    New York, 55-68
Microcar, 132
Middleton, William, 121
Military vehicles, 131
Mitsubishi, 126
MLW-Worthington, 49, 50, 53, 54, 112,
    128
Monorail, 125
Montreal subway contract, 53
Moriset, Antionne, 3
Moss, Bryan, 201, 206
Moto-Ski, 33
Motorized toboggan, 3
Mountain Cat 1000, 219
MTA, 55-68
Muskeg Tractor, 15, 16

National Development Bank (BNDES),
    193
New York subway contract (1982), 55-
    68
Neighbourhood electric vehicle, 218
Newman, Peter C., 241
Niche markets, 129
Nicholas II, Czar, 2
Nortel, 252
*Nortel Networks: How Innovation and
    Vision Created a Network Giant*
    (MacDonald), 252
Northwest Airlines Corp., 247

October crisis, 45
OECD's Arrangement on Guidelines for
    Officially Supported Export Credits, 89
Öhman, Urban, 219, 220
Olive, David, 274
Olivella, Barry, 174, 177
Olympique, 31
OMC, 190, 239, 240
Operating groups
    aerospace. *See* Aerospace
    capital group, 260, 261
    department heads, 266
    international operations, 237, 264,

265
rail transportation. *See* Rail trans-
    portation
recreational products. *See* Recreational
    products
Osbaldeston, Gordon, 172
Otis Elevators, 126
Outboard Marine Corp. (OMC), 190,
    239, 240
Outlook for the future. *See* Future
    prospects

Parizeau, Jacques, 45
Patching, 236
Peary, Robert, 26
Pencak, Marco, 270
Pendolino, 114
People Express, 160
People movers, 125, 126, 263, 264
Personal watercraft (PWC), 213-217
Plaisted, Ralph, 26
Plante, Victor, 4
Polaris Industries Inc., 29, 30, 211-213,
    217
Political environment, 265, 266
Power Corp., 264
Precious, Carole, 26
Pro-ex export financing program, 143,
    193-196
Procor Engineering Limited, 100
Product development, 231, 236
Pullman designs, 88, 96
Pullman Standard Co., 57, 95
PwC market, 213-217

R&D, 66, 88, 89
Rail transportation, 109-126
    automated metros, 121-125, 263
    future prospects, 261-264, 278-279,
        281, 283
    high-speed trains, 110-121, 262, 263,
        281, 283
    people movers, 125, 126, 263, 264
Ravitch, Richard, 56-58, 60, 63, 79
Reagan, Ronald, 63
Recreational products
    ATV, 218

future prospects, 260
neighbourhood electric vehicle, 218
personal watercraft (PWC), 213-217
snowmobiles, 16, 17, 24-31, 211-213,
    218-221
Regan, Donald, 63
Regional jets, 159-197, 255-258
Research and development (R&D), 66,
    88, 89, 276
Reshaping of organizational structure,
    236, 237
Reverse takeover, 50
Richmond, Dick, 163, 164
Robinson, James, 187
Rohr Inc., 95, 96
Roski Ltée, 32
Rotax engines, 27, 260
Rotax 600 cc, 27
Rotax-Werk AG, 32
Royer, Raymond, 59, 60, 66, 68-71, 75-
    78, 88, 89, 91, 94, 99, 112, 227

Saint Pierre, Roland, 12
Schilling Fred, 101
Schroeder, Chancellor Gerhard, 278
Scilipoti, Anthony, 282
Scope clauses, 256, 257, 272-273, 283
Sea-Doo, 213-217
Sea-Doo XP, 216
SGF, 45, 46, 50
Share price, 1
Shinkansen Bullet Trains, 110
Short Brothers PLC (Shorts), 138-141,
    148, 151-154, 156, 166, 177
Sidbec, 46
Siegel, Eric, 120
Siemens, 105, 111
Sifang Locomotive and Rolling Stock
    Works, 264
Six Sigma, 234, 235
Ski-Doo, 16, 17, 24-31, 211-213,
    218-221, 269
Ski-Doo expedition to North Pole, 26
Skiroule Ltd., 70
Skytrain, 122, 125
SkyWest Airlines Inc., 179
Snowmobile expedition across Alaska

Index ◆ 311

(1960), 29
Snowmobiles, 16, 17, 24-31, 211-213, 218-221
Société de Développement Industriel du Québec, 168
Société Générale de Belgique, 99
Sorel, Bernard, 103
St. Louis Car Co., 95
Staley, Kathryn, 22
Strategic governance, 223-240
corporate reshaping, 236, 237
decentralization, 228-230
EVA, 233, 234
financial reporting system, 231
four pillars, 227
Six Sigma, 234, 235
strategic planning, 230
Strategic planning, 230
"Strategic Turnaround as Cultural Revolution: The Case of Canadian National Express (Firsirotu), 224
Subsidy war, 248
Subway cars, 55-91
Succession risk, 266
Super Hikari, 110

Takeover strategy, 129, 130, 147-157
Taylor, Ken, 59
Technical councils, 77
Technology Partnerships Canada program, 195, 196
Tellier, Paul, 181
Terrorists, 269-270, 272, 281
Textron Inc., 211
TGV, 110, 115
Thatcher, Margaret, 139, 140
Theme parks, 125
TML, 101, 102
Track N' Trail (TN'T), 27
Tractor Tracking Attachment, 15
Train à Grande Vitesse (TGV), 110, 115
TransManche Link (TML), 101, 102
Traxter, 218, 260

Tretheway, Michael, 116
Triumvirate at the top, 237
Turnaround operation, 147-157
Twin Otter, 150
Tyco International Ltd., 280
Type certificate, 159

UAL Corp., 282
Union Internationale des Transports Publics (UITP), 121
United Airlines, 282-283
Urban Transportation Development Corp. (UTDC), 122, 123
US Airways, 273, 282
US Surface Transportation Assistance Act, 76
UTDC, 122, 123
Uyterhoeven, Hugo, 128, 218

Valle, Henry, 112
Venus Project, 132
Vertical integration, 32, 43
VIA, 113, 114
Vickers Canada Inc., 87
Vickers Ltd., 46-48
Virgin Rail, 107, 111

Waggonfabrik Talbot KG, 104
War Measures Act, 45
Ward, John, 275
Water skimming, 219
Webster, Howard, 135
Welch, Jack, 235
White, Virgil, 3
Wohl, Bob, 176, 177, 179
World's Championship Snowmobile Derby, 27
WTO rulings, 195-197, 247

Yamaha Motor Corp., 211, 212, 215, 217
Young, Andrew, 83, 84
Young International Development, 83, 84